NATURE AND THE ENVIRONMENT IN PRE-COLUMBIAN AMERICAN LIFE

D0169148

Recent titles in
The Greenwood Press "Daily Life Through History" Series

NATURE AND THE ENVIRONMENT IN PRE-COLUMBIAN AMERICAN LIFE

STACY KOWTKO

The Greenwood Press "Daily Life Through History" Series
Nature and the Environment in Everyday Life

Greenwood Press
Westport, Connecticut • London

Library of Congress Cataloging-in-Publication Data

Kowtko, Stacy.
   Nature and the environment in pre-Columbian American life / Stacy Kowtko.
        p.   cm. — (The Greenwood Press "Daily life through history" series, ISSN 1080–4749)
   Includes bibliographical references and index.
   ISBN 0–313–33472–2
   1. Indians of North America—Social conditions.   2. Indigenous peoples—Ecology—
North America.   3. Human ecology—North America—Philosophy.   4. Indian philoso-
phy—North America.   5. Indians of North America—Social life and customs.   6. North
America—Environmental conditions.   I. Title.   II. Series.
   E98.S67K69   2006
   305.897—dc22   2006012036

British Library Cataloguing in Publication Data is available.

Library of Congress Catalog Card Number: 2006012036
ISBN: 0–313–33472–2
ISSN: 1080–4749

First published in 2006

Greenwood Press, 88 Post Road West, Westport, CT 06881
An imprint of Greenwood Publishing Group, Inc.
www.greenwood.com

Printed in the United States of America

The paper used in this book complies with the
Permanent Paper Standard issued by the National
Information Standards Organization (Z39.48–1984).

10   9   8   7   6   5   4   3   2   1

To my family: Brennen, you inspire me to try and make this world a better place for you; Blake, thank you for being my son and my friend through it all; and Joe, my husband, everything is possible because of you. To all of my extended family in Louisiana and Illinois, thank you for being my network of support.

To my colleagues at Spokane Community College, thank you for your acceptance and support of me, allowing me to be who I am without judgment. Both professionally and personally, I am so much more because of all of you.

To my friend and research assistant, Bekah Kurle, your simple presence makes my life easier in uncountable ways.

This book is dedicated to my father, Thurman Perry Hale, who left this world too soon to see it completed. Thank you for believing in me. And to my grandmother, Wilkie Hale, the strongest woman I know. I can only hope to be a portion of who you are.

CONTENTS

INTRODUCTION

In a modern world of convenience and self-interest, other worlds and cultures that came before often fall to the wayside of popular imagination and memory. When and if they emerge at all, these worlds can appear shrouded by what soothes the conscious or generates the largest profit, giving the past a shaky legitimacy and the present a false sense of security. The disservice is that the reality of the past gives way to the needs of the present, ultimately depriving both of their rightful authenticity and heritage. As distance in time increases, it seems so can the distortion. Therefore, academic efforts focus on correcting and detailing the reality of the past in order to enable understanding of civilization's path to the present. The pre-Columbian or prehistoric truth of North America deserves academic treatment not only to correct false ideas, but also to promote understanding of the role this period played in creating today's world.

Different academic disciplines use many different methods when analyzing the pre-Columbian North America and focus on a variety of issues and debates. Archaeology, sociology, geography, anthropology, history, and other areas look at varied aspects of pre-Columbian history, ultimately contributing to a more comprehensive collection of information. In order to understand the interaction of pre-Columbian peoples with their environments, scholastic examination must consider many different details and debates. Elapsed time, lost evidence, and cultural dissimilarities add to the difficulty in examination. The best efforts at legitimate, inclusive portrayal draw from all disciplines in order to provide the most objective treatment possible.

In addition to the necessity of interdisciplinary approaches, there also exist many controversial and arguable topics. One hotly debated issue in this field is the evidence for trans-Atlantic and trans-Pacific contact with the Americas and its aborigines prior to the arrival of Columbus. The first Western accounts of native societies in North America started with that very "discovery" made by Columbus. The problem with these reports was that the Eurocentric views of the observers distorted their observations because of bias and ignorance. Many believed, for example, the savage natives of the new land were too uncivilized to produce ancient monuments like the ones the Europeans found on the new continent; early Europeans had to have built them. Despite a lack of historical evidence supporting the idea that European cultures made it to the New World before Columbus, most Western historians embraced the idea that the evidence must have been lost. Explorers such as John Lloyd Stevens and William H. Prescott, however, began to study native civilizations in detail, and eventually the Western world came to accept the idea that native populations did build the amazing ancient structures of North America.

The idea that Columbus was the first westerner to discover the continent then dominated the first few centuries of academic interpretation concerning discovery and exploration of the New World. Strong archaeological evidence later emerged in 1961 in Newfoundland suggesting that Vikings crossed to North America by way of Iceland and Greenland around 1000 C.E., almost 500 years earlier. Over the next few decades, scholars also delved into the possibility of other pre-Columbian transoceanic contact and found suggestion for a variety of pre-Columbian visitors. Basque, Muslim, African, Asian, and Northmen are just a few societies who may hold claim to significant interaction with native North American peoples before 1492. Some claims are stronger than others and open up a world of possibilities for academic analysis. There is a strong suggestion, for example, that Muslim travelers landed on North American shores as early as 1312. Some Muslim historical writings suggest that Mansa Abu Bakr traveled to the Gulf of Mexico during the early 14th century. Evidence of linguistic ties between some West African languages and Native Americans in the Gulf area support this idea of pre-Columbian outside contact also. Debates such as these serve to define and detail the reality of a world no longer accessible, the world of prehistoric North America that is infinitely important to today's reality.

What this example shows is that a time's or a people's status as unknown or undocumented does not mean that the culture's history is static or inert. Before the arrival of Columbus, Native American societies lived off the land in a multitude of ways that evolved over decades and centuries. What was true for a Native American in 1550 C.E. was certainly different from the reality of 1450. However, that also differed from the realities of 1350, 1250, and 950 C.E. Their social systems, economic standards, spiritual lives, and aesthetic expressions evolved extensively over the 10,000 to 50,000 years of their residence in North America. No one society very much resembled the next, and this diversity manifested itself in a variety of ways: as small tribes of hunter-gatherers who roamed the plains of the Great Basin, as pueblo-dwelling communities of the Southwest, and as the Mississippian mound-builders in the Southeast who built cities with tens of thousands of inhabitants, just to name a few.

In addition to this diversity across regions, natives in some areas experienced marked change within their own tribes. The Mississippi Valley, as one example, demonstrated drastic political and economic divisions that loosened the tight societal organization that once controlled and directed mound-building societies. By the late 1400s, what were once strong, centralized societies had fragmented into small, wall-enclosed hamlets. During the 1200s, drought and political unrest divided Anasazi society, sending its peoples outward to settle in areas across the Southwest, setting up communities along the Rio Grande and establishing connections with the Apaches and Navajos. Some of these changes brought devastating consequences, and some brought beneficial opportunities for societal evolution. Ultimately, the point is that many societies inhabited North America prior to European contact, none of them mirrored another, and they certainly did not live an unchanging, rigid existence. The distinctive nature of each society commands a need for study and analysis to help define the reality of pre-Columbian existence.

When looking at different disciplinary approaches, other issues surface as well, highlighting various points in pre-Columbian American history in unique ways. For example, recent environmental science efforts suggest it is possible to study ancient American cultures and their transformations through the influence and effects of El Niño. Justification for this approach considers that El Niño is one of the most-analyzed agents of environmental change and also that it is one element that can cause great environmental fluxuations. There can be no doubt that El Niño presented a great challenge to the peoples of prehistoric North America, but only through the combination of sociology and environmental science can a fuller understanding of the relationship between climatic changes and societal reality emerge. This example then highlights the central focus of this work. Environmental issues inextricably intertwine with pre-Columbian North American life, and it is impossible to study one without the inclusion of the other. Ancient American peoples often possessed neither the ability *nor the will* to circumvent or overcome the effects of their natural environment. Everything that defined them centered on their use of, interpretation of, and adaptation to their surroundings. Every representative example in this work focuses on explaining pre-Columbian North America and its peoples in relation to natural history and environs. Comprehensive coverage of every tribe is not possible, but illustrative use of selective examples illuminates major subjects in the study of these peoples and their environments. Ultimately, the goal is to provide a snapshot of pre-Columbian North American peoples from a symbiotic societal and environmental perspective showing both the tribes on the land and the land and environment itself as inseparable.

TIMELINE OF NATIVE HISTORY IN PRECONTACT NORTH AMERICA

The dates in this chronology indicate either the earliest point of cultural development or the time frame in which the culture existed.

65,000 B.C.E.   The earliest suggested migration period across the Beringia Bridge into North America by the ancestors of the Inuit and later Native American tribes.

40,000   A more commonly accepted date for the arrival of early Paleo-Indians from Asia.

15,000   The most popular date for the earliest arrival of Paleo-Indians in North America.

12,000   Archaeological evidence and analysis suggests human habitation in both North and South America.

10,000   IIumans reach the most southern part of the Americas, Cape Horn in South America.

9500–9000   Clovis Culture is recognized by their grooved spear points now called Clovis points. These big game hunters lived throughout the Americas but it is unknown whether Clovis culture originated in one area of North America and spread or if Clovis technology developed independently in different areas. This period is also known as the Early Paleo-Indian period.

9000–8500   Known as the Middle Paleo-Indian period, this
                       500 year span is characterized by a larger vari-
                       ety of spear points, both larger and smaller than
                       Clovis cultures and is considered a time in ancient
                       native history when the populations were adapt-
                       ing to optimal resource conditions.

                       The Folsom Culture develops smaller points
                       than Clovis and hunts big game as their main
                       form of sustenance. They are also the first to use
                       the atlatl or throwing spear as an advanced hunt-
                       ing weapon.

                       Plano Culture lived mainly in the North Amer-
                       ican plains regions. They hunt bison with deli-
                       cately flaked spear points, but come to prefer the
                       mass herding of bison in cliff-drives. Some of their
                       innovations in sustenance technology include the
                       drying of bison meat into pemmican jerky and
                       using grinding stones to grind plants and seeds.

8500–7900   This Late Paleo-Indian period is characterized by
                       Dalton and other side-notched spear points. The
                       adaptation of nonfluted points signifies a move
                       from hunting larger animals to the pursuit of
                       smaller game.

8500   Ancient Northwest Coast natives settle on the
                       ocean shores and develop into a maritime culture.
                       They are unique in their development of high
                       ancient culture without the stability of agriculture
                       or influence of ancient Mexican civilizations. They
                       are also the only ancient culture to develop wealth
                       accumulation and a rigid caste system of social
                       hierarchy.

8000–1000   Often referred to as a "Wide Spectrum Revolu-
                       tion," the Archaic Period represents the transi-
                       tion from Paleo dependence on large game to a
                       broader spectrum of animal and plant resources.
                       Small hand tools and grinding implements char-
                       acterize this period. During this period many
                       cultures evolve and disappear across the North
                       American continent.

8000–6000   The period of the Early Archaic native experi-
                       ences a significant climate warming, which cre-
                       ated an easier living environment. Families live in
                       larger, mobile bands, but as resources become

more plentiful, the range of their nomadic movement shrinks.

6000–2500   The Middle Archaic Period is a time of weapons advancement and tool specialization. The atlatl is used in many areas, mortar and pestles are popular, and nonsustenance oriented tools such as the ax become popular.

2500–1000   During the Late Archaic period, tribal populations are growing, causing people to intensify hunting and gathering practices along with agricultural efforts. One result is that settlement size grows while simultaneously becoming more settled in areas with plentiful natural resources.

1000 B.C.E.–1000 C.E.   The Woodland period on the North American continent is a time when people become more sedentary, begin constructing earthen works, often engage in both hunting and gathering and agriculture, and begin making and using pottery. Just as with other historic eras, the period is divided into Early, Middle, and Late cultural expressions.

1000–500 B.C.E.   The major advancement that characterizes the Early Woodland Period is the invention firing clay cooking and storage containers producing harder, longer lasting pottery.

500 B.C.E.–900 C.E.   The Middle Woodland period exhibits the development of many mound building cultures. The major change that takes place in hunting and gathering societies is the gradual replacement of the spear with the bow and arrow. Detailed artistic expression evolves into a permanent cultural characteristic during this period also. Because of increased trade and the advancement of specialization, social structure within tribes and between tribes becomes more complex, creating social hierarchies in many areas.

500 B.C.E.–200 C.E.   The Adena Culture are hunting and gathering mound-builders that experiment with elementary farming.

100 B.C.E.–500 C.E.   The Hopewell culture live along rivers in central North America as both farmers and hunter-gatherers. They exhibit great skills as craftsmen in pottery, sculpture, and metalworking.

300–1300 C.E.   The peoples that evolve in the Middle Woodland periods often span the bridge into Late Woodland culture.

Hohokam peoples are desert farmers, fabric weavers, and eventually pueblo builders. They also share many cultural similarities with Mesoamerican Indians.

Anasazi cultures live in the Colorado Plateau as agriculturally dependant people. The early Anasazi represent the earliest "Basketmaker" people because of their extraordinary basket work. Some of their cultural traits includes stone carving skills exhibited in katchina, engineering experimentation evidenced by extensive road networks, and scientific understanding evident in the use of astronomical tools.

The Mogollon Culture functions as both farmers and hunters of the North American Southwest. They live in pithouses, then later in pueblos and share many cultural traits with their Anasazi contemporaries.

700   European contact (these dates varied based on tribal location).

Mississippian Culture covers much of central North America and extends into the Gulf of Mexico coastal region. They are mound-builders, astronomists, and skilled bow-and-arrow hunters. They also practice wide-scale agriculture and create great works of art.

900–1600   The Late Woodland period is the full realization of complex prehistoric Native North American societies. At some point during this period, all North American societies reach a peak in complex political, social, and economic development. The richness of individual tribal cultures demonstrates the level of complexity achieved within each society as well as the detailed differentiation between different tribes.

The geographic divisions used in this book fully evolve during this period: the northern and southern woodlands areas that comprise the eastern seaboard, prairie and plains environs, the Great Basin, the northwestern plateau expanse, the West Coast, and southwestern tribes.

1

THE PEOPLE AND THE ENVIRONMENT: WHO WAS HERE BEFORE COLUMBUS

I love to roam over the wild prairie. When we sit down, we grow pale and die.

White Bear, Kiowa Apache

In the study of pre-Columbian Native American peoples and their environments, geography plays a major role. This is one of the most commons ways for scholars to define different tribal personalities and characteristics. During the pre-Columbian period, details of daily life depended on where the tribe lived and how that environment affected the people. Because location was so important, this work divides most of North America into regions: the northern and southern woodlands areas that comprise the eastern seaboard; prairie, and plains environs; the Great Basin; the northwestern plateau expanse; the West Coast; and the Southwest. Each of these regions had distinct characteristics that directly influenced the tribes living in those areas, and this in turn made each tribe unique. Using these regional breakdowns, it will be easy to see how everything about a tribe resulted from its environment.

Geography and culture, however, do not imply levels of historical success or importance. Some environments were more difficult to survive in than others, but it is hard, if not impossible, to "rank" these societies in comparison with each other. History should not judge tribes as better or worse, but simply different. The tribal examples presented here have nothing to do with who history judges to be more important, significant, or successful. The examples instead reflect two things. First, using an order of presentation—such as always talking about woodland tribes first—helps with understanding regional differences and keeping them straight, and second, nature unfortunately leaves behind more information about some tribes than about others. One of the great losses in human history is the amount of evidence lost related to the Native American past. Written evidence concerning these societies is hard to come by, and much of what specialists know, they "dig up" from archeological sites and oral tradition. Looking back on societies that will never exist again is difficult enough, but the lack of direct proof complicates history even further. This means, barring some miraculous discoveries, that some stories are simply lost forever. The present culture's limited knowledge is based on surviving clues, and this is where the journey begins.

NORTHERN AND SOUTHERN WOODLAND TRIBES OF THE EASTERN SEABOARD

In 1620 William Bradford, Plymouth Colony's future governor, stated that the

vast & unpeopled countries of America . . . are fruitful & fitt for habitation, being devoyd of all civill inhabitants, where there are only savage & brutish men, which range up and downe, little otherwise than the wild beasts of the same. . . . And also those which should escape or overcome difficulties, should yet be in continuall danger of the savage people, who are cruell, barbarous, & most trecherous, being contente only to kill, & take away life, but delight to tormente men in the most bloodie maner that may be; fleaing some alive with the shells of fishes, cutting of the members & joynts of others by peesmeale, and broiling on the coles, eate the collops of their flesh in their sight whilst they live; with other cruelt[ies] most horrible to be related.

The problem with the statements in this quotation is that the settlers of Plymouth colony did not arrive at the New World until after this writing. On what was Bradford basing his description? What reports of the New World would give him such a negative view? Ignorance is too simple of an answer for these questions. Religion, fear, prejudice, and visions (or delusions) of superiority all played a role in shaping European expectations and interpretations of North America. When Christopher Columbus landed in the Americas, he held predetermined ideas of what and whom he would find. European records are not the most reliable place to start when looking for the truth about native North Americans. History must look farther back, to physical and oral evidence that came before the Europeans.

Tribes of the eastern seaboard provide a variety of pre-Columbian evidence for analysis and understanding. By the time of European contact, two strong confederations existed in the northern woodland region: the Ouendat (pronounced win-dot) Confederacy and the Five Nations of the Iroquois. This region and much of the continent hosted humans long before 1492, when Columbus "sailed the ocean blue." Some archeological evidence suggests that humans may have lived around the present-day border of the northeastern United States and southern Canada as long as 25,000 to 40,000 years ago. Scholars still question the longer estimates, but many suggest that following the end of the most recent ice age, ancient migrants moved into North America as the ice receded, following the spread of vegetation and animals over from Asia. This began the Paleo-Indian period, spanning from 9000 to about 7500 B.C.E. (before the Common Era, sometimes called "B.C."). History knows little of this period except regarding the growth of widespread tool usage toward the end, which moved the region into the Archaic period—7500 to 1000 B.C.E. The Paleo-Indians of this period used elaborate carving methods to create simple stone tools, and although the Archaic period eventually lost its high level of artistry, tools technology continued to develop. As tribes adapted to their environment, they invented tools to help that adaptation along.

Another development in woodland society was the use of pottery. For the woodlands of the East Coast, this signaled the beginning of the Early Woodland period, which lasted from 1000 B.C.E. to approximately 300 C.E. (Common Era, sometimes called "A.D."). The use of simple, coiled pottery signified a major step in people's use of their environment as collective, coordinated hunting and gathering became popular. However, there is little proof suggesting significant cultural differences between groups of people in the eastern woodlands up until this point. Changing methods of decorating pots suggest that by the beginning of the Middle Woodland period in 300 C.E., regions had begun developing their own cultural identities as a result of changing relationships with their environments. Woodland peoples began to include seasonal hunting and fishing as ways to feed themselves, giving people a more flexible source of tribal sustenance. Then, by the Late Woodland period, beginning in 900 C.E., the more simplistic method of coiling pottery had given way to the paddle and anvil procedure, which created a solid pottery piece more like today's ceramics, allowing for better storage and transportation. This advanced and efficient pottery resulted from, accompanied, and facilitated the growth of advanced agriculture, long-distance trade, cities, and protective fortification. Pottery and tool changes did not directly cause these major changes in society, and in many ways asking which changes came first is like asking if the chicken or the egg preceded the other. The changes do, however, work well as dividing lines of development, like signposts or mile markers indicating larger changes in society and its relationship to its environment.

Although not all woodland societies were at the same level of development at the same time, they all tended to go through the same stages on their own time clocks. Cultural differences became more and more noticeable as societies changed. For example, from artistic and religious perspectives, the Five Civilized Tribes of the South were vastly different from the northeastern tribes. Within the woodland regions, though, there were similarities in larger government and subsistence patterns. All of the eastern societies, both north and south, were more stationary than those to the west. Farming was the major form of subsistence, and hunting and gathering, along with fishing in some areas, supplemented their agricultural way of life. Governmentally, the northern confederacies and southern alliances formed the largest political units on the north side of Mexico, based on the stability provided by their sedentary lifestyle and woodland environments.

The largest common practice of many of the tribes was seasonal hunting and fishing, with the inclusion of simple, yet structured agriculture. The "still-hunting and stalking" season, as many of the Algonquian-speaking tribes called winter, saw the splitting of tribes into hunting parties or families that spread out across the eastern seaboard. When the first thaws arrived, these small groups migrated back to summer camps to exchange stories of the hardships and miracles of the past winter. They then spent the spring and summer planting and nurturing crops suited to their specific climates. Each tribe's experiences differed greatly, given that this region encompassed every natural environment of the North American East Coast. Its boundaries stretched from the Atlantic coastal plain on the east to the present-day Missouri and Mississippi rivers on the west, across today's Canadian border, and into southern Ontario and along the St. Lawrence River to the north. The southern border ran through the Blue Ridge Mountains and down into pine woodlands, eventually ending at the swamps of the Florida peninsula.

The best phrase to describe the natural environments in this expanse of land would be "microhabitats." These areas hosted extremely diverse collections of plant and animal life. Ecologists suggest that as much as 80 percent of the East Coast was "late successional" or old-growth forest. The size, structure, and permanence of the forest patches depended on environmental and human factors. The term *late successional* indicates forests shaped and affected by centuries of influences, disturbed little by man. Ancient trees, woody debris, and centuries of climatic events created flexible, sustainable microenvironments that were apparently suitable for a wide variety of plant and animal species. As discussed in the Wilderness Society's work on the present-day conservation of biodiversity in the East, some species of fowl, insect, and reptile were relatively unsuited for life outside of the canopied environment of old-growth forests.[1] Heightened soil productivity and plentiful nutrients encouraged greater vegetation diversity than is possible in a man-managed environment. Many of these species did not adapt well to change, making them dependant on more mature, unmanaged, heavily grown forests. Even though natives practiced limited seasonal agriculture, the effects were minimal and relatively noninvasive, especially in comparison to the European farmers that came later. Although the details varied along the coast, most native agriculture intruded little upon the wild woodland environment.

Some standard government features evolved from the semi-nomadic lifestyle of seasonal agriculture coupled with hunting and fishing. Most eastern governments set up different offices or positions to deal with different tribal experiences. The separation of leadership between the war chief and the civil chief is a perfect example of division of power. A man could not be both civil chief and war chief at the same time. Most tribes saw the two positions as a conflict of interest. Socially, young men had to win war honors to be eligible for full citizenship and participation in the tribe and its government. This was necessary if the young man hoped for tribal counsel membership and perhaps eventual chiefdom. Many societies felt that only through war experience would their younger generations come to value peace as the ultimate goal. If a sitting chief chose to go on the warpath, he was required to resign his civil or peacetime control. The understanding was that civil chiefs would stress peace within their own tribes and discourage young warriors hungry for war honors from moving too hastily to violence. A war chief would and should have different goals. Territorial issues concerning both agriculture and hunting or fishing often required a war chief experienced in the needs of his tribe as well as knowledgeable about the nature of surrounding societies. When there was peace among tribes, the civil chief guided the people through the challenges of migration and survival. These tribes' semi-nomadic lifestyle made the position of war chief necessary because of the inevitable clashes over territorial rights. This environment also made the office of civil chief necessary for the tribe's survival and growth.

History now calls these societies the Eastern Woodland tribes. The first explorers and settlers did not consider these peoples a major presence, and within 150 years of their first arrival, that perception became fact. The population count in 1650 was only 10 percent of what experts estimate the population count was at first contact. The environment in which the native people lived changed drastically as well. What used to be small areas of native farming lands bordered by wild forests became overgrown woodlands as the native populations began to die off as a result of disease and confrontation with Europeans. This led many Europeans of the 1500s and 1600s to describe the land as wild, untamed, and uncivilized when, in reality, had they been able to step back in time, they would have found a coast teeming with diverse human, animal, and plant life. History continues to explore the reality of this vanished forested region, its animal life, its vegetation, and its peoples.

THE PRAIRIE SOCIETIES

The East Coast served as the earliest meeting place of Europeans and native North Americans. The further west across the continent a native society lived, the later the contact with Europeans usually came as a result of the natural progression of European westward expansion.

In some ways, the effects of white contact were like a wave washing across the continent. In the case of more western American Indians, delayed European contact has meant fewer early European records of their society. European perception of prairie culture and society still today skews analysis of the Midwestern native reality. "The people of the Great Plains Culture Area are unique because their lifestyle evolved after contact with the Europeans."[2] This excerpt, taken from a high school learning project and accompanying Web site, suggests that the prehistoric peoples of the plains were a static, uninteresting society just waiting for European contact to help them become a fully developed culture. Nothing could be further from the truth.

Because of the nature of prairie environments, pre-Columbian societies further west evolved very differently than the East Coast tribes. With their region bordered on the east by the Mississippi River and the west by the Rocky Mountains, while stretching from southern Canada all the way to Texas, the American Indians in the prairie faced different hardships, enjoyed different advantages, and developed different survival methods. Although they were farmers, like their cousins to the east, a larger percentage of their food came from hunting buffalo and other wild animals on the wide, flat prairie expanses. Swirling like an immense sea of grass and wildflowers, prairies provided herd animals for food, little protection for natural shelter, and danger when lightning struck. Long, dry summers and cold, blustery winters shaped the prairie peoples into societies that embraced, appreciated, and respected their rugged environment.

The prairies themselves have different characteristics in different areas of the region. Shortgrass, which only grew to be a foot tall, flourished in the drier areas around present-day Iowa and Oklahoma. Where there was more moisture, prairie grasses grew longer and taller. Further east, the grasses grew as high as 8 to 10 feet tall. Fire also played a major role in establishing and maintaining prairie environments. Natural burning prevented the encroachment of woody growth that might choke out delicate prairie grasses and it helped the grasses develop survival mechanisms. The main root structure of the prairie grass plant existed entirely below the soil, where fire could not damage it. Prairie grasses evolved this survival feature as a result of regular seasonal fires. Nature took care of this balance process through lightning strikes, creating a yearly cycle of fire that forced prairie grasses to develop deep, resilient roots. During the Paleo and Archaic Indian periods, grasslands were the most predominant vegetation environments in this region. Grasslands covered approximately 7.5 billion acres of the 19.25 billion total acres in prehistoric United States. Modern human habitation changed that, but for thousands of years, natives worked with the environment instead of against it.

bozho nikan! ahaw nciwe'nmoyan ewabmlnan. iwgwien e'byayen ms'ote'. This typical greeting in the Powtawatomi language—translated as "Greetings, friends, I am glad to see you. Thank you for your visit here"—represents the hospitable attitude of many prairie tribes. Faced with environmental challenges, prairie societies tended to be strongly interdependent units. Although little early agricultural evidence survives today, there is proof that many prairie tribes developed farming methods about the same time as eastern cultures. The earliest evidence of maize or corn cultivation in all of North America by humans is in prehistoric Mexico around 3500 B.C.E. These practices eventually reached prairie tribes around 400 C.E., whereas eastern tribes showed elementary farming practices as early as 100 C.E. Then within 500 years, evidence suggests, that new growing practices allowed the planting of beans, pumpkins, squash, and melons as well. Archaeological evidence of dwellings, deep pits, pottery, and bone hoes testify to the complex reality of native prairie life during this period. Cahokia, a Mississippian archaeological site near present-day St. Louis, functioned as a major trade center, and evidence of temple mounds and other structures suggests a complex culture. Cahokia began its growth around 800 C.E., experienced a golden age between 1000 and 1250 C.E., and continued to house perhaps as many as 30,000 inhabitants until almost 1400 C.E. The Cahokia archaeological site offers the most complete picture of a large prehistoric prairie trading and civilization center north of Mexico.

Evidence from sites outside of Cahokia indicates that ideas and items traveled great distances to and from this trading center. Copper, obsidian, gulf-shell, and turquoise jewelry, along with various cultural styles of pottery, are some of the artifacts found at many sites where they could not have originated, but were connected in some way to Cahokia. This suggests that Cahokia was a major trading center, as does its strategic positioning at the meeting point of the eastern woodlands, the northern prairies, the Ozarks, and the Mississippi valley to the south. This area offered a collection of natural resources unavailable to most societies of this time. The prairies to the north provided grasses for buildings and furnishings. The eastern woodlands offered foraging and hunting opportunities, as well as hardwoods for the construction of canoes, tools, weapons, and buildings. The Mississippi Valley provided game for hunting, rich waterways for fishing, and fertile soil for planting. The Ozarks offered rocks and minerals unavailable anywhere else: sandstone, limestone, granite, and chert used in toolmaking, without which the Mississippian society would not have been able to evolve. Few pre-Columbian societies enjoyed so many natural resources within such easy reach.

The Mississippi, Illinois, and Missouri rivers meet here as well, creating an extremely fertile flood plain. Now called the American Bottom, the area stretches approximately 70 miles along the Mississippi, close to Cahokia. Streams connected to the Mississippi flooded in the spring, bringing riverbed silt to fertilize the land and providing the opportunity for extensive, successful farming. These waterways served a dual purpose; they also gave Mississippian tribes access to travel for hunting, trading, and cultural exchange. These societies may have been the most socially advanced of any north of Mexico, and this resulted directly from the environmental advantages these Mississippians enjoyed.

This diversity had to begin somewhere, and the origin of the prairie peoples is hotly debated. Scientific evidence suggests that the migration route from Siberia through Alaska and into Canada carried a major strand of early inhabitants right into the crux of the North American continent. How early this occurred is still in question, but the most recent possible date for the Mississippi flood plains would be 10,000 years ago, with some scientists suggesting that it could be as far back as 25,000 to 40,000 years ago. Some spear points found in the fossilized remains of mastodons suggest that paleo-hunters killed the animals over 12,000 years ago, and there are a few evidence claims dating prairie habitation much earlier. There are two sites in South America that date much earlier than these suggestions. One site dates back to 12,500 years ago, and the second, 33,000 years. For either of these dates to work, assuming that humans walked across the Bering or Beringia Strait, they would have had to have been living in North America a minimum of 14,000 to 15,000 years ago, and most say this is not possible. An alternative suggestion is that prairie tribes were related to tribes further south around the Florida peninsula, rather than being direct descendants of ancient migratory humans. If this is the true connection, it suggests that the development of Mississippian culture did not take place independently in the prairie environs, but rather as an expansion off of an already-established native culture further to the south.

Another challenge prairie peoples adapted to was a climate that began to warm around 9000 B.C.E., causing changes in plant and animal life. The Paleo-Indian way of life adapted to these changes, eventually moving into the Archaic period around 7500, like the eastern tribes. Larger game animals began to die off, and smaller mammals, fish, and fowl flourished. They did not discard migratory hunting just yet, but rather adopted a more seasonal approach to sustenance, using what food sources were available as the seasons changed. Evidence indicates that small-scale trading began at this point, greatly predating, but also setting the stage for, the massive trading complex that Cahokia would become. The best word to describe these people would be "experimenters." They seemed to experiment with everything, looking for better ways to interact and deal with their environment. Tool quality, variety, and use grew greatly during the Archaic period of the Mississippians. By watching the growth cycles of food plants, they experimented with elementary farming in small garden settings. Little evidence remains from the period between 8000 and 1000 B.C.E., but apparently the years between 1000 and 600 B.C.E. saw growth in many prairie cultures as the people began to settle down on a seasonal basis to the business of building a civilization. This is where and when researchers can trace the more recent ancestors of Cahokia and its tribes. The now-native peoples became tied to their lands more than ever. For example, the earliest evidence of mound-building, a unique cultural indicator of prairie and Midwestern people, is from around 500 B.C.E., when the Adena constructed some of the first-known small mounds in the Ohio River Valley. The idea spread quickly, and societies throughout the prairie lands began constructing mounds for religious, social, economic, and governmental purposes.

Enter the Mississippians and the period of Cahokia's success. They based their government system on chiefdoms, with a chief's territory based on distinctive floodplain regions. The best assumption concerning the chief's main duties is that they involved controlling the distribution of food to his main community as well as to outlying settlements. There is evidence that hints at other responsibilities as well, such as religious roles, artisan employment, and political leadership, but the proof is too unreliable to result in definite conclusions. The most popular opinion is that agricultural and climatic changes affected the powers of chiefs so much that their influence was probably very limited. This form of government stretched through Mississippian areas all the way from the prairies and down the Mississippi River itself.

Considering the tribes that occupied the lands to the north of Cahokia, the earliest dated inhabitants lived in the Illinois prairie environment around 10,000 B.C.E to 9,000 B.C.E. Human habitation existed continuously in this area for about 3,000 years before the development of rudimentary agriculture, suggesting that prairie hunting and gathering societies were already somewhat stationary prior to fully settling into a more agriculturally dependant lifestyle. The Archaic-period prairie dweller was peaceful. He apparently enjoyed leisure time, but spent little energy in creative efforts. Surviving evidence does not suggest art was one of his pastimes. In 2500 B.C.E., the average life span was only 32 years, but this was long enough to construct what may be the oldest houses in the United States. Physical remains suggest that common diseases were tuberculosis, arthritis, and syphilis. Surprisingly, despite an abundant food supply, the population numbers appear relatively stable, and growth of the prairie populace was fairly limited through the early centuries of the Common Era. Although not complete, this snapshot offers an insightful glance into the life of prehistoric prairie humanity.

When examining the western prairie lands, the Pawnee offer interesting opportunities for study and analysis. "Pawnee," derived from *parika*, or "horn," identifies tribes who settled in the present-day Nebraska area, having migrated north from the Texas region. "Horn" is an appropriate name; it was a term used for the wearing of a "scalp-lock," in which the hair was stiffened with paint and fat and made to stand curved like a horn. They called themselves the *chahiksichahiks*, or "men of men," and lived in earthen houses along creeks and streams for over 500 years. Because they relied largely on the cultivation of beans, maize, squash, and pumpkins, much of their existence resembled their prairie cousins to the east. Introduction of the horse by the Spanish to Pawnee society mobilized the Pawnees later on in their development, giving them a cultural connection to Plains natives, but ultimately their dependence on agriculture and relatively sedentary lifestyle keeps them in the prairie category. Prairie tribes, faced with difficult environmental obstacles, developed unique shelter, sustenance, and societal aspects that allowed them to thrive in an environment of extremes.

THE PLAINS OF NORTH AMERICA

The Plains Indians represent, visually, what most people around the world think of when they think "Native American." They hunted and ate buffalo, rode horses after contact with the Spanish, and lived in tepees. Unlike the Woodland and Prairie tribes, Plains Indians did not develop extensive agriculture as a form of sustenance. They were much more migratory, basing their society on hunting and gathering. The plains of North America span the continent from the border of Alberta, Canada, down to northern Mexico, and they sit between the Missouri River and the Rocky Mountains. Although the plains are basically covered in grass, the vegetation is different from prairie grasslands and is interspersed with groves of cottonwood and willow trees around water sources. Low, rolling plains make up the contour of the landscape and contain several extensive river systems. The soil of much of the lower and eastern plains areas would have been rich for farming, but the nature of animal life and wide open expanses encouraged a dependence on hunting. It did not rain much, and when it did, the storms, which occurred in the summer, were often short and violent. The winters were cold and dry. Wild-growing edible flora included many low-growing plants such as ground turnips, berries, nuts, sunflowers, and beans, giving the natives the ability to supplement hunting with gathering. Antelope, deer, bison, and elk populated the land, and this combination set the stage for the development of migratory peoples.

Specialists commonly accept the idea that humans came to North America approximately 10,000 to 12,000 years ago. Some more recently discovered evidence in the plains implies, however, that humans may have lived there as long as 14,000 years ago or more. Many scientists agree that the inhabitants known as the "Clovis" culture represent the earliest known peoples of North America, named for the location in New Mexico of the first discovery of what is now called the Clovis point. This is a spear point sometimes called a prehistoric "weapon of mass destruction." Because it was apparently very effective at killing large mammals, scholars credit the Clovis point with the extinction of mammoths and the decimation of other large species. Evidence of Clovis inhabitance in the plains is rather widespread. Archaeologists have found artifacts in different areas across North America that suggest there were peoples here long before the accepted Clovis period of 11,000 to 10,000 B.C.E. One site in Texas, directed by Michael Collins, suggests that an older Clovis culture goes way beyond the simplistic picture of prehistoric survival. Evidence at the Gault, Texas, dig shows a complex culture, complete with a well-rounded diet, complicated trade network, a multitude of tools, and perhaps the oldest art in North America. Collins suggests that

the longstanding notion of the rapid spread of Clovis across the continent has been taken to mean the spread of a people across the continent. An alternative might be that the spread of Clovis is actually the expansion of a technology across existing populations—analogous to the fact you can go anywhere in the world and find people driving John Deere tractors. (NOVA's "Stone Age Explorers")

In contrast with the idea of people moving across a continent taking the tool with them, this would mean that people were here for much longer than previously believed and simply developed a tool that caught on.

Eventually, the Plains people moved out of the Paleo period and into the Plains Archaic, a period dominated by hunting. Regionally, some tribes included major gathering efforts as well, but for a while, hunting bison was the most popular method of feeding society. By 5000 B.C.E., most Plains tribes had incorporated some gathering into their subsistence patterns as well. Some areas also began hunting smaller animal and fowl. Few archaeological sites show that camps were reoccupied on a regular basis, suggesting there was no predictable pattern to tribal migration. This makes sense, though, given that following grazing herds and utilizing plant growth along the way would require moving where the hunting and gathering was best, rather than repeatedly staying at sites where the resource supply could be used up. Sites that did see repeated use were most often located near "jump-off" points, where tribes would herd bison to cliffs and force a jump to their deaths. After the beginning of the Middle Archaic period, the climate began to improve, leading to larger herds because of increased growth in ground forage for them to eat. In human society, cultural diversity became apparent as well, as evidenced through medicine wheels, for example. These wheels, which are stone circles of varying size, may have had more than one function. Ceremonial and religious purposes and the honoring of fallen warriors are just a sampling of suggested roles. These constructions, along with the discovery of diverse tools and pottery, show that Archaic Indians were in a dynamic state of societal and cultural development.

One such tribe was the Blackfoot of the northern central plains. These Algonquian-speaking tribes were largely located in Montana and Alberta. The name Blackfoot was probably a reflection of ash-stained moccasins worn by the people. They are representative of Plains Indians in that they were nomadic hunter-gatherer societies who lived on bison and low-growing plants and lived in tepees. They also hunted small animals, but their main fare was the buffalo. Almost everything they needed could be provided by that one animal. Besides being cooked, the meat could also be dried into jerky or pemmican, a protein-rich food that would store for years. Bones became tools, horns turned into liquid containers, muscle sinew stretched into thread, and hair proved to be perfect braiding for clothing. Hooves served as musical instruments or were boiled down for glue. Tanned hides were perfect for protective clothing as well as for tepee skins. Few areas of North America enjoyed such a singular resource treasure like the buffalo.

Blackfoot dependence on the bison also created different gender relationships and responsibility than in other tribes. Women were in charge of skin tanning, which was a long, tedious, tiring process. They often measured a woman's worth by the quality and quantity of her hide production. In addition to making clothing and moccasins, women also tanned the skins for tepees, giving them ownership of family dwellings. This twist in gender role and responsibility was rare in Native American life. The women of the tribes produced just about everything else as well, including tools, drums, pipes, shields, and weapons. Men were the defenders and the hunters, but the women were fully in charge of making that happen, giving them a voice and power that not all native women enjoyed.

Another "typical" and highly recognizable people of the plains were the Siouan people. Among the Siouan descendants are the Sioux of the Dakotas. The oldest evidence of human habitation in the Dakotas reaches back to 11,500 B.C.E. The language and customs of the oldest Siouan peoples are lost to history, but scientists do know that early migrants camped in the Dakotas, following bison, mammoths, mastodon, and other large game animals. Climatic changes indicated the beginning of the Archaic era of the northern plains, and warming temperatures brought vegetation, animal life, and landscape changes. Then for 3,000 years of this period, the Dakota area experienced long, hot droughts sometimes interspersed with heavy, torrential rains. The droughts dried out most chances for successful habitation or plant growth, and the rains washed away massive amounts of soil, leaving the area with few resources. The nature of these drastic weather patterns required both humans and animals to be constantly on the move. Eroded areas could provide some temporary shelter, but not for long. Small bands of nomadic hunters became very good at what they did out of necessity. It would take many generations before the Dakota lands would become more permanently habitable.

By 400 B.C.E., the massive weather movements had subsided, and new, more hospitable conditions took over. Rainfall became less destructive and more predictable, producing lush forests and larger herds of big game animals such as the bison. Hunting and gathering became the Dakota mainstay, but limited agriculture made an appearance also. Natives added smaller animals, such as fox, beaver, and squirrel, along with fish and waterfowl to their diets. These changes in hunting, along with two specific cultural developments, mark the dividing line between the Archaic Plains and the Woodland Plains, which lasted for these people from 400 B.C.E. to 1000 C.E. The use of ceramic pottery and distinct burial mounds signifies cultural development in the Plains tribes and significant advancement in societal complexity.

This led the Dakota peoples into the Village Plains era. By 1000 C.E., Native Americans settled into what most think of as a typical native lifestyle. Hunting and gathering were already part of the plains culture, and now limited farming was added. Farming was the development that permitted the growth of more long-term, seasonal settlements. The harsh nature of winter on the plains required tribes to move in late fall to winter camps that were more protective and that offered suitable natural resources for winter survival. Family crops of the spring and summer were small one- to five-acre fields of sunflowers, corn, beans, and squash. Families in the northern Dakotas often lived in earthlodges constructed of frames covered with sod and grasses, providing good protection from an often-hostile climate. In the southern Dakota areas, tepees were more common, resembling the Blackfoot mode of housing. This was the basic way of life in the Dakota plains for over 700 years. European contact came in 1738 when Pierre Gaultier de Sieur de la Verendrye arrived in the northern part of the Dakotas. He was the first known white to come in contact with Dakota natives and provided the earliest known accounts of the people. The arrival of this Frenchman closed the door on plains pre-history and ushered in the age of European contact, putting the Dakota Sioux and many other Plains Indians on an entirely new historical path.

INDIANS OF THE PLATEAU

Fifteen million years ago, lava welled up from inside the planet and formed the plateau that constitutes present-day Oregon, Washington, and southern British Columbia. Thirteen million years later, glaciers moved in to cover the region and did not recede until 15,000 years ago. Sometime between 12,000 and 30,000 years ago, humans traipsed across the Beringia land bridge between Siberia and Alaska, but they were probably prevented from traveling into the plateau area by the expansive glaciers. The ice did eventually melt, unleashing ice dams, which created the "Spokane floods" that carved Grand Coulee and Puget Sound out of the landscape. This fashioned a "shrub-steppe" environment scattered with forested areas that sits between the Rocky Mountains and the Cascades. It is named for the most common vegetation—the shrub—and the Russian word *steppe*, which means "vast, treeless plain." The winters in this area were cold and wet with blowing, blustery snow and hot, rather dry summers, with cooler nights that provided a welcome relief from the blistering heat of the day.

Grasses and shrubs were the most common ground cover. The landscape was littered with sagebrush that had completed its growth cycle, becoming the rolling tumbleweed so many associate with the Wild West. Mixed in with the shrubs and grasses were a variety of wildflowers as well, adding color to the earthen-hued scenery. Small birds, mammals, reptiles, and amphibians lived amongst the low-lying vegetation. Many mammals were burrowing animals out of necessity; living underground provided convenient, effective cover from the extremes of the climate. Pocket mice and ground squirrels provided a food source for larger predatory animals such as coyotes, hawks, and bobcats. Elk and mule deer were common, along with badgers and a large variety of birds. A few species of lizards and toads made their home on the steppe, as well. Northern Pacific Rattlesnakes rounded out the steppe's small complement of reptiles to create a diverse population of wildlife.

There were not enough large game animals to support a fully developed hunting culture, though. The rugged soil of the plateau did not lend itself to farming either. Instead, many plateau tribes perfected the art of fishing and supplemented that with gathering wild plants in the river valleys and grasslands. The key to survival was the salmon that swam up from the ocean during the spring and summer to lay eggs. Natives perfected different fishing techniques, depending on culture and location. They used long spears, handheld nets, weighted nets, small traps, and large underwater corrals called *weirs*. The fish were most useful dried, so that the people could eat through the winter. Fishing affected everything in their lives, from gender roles and government structure to art and leisure. Once again, strategies of survival necessitated by environmental factors shaped a group of people into unique society units entirely tied to their natural surroundings.

One of these unique societies, the Nez Perce, knew themselves as the *numipu,* or the "real people." *Nez Perce,* in French, means "pierced nose," which comes from the Shoshone description given to Lewis and Clark of the land their neighbors lived on as the Land of the Pierced Nose. This was actually a mistake; the tribes that practiced piercing were further to the west and south. *Numipu* land was situated in the valleys of the Clearwater and Snake rivers in present-day Washington. The prehistoric residents of the Nez Perce were highly mobile people who utilized forest resources until the time came to winter by the rivers. When settling down for long, cold snows, the ancestors of the Nez Perce were just as adaptable as when using forest resources. Using what was available, they often built partially subterranean houses framed with wood and covered with sod and grass. This made the homes easy to keep cool in the summer and warm in the winter, if they chose to use them year-round. The short stature of the houses protected them from winds as well. As the ancient natives moved through the Archaic period and into their Woodland period of development, the houses became larger and grew more permanent. Several family groups lived together in one building, and the tribal groups grew in size. Situating themselves next to a river provided a source of fresh fish through the winter, although fishing catches diminished greatly when the weather turned colder. These Plateau natives adapted perfectly to their environments, finding the most efficient and effective ways to live not in spite of, but in conjunction with, environmental gifts and challenges.

An interesting discovery in 1996 that received national attention came out of the Columbia Plateau. Scientists have not had the opportunity to draw many conclusions yet, but the discovery of the "Kennewick Man" created uproar in governmental, native, and scientific communities. Boat-race spectators discovered skeletal remains at a park in Kennewick, Washington, and in trying to decide who had the right to determine Kennewick Man's fate, many court battles have taken place. The Army Corps of Engineers had initial possession, but according to the Native American Graves Protection and Repatriation Act, if there is a connection between discovered remains and a living tribe, the tribe is the rightful owner with full decision power. The problem is that discoveries like this do not surface very often, and scientists considered this a rare opportunity to look at a little-understood period in time. Carbon dating showed Kennewick Man had lived approximately 8,400 years ago, making him one of the oldest, most complete skeletons discovered in the Americas. He was in his early 40s when he died and suffered many serious wounds during his lifetime. In addition to the carbon dating, there is evidence that culturally distinguishes him from more recent native tribes. First, his people used no cradle boards to flatten the front portion of the skull in childhood. Next, later Native Americans tended to experience significant arthritis and develop heavy wear on their teeth as a result of their diet. Kennewick Man experienced neither of these physical factors. The bone structure itself fits neither typical native nor Caucasian patterns, and the best current speculation is that he could be of South Asian origins. The debate he ignited is an important one. After all of the suffering of and injustice experienced by the Native Americans in North America, shouldn't they have the right to claim their ancestors and bury them as tradition mandates? Do scientists have the right to discoveries, regardless of their connections, so that people may learn more about human origins and ancient history? Should it be a case of "finders, keepers"? Kennewick Man potentially holds many secrets about human history in his bones, and the jury is still out as to whether those secrets will see the light of day.

NATIVES OF THE GREAT BASIN

Geographically, the Great Basin includes parts of Wyoming, Idaho, and Oregon, inland California, and most of Nevada and Utah. The physical borders are the Columbia Plateau to the north, the Colorado Plateau to the south, the Rocky Mountains on the east, and the Sierra Nevada Mountains

on the west. Current ecological conditions differ greatly from what earlier natives would have encountered. Today the region experiences less
than one foot of rain per year, and much of this the soil cannot absorb, so
instead it runs off in flash floods. *Playas*, or wetland lakes, are a common
geographical feature of the basin because of recent geological activity.
Although today this is generally a drier area, in the higher altitudes more
microenvironments thrive, such as areas of low-growing plants or alpine
forests. Dry lakes and riverbeds suggest that during earlier centuries,
there were rivers and lakes with more plant and animal life than exists
today. During the Pleistocene Epoch (more than 11,000 years ago), much
of this area was covered by Lake Lahotan and other large bodies of water.
Over the last 11,000 years, those waters evaporated, leaving some of the
larger lakes behind, such as the Great Salt Lake of Utah. Some of the plant
species found in the Mojave Desert of the Great Basin are some of the oldest living organisms on earth. In the 1960s, scientists cut down for study
a Great Basin Bristlecone Pine, finding that it was almost 5,000 years old.
There is also some suggestion that there are creosotebush plants (ever-
green, multibranched, open shrubs) in the Mojave that top 10,000 years of
age. In some ways plants and riverbeds can speak to future generations,
revealing secrets of landscapes gone by.

The next geological age was the Holocene of the last 11,000 years.
A warmer and drier climate began to develop as mountain glaciers
receded from the area. During the earlier epoch, climate conditions
pushed many species to adaptation, extinction, or most often, migration
upward in altitude or south. In the process, many adapted to drought and
heat conditions, and as the glaciers melted and receded, different species
moved back into the Great Basin area as it dried out. This major climatic
change set up the desert-like conditions we associate today with the Great
Basin. It is important to remember that although the major geographic
feature associated with the Great Basin is desert, scattered throughout are
higher- and lower-altitude microenvironments that bear no resemblance
to the desert norm. Some scientists (Gould 1992) suggest that this period
was simply another interglacial period and that glaciers will again form
and take over the region. The only two environmental choices for the
future seem to be renewed glaciation or adaptation to global warming
produced by a technological society.

The northern Great Basin showed the first signs of human habitation
around 9000 B.C.E. Because it was a drier area of the continent, the conditions favored preservation of artifacts that would normally disappear
over time. Archaeologists have found nets, textiles, baskets, and other
containers, as well as complete arrows and wooden pieces of art. These
types of artifacts provide societal insights normally lost to historical study.
Because of limited vegetation and animal life, these hunter-gatherers
lived on a rather narrowly defined diet. Pine nuts, acorns, wild beans,
wheatgrass, and berries were typical gathered foods. There were a few

tribes who employed limited agrarian efforts, growing corn, beans, and squash, but the harsh nature of the environment limited these attempts. For meat, the easiest, most accessible source was fish. Small game supplemented their protein intake; rabbits, rodents, snakes, lizards, small desert antelope, and birds were not abundant, but definitely provided valuable nourishment when available.

The most precious resource to Basin Indians was water. Food sources were not plentiful, but fresh water was even harder to come by. Wood was scarce, and as a result of resource hardships, Basin societies highly valued skilled toolmakers. One way to overcome the obstacle of limited resources was developing a strong dependence on family groups. Combining the efforts of many to search out new resource reservoirs made the job much easier and more productive. In hunting, small family groups would participate in animal drives, in which they drove large animals (such as antelope), smaller mammals, and even grasshoppers into corralled or trapping areas, providing more sustenance for the tribe than would be possible if they worked as individual hunters. Everything these natives did was strictly tied to the environmental advantages and disadvantages of the desert lands. Their housing especially reflected this dependence and adaptation. Housing types changed with the extreme swings of the seasons in order to provide the best shelter possible in a harsh environment. In the summer, lean-tos or windbreak constructions made of desert brush worked best to give protection from wind and sun, while allowing for alternating ventilation for the hot day and insulation (by lowering the sides) from the cooler nights. During the winters, cone-shaped *wickiups* made of poles covered with sod, grass, brush, or animal skins provided a more insulated, moisture-proof shelter against the heavy rains of late fall and early spring and snows in the winter.

Around 2000 B.C.E., desert natives moved into their Archaic period and showed significant cultural advancements. Natives developed a coiled pottery that was almost waterproof, perfecting their ability to carry and store perishable goods. Archaeologists have found duck decoys, suggesting developments in hunting techniques. Sickles for harvesting wild grass show a technological adaptation to the tribe's surroundings. In order for these people to survive, their methods of hunting and gathering had to improve greatly. To provide necessities for the people, groups had to be prepared to move frequently as they exhausted local resources. Toward the end of the late prehistoric period, limited agriculture caught on, but lack of water sources kept this development from spreading. In the eastern and southern portions of the Great Basin area, natives increased their agricultural activities to include regular planting and harvesting cycles on a small scale. Most often, the food plant of choice was a root-type food. Tribes in the western areas experimented with root foods also, but the environmental challenges of climate and water supply prevented western tribes from developing a more advanced farming culture.

In fact, the often scarce availability of resources also regulated the size of the tribes, keeping them smaller than in other areas of the continent. Population density during the late pre-Columbian period ranged from 25 people per 40 square miles to less than 10 in harsher areas. The entire Great Basin housed probably 45,000 people total, and that population count did not vary much up or down, despite often unforgiving climate conditions. As an interesting historical aside, it was only after European contact that population numbers dropped dramatically—in less than 200 years, the area native population had dropped to 12,000 in 1930, the known record low, because of disease and conflict. Precontact populations relied heavily on seasonal settlement patterns, which differed across the region. River zones offered good hunting and low-growing food plants for gathering. Valley floors provided grass seeds and some successful hunting environments. Lakes and marshes supplied fish and waterfowl for meat and cattail and other water plants for roughage. In the more mountainous areas, berries and roots were plentiful, and mountain animals proved good for hunting. Depending on the character of the often harsh environment, Native Americans of the Great Basin adapted their society to best survive in conjunction with nature.

Two tribes stand out as representative examples of late pre-Columbian Great Basin cultures: the Shoshone-Bannock and the Paiute. Coming out of the desert tradition, these people stand out as representative desert natives with their use of baskets and grinding stones. They collected seeds and carried, stored, and boiled them all in advanced, almost-waterproof baskets. They made their weapon points wider and generally smaller than their big-game–hunting cousins to the north and the east. Hunters often mounted these points on the ends of spears and threw them with the aid of a spear-throwing device. They did not need bigger tips because the largest animals they usually hunted were wild sheep, antelope, and deer. The lifestyle described here was prevalent in the Archaic Desert era and began over 10,000 years ago, continuing and evolving until European contact in the early 1800s. The Shoshone and Paiute are the cultural descendants of the Archaic Desert traditions. This culture is a good example of what results when people must adapt to their environment. There were no desert areas in Alaska, Canada, or the areas of Asia that early migrants might have come from, so this culture must have developed after the people reached the desert areas. In the 1700s and 1800s, these cultures showed their adaptive tendencies again by assimilating Plains culture into their own through the adoption of horses and tepees. These are only some examples of survival and adjustment techniques embraced by Native Americans living in some of the harshest environments in North America, second only to the Arctic and sub-Arctic regions of present-day Canada.

SOUTHWESTERN NORTH AMERICA

Native southwestern North America includes most of Arizona, New Mexico, and the western Mexican states of Sinaloa and Sonora, as well as the western parts of Durango and Chihuahua. Most of this area is truly desert land, unlike the plains region that, although it is a rather dry climate, is not a desert in the truest sense of the definition. Settlements here formed around oasis spots of water and vegetation. Agriculture was very important to all southwestern tribes, but settlements did not spread out to use vast tracts of land and water resources. They instead centered in towns or villages known as *pueblos*. Among these tribes are the Zuni, Hopi, Navaho, Mohave, and Apache. The Mexican tribal names are less well-known, but some enjoy a bit of notoriety: the Yaqui and the Tarahumara are two examples. One unique feature of these tribes is that out of all of the Native American groups in North America, this region and its people is one of the least disturbed by contact with Westerners and Europeans, following only the Inuit of the Arctic areas in their seclusion. This means that present-day groups still exhibit many traditions beliefs, attitudes, and customs somewhat less influenced by Western contact. This gives us a window into what other native communities might have evolved into had they been left more to their own historical devices.

Consider the following question: would agriculture have evolved in forested areas or desert areas first? Although forested areas might have offered *easier* farming opportunities, anthropologists suggest that the first areas of civilization to see the advent of farming were often the desert lands. Look at it this way: necessity breeds invention. The Southwest, out of necessity, forced the people who chose to live on its lands to find alternate, reliable, and sustainable ways of providing food for their communities. The oldest civilizations in the world, Egypt and Mesopotamia, based their lives around agriculture. In harsh climates, early people gravitated to fertile river areas, quickly adapting through observation and experimentation to provide a consistent food supply. Archaeological evidence implies that farming first took root in the American Southwest about 4,000 years ago. For 1,500 years, hunting and gathering supplemented the growing agricultural lifestyle, but slowly desert peoples mastered the art of farming and became completely dependant on it. Corn, specifically, was largely responsible for this development and solidified the sedentary lifestyle that had been budding for almost two millennia. The *pueblo* peoples built some of the most unique North American dwellings in the process of settling down to agricultural pursuits, creating monumental cliff, cave, and desert cities unlike anywhere else on the continent.

Based on their individual environments, several major cultural strands emerged from the desert heat. The Anasazi, Hohokam, Mogollon, and Sinagua are traditions of the desert Archaic period. More is known about earlier expressions of desert culture than about other areas of North

America, and the arid, dry climate is the surprising ally. Deserts provide a perfect atmosphere for the preservation of organic artifacts. One of the most dangerous elements in the process of preservation is moisture. As one of the most destructive forces on the planet, its virtual absence in the Southwest helped save a wealth of artifacts for historical study. One such site, Pendejo Cave in southern New Mexico, preserved evidence that fuels archeological controversy. It may be one of the oldest examples, if not *the* oldest example, of evidence of human habitation in North America. Most of the easily dated artifacts reach back 13,000 years, but some of the deepest layers may be as old as 50,000 years. Should this latter number be proven and accepted, it would overturn many theories about the length and nature of human occupancy on this continent. By now, it seems that all regions have at least one site that is in the running for the status of oldest known human presence in North America. Can they all be right? The answer to that is yes and no. Despite the focus on who has the oldest or most legitimate claim, the important questions ask what we *do not* know. The fact that these sites keep offering new evidence and information suggests that the hunt is far from over. If nothing else, it guarantees lifetimes of study for future generations.

One relatively recent deduction is that the climate was a good 10 degrees cooler with a higher average rainfall than what the American Southwest experiences today. Typical desert vegetation grew only at the lowest elevations, with significant caches of vegetation growing as low as 1,000 feet. This was the time of desert Paleo-Indians, lasting through 6500 B.C.E.. The desert Archaic period took over then and lasted until 1200 B.C.E. What followed was a patchwork quilt of overlapping cultural time frames in different areas of the Southwest. The Anasazi ancestors of the modern pueblo peoples existed from 1200 B.C.E. through 700 C.E., when the modern pueblo culture took over. The Mogollon predecessors of the Hopi and Zuni tribes appeared in 0 C.E., lasting through 1500, and their era overlapped with the Hohokam culture, which began in 100 B.C.E. and then became the Pima in 1300 C.E. The Fremont, Patayan, Sinagua, and Athapaskan cultures evolved during the Common Era as well, adding to population diversity in the desert lands. Because of the more isolated nature of many of these societies, the cultures effectively existed independent of each other, developing and exhibiting very different characteristics as a result.

Archaic Indians in this region provide the best example of change and adaptation to their environment. As the climate warmed, the Paleo-Indians found that they would have to change their dependence on game hunting and foraging to match the changes in the weather. Eventually they would need to function in a complete desert environment. These societal changes happened slowly over generations, but the weather did not change overnight either. The nature of climatic shifts often gives people, vegetation, and animals lifetimes to adapt. During the early Archaic period, natives moved in small family groups that reflected seasonal changes. Although hunting and gathering was often still easy, they frequently moved to follow long-term sustenance sources. Somewhere around 4000 B.C.E., during the middle Archaic period, desert societies began developing villages. Everything from the size of the settlements and types of houses to the tools they used as they evolved suggests larger populations and longer stays in one place. Property and supplies were harder to come by for migratory populations, and because of this, specialists believe early agriculture found its beginning here. By the late Archaic period, agriculture was in full swing, helped along by a relatively brief period of climatic warming and higher moisture. By the time the climate settled into what is recognizable today as the southwest desert, Archaic Indians had a good grasp of what it would take to keep farming efforts successful for their now-settled societies.

Out of the many cultures that evolved from the desert Archaic tradition, one of the best known is the Anasazi civilization. Most concrete evidence suggests that Clovis culture appeared in the Southwest around 11,500 years ago, but within 3,000 years, that culture disappeared, apparently connected to the loss of the southwestern mammoth. Overhunting and a drying climate forced the development of new traditions. The next in line, the Folsom and Cody traditions, remained migratory, hunting smaller herd and range animals that survived the climatic changes, such as bison and antelope. The early Holocene period also witnessed more drought, and by 5000 B.C.E., the climate was much like the climate of today's Southwest. Because resources became less and less widely available, many peoples became less mobile. This developing isolation also created the first signs of cultural distinction. The Oshara Culture in the Four Corners area (the meeting of Utah, Arizona, Colorado, and New Mexico) is one example of a people that eventually evolved into another; they became the Anasazi tradition, and although the Oshara's lifespan of several thousand years was nothing to sneeze at, time and environment cannot be ignored.

Four thousand years later, the Terminal Archaic period began for Southwestern natives. They experienced some increased moisture and stability in the climate and environment, which allowed for a brief period of rest from the harsh climate of the recent past through a period of gradual but steady change. These early Anasazi people experimented with domesticated plants such as beans, squash, maize, and the bottle gourd. Minnis (1985) describes this as "a monumental nonevent with little immediate impact on native human populations." Prehistoric domesticated "crops" were highly unpredictable and not very useful, so the assumption is that native people would not have developed a dependency on them. Instead, the purpose seems to have been the desire to create a wider variety of plant life for foraging. As the climate continued to change and experimentation with farming increased, however, so did dependence on those farming efforts. Evidence such as pottery and grinding tools suggests a greater reliance on agricultural produce. One mistake scientists have made is assuming that agricultural development and structural remains suggest permanent settlement. New evidence implies that although the villages themselves may have been permanent, tribes still used them on a seasonal basis. At many sites, the pithouses used by natives actually predated the crops in the area, insinuating earlier use and eventual reoccupation. The southwest peoples continually changed as necessary in reaction and response to their environment, but they tenaciously held onto cultural patterns and traditions.

Between 200 and 400 C.E., climate changes began to make agricultural pursuits nearly impossible. It does not seem, though, that these changes posed insurmountable obstacles to native populations. They apparently relied heavily on flexible traditions rather than on permanent, ingrained dogma. Population density was generally low throughout the region and into the Colorado plateau, which made it possible to extend both the stay and the range of mobility. This encouraged a continuing reliance on seasonal agricultural movement. The smaller the nomadic groups were, the easier it was to provide for them. After 400 C.E., the climate leveled out, providing more precipitation on a constant basis. The Anasazi culture had been fully developed for several hundred years, and the new climatic stability helped solidify their cultural personality. One predominant feature of the Anasazi was their practice of basket making. During this period, Anasazi basket weavers elevated the art of weaving to its highest expression, producing everything from baskets and sandals to clothing and utensils. Despite the relative stability of the weather and their highly developed material culture, it does not seem that they were a fully sedentary society, another important cultural aspect. They often exercised occasional seasonal movements within a smaller, well-defined territory. The weather changes during this period affected the tribes little because they were a small population that adapted quickly. By the 600s, the Anasazi had grown a more reliable, productive variety of maize, and this is the element that really shifted the Anasazi toward more permanent settlement. Although scientists originally thought that Maiz de Ocho originated out of Meso-America and found its way north, new evidence says this is not the case. Over long periods of time, native peoples in the Southwest consciously chose plants that would produce larger kernels and flower earlier. Large kernels were much easier to grind, and an earlier flowing season allowed natives living in areas with shorter growing seasons more success in their farming efforts.

In response to these new, more productive agricultural methods, the Anasazi began building above-ground structures: they needed storage space for all of the extra food. Prior to the building of pueblos, food stored in pithouses was susceptible to ruin by small mammals and moisture. As dependence on agriculture grew, the flexibility and mobility of past generations decreased while the need for enough crop surpluses to weather environmental crises increased. As the population settled down, it also grew, which made increasing the range and duration of migration no longer effective in dealing with food-supply problems. The nature of the shift from pithouse to pueblo dwelling suggests a long period of combination of the two, with families living in pithouses while masonry buildings behind them provided the long-term storage they needed. During this "Basketmaker III" period, positive and negative environmental changes, the development of new crops, and population growth all played a role in creating stationary Anasazi communities.[3] Simply having more storage available helped pin down the peoples; who would store their food supplies and then leave those stores unguarded? And when it was necessary to stay in one place, experimentation with crops continued, increasing the need for storage and so on, creating a self-sustaining circle of advancement. The end of the Basketmaker II period is critical to Anasazi history. It stabilized their highly mobile society and just in the nick of time—because the changes after 700 C.E. set the path for more swift developments.

During the Pueblo I period from 750 through 900 C.E., the Colorado Plateau experienced drastic climate changes. The effective, available moisture decreased significantly, erosion increased greatly, water tables shrank, and rainfall became extremely unpredictable. As a result, population density changed, with marginally occupied areas all but disappearing and arable riverbeds experiencing large influxes of people. This era of history shows how natural environments affected cultural development. Anasazi of this period are divided into subgroups based on where they lived, which affected everything from farming techniques and how their villages looked to how they interacted with each other on a societal level. There are some generalizations that can be made, though. Farming was rather conservative, depending on dry farming (rainfall only) techniques and already-established crops. Pithouses began to take on *protokiva*, or ceremonial, aspects. Additionally, surface structures, initially used for storage, appeared attached to the pithouses, but eventually expanded to include more domestic quarters as well. As these societies added population and crowded closer together, positions of leadership emerged, resulting in larger houses with some signs that people were concerned about the security of their property. One specialist, Fred Plog, suggests that alliances formed between neighbors and friends based on surplus-sharing and exchange contributed to complex political and social structures of the Anasazi in later periods.

Environmental conditions improved during the Pueblo II years (900—1100 C.E.), with a slow but steady increase in effective moisture. As a result of this gradual climatic improvement, Anasazi groups strengthened and expanded their agricultural economies. In most areas, they continued to use dry farming systems as well as *akchin* fields that took advantage of the runoff and deeper soils of alluvial fans. In some areas, farmers looked to supplement these traditional farming methods. For example, in Chaco Canyon in northwestern New Mexico, they built irrigation systems that directed rainwater running from the canyon walls into the fields. Anasazi also used extensive water-control systems along the river basins of southwestern Colorado. A group known as the Virgin Branch Anasazi constructed check dams and canal-irrigation systems to give them more complete control over their water sources. Adaptation, experimentation, and differentiation were at their height for the Anasazi peoples of this period. Archaeologists use these differences to divide the Pueblo II Anasazi into groups identified by distinctive material culture. The reality is that hard and fast cultural boundaries did not separate these peoples, and artifacts and ideas migrated and were exchanged on a regular basis. But there are cultural characteristics that can help scholars define and understand the complex differentiation that resulted from individual environmental conditions.

No matter what culture they belonged to, villages only housed inhabitants for maybe one generation before natives might be forced to move on. Some reasons for this could include natural-resource availability, environmental challenges, social or political strifes, or outside threats. One exception to this is Chaco Canyon, a 10-mile portion in northwestern New Mexico. Given that it was one of the largest known Anasazi settlements, it is somewhat surprising that it was abandoned within approximately 200 years, and the reasons for this remain unknown. From this center point, the Anasazi spread out, building other pueblo and cliff-dwelling villages in their wake. It was these types of buildings that greeted Spanish explorers in the 15th century. What remains of these villages are monuments to the individualism, creativity, adaptability, and endurance of the many Anasazi peoples. Each environment and society was unique. How they adapted to the natural challenges around them made them who they were until European contact. Following that environmental change, natives no longer had control over the adaptations to come.

WEST COAST NATIVE AMERICANS

The North American West Coast is defined as the stretch of land from British Columbia to Southern California. Some anthropologists differentiate between northwest American Indians and California coastal tribes, but for purposes of this treatment, the two areas will be presented in a combined, but comparative, examination. The northern coastal region was more homogenous; most tribes lived in plank houses, developed advanced economic and trading systems, and exhibited an unusual sense of the aesthetic in their art. The northern tribes developed the most distinctive societal and cultural traits, second only to Arctic peoples. This development resulted from their unique environment as well as from stronger Asian influences.

Traveling down the North American coast into California, Native American societies produced a greater diversity than their coastal neighbors to the north. Culture and language differed greatly from tribe to tribe. This area experienced a greater population density comparable to eastern agricultural tribes, but they did not develop advanced farming themselves. The availability of natural food resources was so great that it negated the need for controlled production of food. Despite population density and diversity, names such as Wintun, Maidu, Miwok, and Yokuts are relatively unknown today, yet these were major tribes in this area. Their contact with Europeans was the latest, not coming until the end of the 1770s, and their independence in the face of that contact was the shortest; the Gold Rush of the 1840s effectively ended it. Also, their reality is probably the hardest to tease out of historical records. One assumption is that many archaeological finds concerning these peoples are buried not only in the ground (because of the area's geological instability), but also under the Pacific Ocean (because of rising ocean levels). It does not help that the short time between initial European contact and widespread white settlement limited the historical evidence often produced by earlier interaction, observation, and recording.

Just as with other regions' histories, the history of North American coastal people most likely began with the migration of humans across the Beringia Bridge. Those who accept the migrating Asian peoples as the direct ancestors of all native North Americans rest their conclusions on two points. First, they recognize that biologically the two groups are very similar in blood type, hair consistency, dental characteristics, and skin color, among other physical traits. Logistically, the point between Siberia and Alaska seem to be the only feasible path of migration. The two locales are less than 50 miles apart, and scientists know that north Asian people did boat, walk, or dog-sled across at various times in history. For the North American continent to have been populated any other way, people, it is assumed, must have had large sea-traveling vessels. Conclusive evidence for this theory does not exist, but there is the suggestion that Asians migrated to North America in smaller seacraft. Archaeological studies of the California coast offer the best opportunities to prove or disprove this theory, and many scientists are engaged in that very activity.

Looking at the environment nomads would have faced, Beringia (the regions to either side of the strait, including most of modern northwestern Canada) was different than today's cold, rather barren landscape. Unfortunately, specialists do not agree on what that environment was. One school of thought suggests that despite vast expanses of valleys, significant mountain ranges, and a colder, drier climate, these lands must have sported some dense vegetation in order to support the animal life evidenced in North America. Horses, mammoths, and bison all had dental characteristics that suggest leafy vegetation, not the moss and lichens of today's Beringian area. It must have been a windswept environment as well, considering that animals such as the prehistoric horse and bison were not biologically adapted to trudging through snow on a consistent basis or digging vegetation out of deep snow build-up. Dale Guthrie calls this environment the "Mammoth Steppe."

However, there is another theory. Paul Colinvaux bases his environment hypothesis on analysis of pollen found in lake sediment and deposits. He suggests that the pollen content of the soil was so low after the last ice age that widespread vegetation could not have existed. He calls the landscape a "polar desert." The nature of this polar desert could not have supported much animal and human life. Recently new evidence emerged related to this debate. Apparently, both of these theories could be somewhat correct. A completely preserved patch of Beringia vegetation dating back 17,000 years was discovered under a volcanic ash layer. The area was completely covered with various types of vegetation, supporting the Guthrie theory of plant coverage after the last ice age. The root structures of these plants, however, showed few signs of strength or permanence, suggesting that although the coverage at this time was fairly complete, the light root structure meant there would also be periods of little vegetation, as Colinvaux suggested. Concrete evidence of pre-Columbian history is hard to come by, but every once in a while, a volcano explodes or a flood washes in natural preservatives, and like magic, a window to the past remains open.

So who lived in this apparently quick-changing environment, and how did they get there? By the time of the earliest evidence of human habitation, the windswept lands with lighter vegetation had given way to a warming climate and woody growth. This was important because without woody growth, humans would have had no materials for shelter or fires. This warming and growth trend began around 15,000 years ago. Additionally, core-drilling analysis suggests that the land bridge was available to ancient peoples perhaps as late as 9000 B.C.E., much later than previously argued, potentially changing understanding of migration patterns again. The path of migration is up for debate as well. Some scholars suggest that as the ice receded, a corridor opened through the center of North America, allowing humans, plants, and animals to travel down the continent and into South America. Another theory is that people traveled south along the West Coast, circumventing the major sheets of ice covering areas of British Columbia and Washington State, with the Columbia River providing the first path inland to the rest of the continent. The events of both theories could have happened, but once again, not enough evidence survived to allow scientists to come to a definite conclusion.

The Clovis period (ending in roughly 10,000 B.C.E.) represents the earliest inarguable evidence of human habitation in North America. Clovis evidence is widespread across the continent except in the Northwest and on the West Coast. There have been discoveries of isolated examples of Clovis artifacts found in the coastal areas of Washington State and British

Columbia, but so far, this is the extent of early evidence. One site on the Pacific Coast, around Vancouver Island, produced evidence that dates human habitation in this area back to 10,800 B.C.E. In the remains of a mastodon, archaeologists found a bone point that had penetrated a rib and had then been healed around. Although this evidence is not completely accepted as reliable, it is the closest scientists have come to proving early human inhabitance on the West Coast.

What would these people have been like? Current analysis says that, although there may have been some reliance on land mammals for sustenance, most evidence suggests the eventual full-time, year-round adaptation to coastal resources. Fish and shellfish dominate many site remains. Coastal natives in the Northwest used sea lions, seals, and even porpoises as food sources as well. Although there are not many surviving tools as artifacts, knowing that these peoples utilized such a wide variety of coastal animals for subsistence suggests a higher level of technological advancement than commonly assumed for this early period. Old Cordilleran culture of the coast (the period between 10,000 and 6,500 B.C.E.) shows an amazing amount of continuity among coastal tribes, in contrast to other cultures in North America, especially regarding subsistence patterns. Following this period were the Charles (6500–3200 B.C.E.), Locarno Beach (3200–2400 B.C.E.), Marpole (2400–1600 B.C.E.), Strait of Georgia (1600–200 B.C.E.), Salish (200 B.C.E. through 1700 C.E.) and Developed Coast Salish (post–European contact) periods. Much of that continuity has extended through the subsequent periods, although the cultural level of complexity continued to grow.

The Salish people are one good example of northwest coastal culture. Relying predominantly on fishing and water resources, they often supplemented their food stores with hunting and gathering. When fishing, they often used harpoons, gaffhooks, spears, basket traps, and dip nets as individual fishermen, or larger *weirs,* underwater barriers, and trawl nets in group fishing efforts. Coastal hunters must have used simple spears early on, but as their culture developed, they adopted harpooning technologies that allowed them to hunt seals and other water mammals more efficiently. In hunting land animals, traps were most often employed. Gathering played its role as well, and women of the tribes gathered everything from mussels and crabs to berries and carrots. The containers used to carry these foods were woven, with patterns distinguishing coastal cultures from each other. Carving was another cultural feature that separated northern coastal tribes from other Native American groups. This feature is one of the most predominant traits that make them seem almost foreign in comparison to the rest of the continent. Carving decorated the front of houses along with totem poles, one of the most recognizable images associated with this area. The paths that tribes such as the Salish, Chinook, and Tillamook took in adapting to their environment made them successful in a unique landscape, but also made them one of the most culturally unusual.

The southern coastline presents a region with the most natural diversity in North America. California's many coastal communities employed extensive fishing, much like the natives of the northern coast. During their Archaic Era, which lasted from 6000 B.C.E. to 500 C.E., many California tribes established more permanent settlements. In the process of developing a settled society, West Coast tribes experienced a unique change. By the late Archaic period, wealth accumulation was a major focus for many individuals and tribes. In fact, by the Emergent period, 500 to 1800 C.E., many communities exhibited strong class distinctions based on wealth. This development makes these southern societies stand out culturally in comparison to other native regions. Their economies were based on a shell currency, helping create extensive trade networks up and down the coast. Many of these communities would properly be considered island societies, a social and physical setup that would encourage trade relationships to ensure resource availability to everyone. The Chumash, for example, were a maritime dependant society that developed rather extensive trade networks with their neighbors. Transportation was little problem because necessity forced the utilization of canoes, fashioned out of planks. Artistic expression was also common, taking many forms such as shell jewelry and wood carving. Additionally, they developed diverse tools to help facilitate maritime living. In short, unique challenges produced a unique wealth-based people who traded heavily, ultimately allowing individuals to develop a level of specialty more advanced than in other areas of the continent. The coastal environment produced what were perhaps some of the most unique societies of North America.

THE "FINAL" PRE-COLUMBIAN PEOPLE: NONNATIVES BEFORE COLUMBUS

There were other people not mentioned so far on the North American continent before Columbus, and they were not native residents. Scattered archeological evidence suggests a variety of Eastern and Western explorers walked these lands much earlier than 1492. The most well-known is probably Leif Erickson, a Viking who arrived around 1000 C.E. But before him, the host of travelers included Mediterranean, European, Middle Eastern, and Chinese adventurers. Some scholars suggest that Egyptians and Nubians reached the Gulf of Mexico between 1200 B.C.E. and 800 B.C.E., bringing with them written language and pyramid technology. The Olmec stone heads of Mexico exhibit African facial features, leading to the conclusion that the Mande people of West Africa came here in the early 1300s. Recently, historian Gaoussou Diawara has suggested that the African king Abubakari II came to Brazil in 1312, leaving archeological and linguistic evidence behind. Some scholars scoff at the suggestion that Africans might have "discovered" the New World before Europeans, causing their opponents to accuse them of ignoring historical evidence simply to maintain Euro-superiority over early sea travel and exploration. The argument still rages, waiting for more evidence to sway the conclusion one way or another.

Leif Eriksson is definitely the most well-known and most widely accepted pre-Columbian visitor to North America. One story suggests that after landing in Greenland in the late 900s, Leif traveled farther west, landing in an area he named *Helluland*, or Flat Rock Land. Scholars now believe this is Baffin Island in Northern Canada. He sailed on, landing in *Markland*, now believed to be Eastern Canada. His last stopping point was a rich, fertile land he dubbed *Vinland*, Wineland or Pastureland, and he stayed the winter there. Few Norsemen, however, ever returned to the continent, despite its wealth of resources. Norse sagas tell of the lands explored by Leif but provide little explanation for why more people did not venture here. Various sagas also contradict each other and give no definitive clues for determining where in North America Leif actually landed. Some have said it could be as far south as Virginia. With only the sagas to study and precious little material evidence, history may never have a complete picture of Leif Eriksson's odyssey.

A variety of other visitation claims include such personalities as a band of medieval Irish monks, Prince Henry Sinclair of England, Prince Madoc of Wales, and Hoei-Shin from China. Most evidence claims rest on tools, technology, art, architecture, and linguistic legacies. The beauty of history is that although many of these claims are still questioned, the *possibility* exists that there is a buried treasure of historical evidence just waiting to be discovered. Every encounter left inerasable marks on native cultures, which is just the type of teaser necessary to fuel continued curiosity.

NOTES

1. For more information on late successional forest biodiversity, see Cynthia Fleming's Science and Policy Brief titled *Conservation of Biodiveristy in the East: The Role of Early Successional and Mature Forests* published by The Wilderness Society and located online at http://www.wilderness.org/Library/Documents/upload/ScienceAndPolicyBrief-6-ConservationInTheEast.pdf.

2. As part of the Out West Natural History project, *Great Plains Culture Area* is included in a collection of Web sites that provide information on the information utilized in creating the natural history project. Located at http://www.scsc.k12.ar.us/2002Outwest/NaturalHistory/Projects/LachowskyR/Great_plains_culture_area.htm.

3. The term *Basketmaker* designates an era of cultural characteristics and differentiation of the Pueblo people. There is no Basketmaker I period as there is no physical evidence to support it, but Baskmaker II and III designate periods of early efforts at seasonal settlement and development of increasing storage, construction, and weapon technology. The era begins in 1200 B.C.E and ends in 750 C.E.

2

ANIMAL AND HUMAN INTERACTION: NATURAL COOPERATION IN THE ENVIRONMENT

In the beginning of all things, wisdom and knowledge were with the animals, for Tirawa, the One Above, did not speak directly to man. He sent certain animals to tell men that he showed himself through the beast, and that from them . . . should man learn.

Eagle Chief, Letakos-Lesa Pawnee

Prehistoric Native Americans' relationships with their animal cousins looked little like what today's Western mind imagines when thinking of human–animal interactions. The relationships were unique, intricate, intimate, and spiritual. The most obvious connection was the use of animals for food. This relationship, however, barely scratched the surface. All animals, even the ones that posed a threat, were treated with respect, honor, and kinship. Animal figures also often functioned as spiritual totems or representations of the inner soul of a human being. Domesticated pet relationships did not really exist until contact with Europeans, and then the introduction of animals such as cattle, pigs, and horses as domesticated animals often served as a tool for Westerners in their efforts to civilize the "savage natives." The closest "pet" relationship would have been with indigenous dogs, although this relationship did not mirror today's pet definition. Often when the dogs had outlived their usefulness as pack animals, for example, they were eaten so as not to waste a food source. A Westerner's stomach would turn at the thought; the relationship is simply too different. In addition to these issues, looking at animal relationships over long periods of time is difficult. Most of what can be assumed about prehistoric beliefs survives in drawings and oral tradition. Native religion offers great insight, and although spiritual beliefs surely changed, becoming more intricate over time, the larger details remained virtually the same until contact with Europeans. These complex connections between humans and animals in prehistoric North America offer an exceptional window of opportunity for analysis and understanding.

THE CIRCLE OF LIFE: ANIMALS AS THE GODLY GIFT OF FOOD

In readings about Native American hunting, the word "gathering" often follows close behind. It is difficult to separate the two, no matter which regional environment is being examined. Communities from the woodland East Coast to the desert Southwest and everywhere in between relied on some form of hunting and gathering for survival. Usually the term "gathering" suggested the collection of wild-growing plants for food, but people often collected small reptiles and mammals as well in a gathering process unlike hunting, although animals were involved. Rounding up these smaller creatures required practice, skill, and technique, but the term "hunting" usually referred to a different process of chasing and ensnaring such larger grazing animals as the bison or mammoth and bigger carnivores such as the cougar or bear. Hunting was often a group activity done for the benefit of the community, not for just one individual or family unit. However predatory and one-sided this human–animal relationship may seem, even this interaction was just that: an *inter*action. Many societies believed that the spirit of the animal made itself available to humans only if properly respected and revered by the hunters. Correct treatment ensured that the spirit would return to its spirit realm with favorable stories about the tribe and its people, guaranteeing future hunting success. Of course, this could be turned around, and following unsuccessful hunting trips, hunters often blamed some intentional or unintentional disrespect as the culprit. As a result, respecting the animal spirits took on a professional character in most native societies. Organized, practiced, and perfected rituals and procedure dominated native hunting.

In order to help ensure success, holy men or shamans often led the hunting parties. In the Shoshone tribe, for example, if an antelope-spirited shaman was not available, trapping the pronghorn herds was postponed. In Plains buffalo jumps and trappings, the holy man exerted his spiritual influence to direct buffalo herds over cliffs to their deaths or into corrals for the slaughter. No one but the shaman attempted this dangerous essential duty. Spiritual guidance was not used in all types of hunting, however. The Shoshone also used nets and large groups of people to herd and capture rabbits without the benefit of a shaman. The nature of this method and the rabbits' behavior virtually assured success, so there was no spiritual ritual connected to the communal hunt. That does not mean that those participating in the capture and enjoying the fruits of the hunt did not honor the rabbits' spirits. They did so in other ways during and

Drying buffalo meat on the plains using a traditional centuries-old hanging method. National Archive Photo number 518892.

after the hunt, when killing, preparing, serving, and consuming the animal, giving thanks to the spirits at every step. The practice of thanksgiving varied depending on the nature of the hunt, but the level of respect stayed the same.

Another method of raising the chances of success when hunting larger game was the development of specialized skills and knowledge by prehistoric hunters. Understanding the behavior patterns of the animals was one of the most important steps in a successful hunt. Hunters also needed extensive familiarity with the surrounding territory and an in-depth understanding of the pros and cons of their weaponry. Last, mental and physical conditioning and agility kept the hunters in a constant state of preparedness, even when hunting season passed. The list of factors about which hunters had to be aware in the learning and preparation process is impressive: animal age, sex, breeding habits, and body condition could all affect the process and outcome of the hunt. Then add consideration of the time of year, time of day, climatic conditions, foraging conditions, distance to water, and size of the herd. The hunters had a virtually insurmountable body of knowledge to learn and master. It was also important to consider the prey's relationship with other species around them, in order to predict their interactive behavior. Additionally, the reactions of birds and other animals could provide important information, such as location and movement of prey. Because of the importance of their role in native society, prehistoric hunters began training at young ages to help ensure the survival of their peoples.

For a young male in native society, preparation began early for the responsibilities of adulthood. One of the many skills he needed to master was weapons manufacture and maintenance. Often, young men first used these weapons in the killing of an animal as a rite of passage. Many tribes across the continent practiced some form of vision quest for their young men. After traveling into the wild for days, often without food or water, the young man would return with vision tales of his spirit guide, his totem. For some tribes, including several on the West Coast, performing the proper rituals of respect paved the way for the hunting and killing of a flesh-and-blood member of the boy's totem animal. Prior to the arrival of Europeans, hunters valued their weapons above all else. It was not just quality and workmanship that made these tools valuable; there was a spiritual connection between hunter and weapon that is difficult to define in modern terms. The relationship was so close that most hunters would not consider using another's weapon. At the very least, the unfamiliar weapon would be ineffective, and in a worst-case scenario, the hunter might actually be harmed through the use of another's weapon. Decorated with love and care, a hunter's weapon felt nearly as indispensable to him as an arm or a leg.

Traditional North American weaponry took one of three forms. The oldest was a simple spear with a long, wooden shaft and a stone or bone point on the end. The hunter could use this spear for hand-to-hand killing, or he could throw it over short distances. This type of weapon was most effective in close combat, in which the hunter could use his strength and agility to make the spear an effective weapon. The second type of weaponry revolutionized prehistoric hunting. A spear launcher called an *atlatl* (at-LAT-ul) greatly increased the distance and force of a spear. By using a whip-like motion, a hunter could hurl a spear with deadly force from a safe distance with great accuracy. There is no evidence as to the first development and use of this device, but evidence does suggest that by 8000 B.C.E., it was in widespread use around the continent. The best guess is that the earliest Clovis cultures brought the weapon with them from the "Old World" across Beringia. These weapons made up the early Native American arsenal until about 2,000 years ago. The bow and arrow made its first appearance in the early years of the first century of the Common Era. Arriving from northeast Asia, this ensemble quickly replaced the atlatl. With the shorter and lighter shaft of the arrow and the weapon's accuracy, flexibility, and portability, the bow and arrow proved to be the most effective Native American hunting weapon. Each weapon system required relearning and refining of skills, but true to form, Native Americans rose to the challenge and adapted successfully to changes in and additions to the natural environment.

One interesting feature of many hunting efforts was that "territorial boundaries" were not always considered important. After European contact, tribes began to define their territories more strictly, but prehistoric groups often combined efforts and shared territorial rights. Especially in larger endeavors, such as the buffalo jumps and pronghorn traps, there were often more meat and animal resources than one band or tribe could use. Buffalo were the most useful to native communities. Besides the use of buffalo meat as a major food source, buffalo hides could be made into everything from tepees and shoes to shields and drums. Bones and horns became tools and cooking utensils. Buffalo fat became soap, and the dung functioned as fuel. Women even used the brains to tan the hides and soften the skin. Nothing went to waste, and if one tribe was lucky enough to kill more than it needed, it would not only be inefficient to leave surplus to rot, but more importantly, it would also be highly disrespectful to the animal spirits, condemning the tribe to future hunting failures. A few extra buffalo would go a long way in providing necessities and luxuries for many people. Cooperation between tribes ensured future hunting success and the survival of many, while cementing alliances that could come in handy in times of need.

Now back to the animal gathering. Small mammals, such as beaver, squirrel, muskrat, raccoon, and rabbit, combined with reptiles including snakes, turtles, and lizards, supplemented natives' meat diets. Depending on where the tribe lived, birds, sea mammals, fish, and insects could be added as well. These foods are relatively high in protein, which helped assure that Native Americans enjoyed healthy lives. Many of these animals also supplied a significant amount of fat, giving the Indians stores of warmth and energy when the weather turned nasty. Some primary sources suggest that tribes selectively hunted certain animals for their *high* fat content, a practice that contradicts present-day dietary wisdom. Vilhjalmur Stefansson, an explorer of the late 19th century, wrote that natives seemed to prefer

the flesh of older animals to that of calves, yearlings and two-year olds . . . It is approximately so with those northern forest Indians with whom I have hunted, and probably with all caribou-eaters.

Scholars use postcontact sources such as these to suggest that many Indians preferred a diet high in fat. The problem with this assumption is that Stefansson traveled and lived among the Inuit, an Arctic tribe of Northern Canada, where extra stores of fat were necessary in the harsh, cold climate. These people could experience what Stefansson called "rabbit starvation": if there was no fat from other sources, diarrhea, headaches, fatigue, and discomfort could develop. The Arctic's extreme climate required a different nutrient list for healthy survival. In many other areas of the continent, it was much more common to rely on small animals as a food source, even though their fat content could not match the larger game. Regardless of the region studied, native North Americans enjoyed good health and strong bone structure based on a diet high in both fat and fiber. The environment provided for natives' nutritional needs, and they utilized their natural riches to maintain exceptional health and vitality.

Other dietary inclusions were fish and sea creatures. American Indians living in coastal areas greatly utilized their abundant fish resources. Like other animals used by natives, fish provided more than simply meat; the oils in fish proved useful for cooking and making dressings. This food source was especially useful for providing fat-soluble vitamins in native diets. Animal fats and organ meats also fulfilled this need, specifically supplying vitamins A and D. These nutrients allowed the human body to effectively use protein and minerals, making people taller with stronger and more predominant bone structures. Natives knew nothing of vitamin combinations and nutritional guidelines but through observation, experimentation, and flexibility, they found the natural resource balance for healthy living. In order to provide communities with sufficient amounts of fish, native people developed specialized fishing techniques and employed scientific observation to ensure successful fishing. They used spears, hook and line, harpoons, arrows, traps, nets, lures, and even poison. When combined with the knowledge of habits and habitats, native fishermen perfected fishing to an art. The Nootka, a northwest coastal people, offer a perfect example of successful observation and development of vital fishing methods. The life cycle and patterns of salmon offered them this opportunity. The Nootka knew that the salmon would return every spring to spawn in freshwater springs. Nootka fishermen would build fences called *weirs* that stretched across the entire river to prevent their upstream migration. Then the Nootka employed a variety of traps, harpooning, and nets to harvest their catch. They often whaled also, and this was considered one of the noblest of pursuits. The water and its inhabitants shaped and directed the rhythm of people's lives.

Another region of the continent that relied heavily on water ecology was the Southeast Woodlands. Fish and waterfowl were abundant around the rivers and swamps. Some tribes in the Florida area lived entirely off of the fish and shellfish they caught while developing absolutely no agricultural skills or knowledge, which was completely unnecessary. The peoples of the Northeast Coast enjoyed fertile plains that were coincidentally one of the continent's richest fishing areas. Because of the plentiful rivers, weirs were popular on the eastern side of the continent as well. Several weirs still remain as archaeological sites, with one close to Hackensack, New Jersey—the Fair Lawn-Paterson Weir. As described before, a weir is a structure designed to hold fish. The Fair Lawn-Paterson Weir in New Jersey, which spans nearly 100 yards in the Passaic River, is made of boulders and smaller rocks, is shaped like a V, and has an opening at the point known as a sluice. People used nets and baskets to catch fish at the sluice. Some of the earliest historical references to weirs come from Dutch sources in the late 1600s out of Sloterdam, which means "sluice dam." These weirs reminded the Dutch of similar structures at home in the Old World. They were there when Europeans arrived, but how long had they been there? There is no evidence to suggest that any colonial populations used weirs in their fishing efforts, so the weirs must be of native origin. The one colonial example that does exist was a commercial fishing enterprise that used construction methods and materials completely unrelated to the Fair Lawn-Paterson Weir. Widespread use of stone weirs by Native Americans on the East Coast was well known and documented at the time of European contact, so the assumption is that Fair Lawn-Paterson is pre-contact or prehistoric in age. Because of this, many experts are currently trying to protect and preserve these ancient structures. Little is known about inland weirs, and study of these dams can shed light on prehistoric living patterns in an area of the continent where heavy urbanization and modern development has destroyed much of the archaeological record. Examination of this one relatively small environmental adaptation could open a window on entire civilizations.

Other game also supplied some of these needed substances to the Native American diets. Vitamin C could come from fatty glands in certain animals. Specifically, the adrenal-gland fat from the moose prevented scurvy, and all members of the tribe were protected by sharing just a small amount from each moose killed. By consuming the animal diets described, combined with fresh fruits and vegetables, native communities experienced a high degree of personal health. Tuberculosis, arthritis, and even cavities were virtually unheard of in most communities. Only when the Western world introduced human-managed foods did health begin to decline in predictable, wide-spread patterns. Foods like raw liver, dried lung, and sour porridge gave way to cultivated meat, skimmed milk, and sugared cereal. Changes in environment forced adaptations in community behavior once again.

COMPETITIVE ENVIRONMENTS: SURVIVAL OF THE FITTEST?

Another important human–animal relationship involved competitive or dangerous animals. Every natural environment contained creatures that posed a threat to the human residents. Roughly 12,000 years ago, "mega-fauna" began crossing the Beringian Bridge to roam the North American continent. Animals such as lions, camels, woolly mammoths, mastodons, and tigers preceded ancient homosapiens into northern Canada, beginning the long trek that would lead toward today's reality. Although they were strictly herbivores, animals such as the woolly mammoth, mastodon, and eventually the bison presented serious dangers when hunted. Herding the animals off cliffs or into thick swamps gave prehistoric Native Americans a significant advantage over creatures much larger and more numerous than their hunting parties. The last section detailed the reverence for and uses of the bison, but what about animals that posed a threat even when left alone? How did natives react to and interact with large dangerous animals such as the cougar and bear and such smaller ones as scorpions and poisonous snakes?

Take the puma, for example, also known as the panther, mountain lion, cheetah, and leopard, among many other names. Although these animals were powerful, strong, fast, and deadly, Native Americans lived along side the puma largely in respect, rather than fear, of the awesome presence of these large cats. Of all of the cats' qualities, Native Americans held the creatures' silence in the highest regard. The Manataka American Indian Council in Arkansas captures how the natives felt about their imposing neighbors: the puma's silence was seen as "a holy state of consciousness as [Native Americans] quietly [beheld] the grace and glory of the Creator. It [was] said that silence [spoke] words of the Great Mystery," and the large feline was the animation of this wonder. Many examples exist regarding respect of the puma as the natural environments that hosted puma spanned the entire continent. Forests, mountains, and deserts alike housed different varieties of large, graceful cats. At six to eight feet long and 100 to 150 pounds, they were anything but cuddly. As a carnivorous, stalking predator, the puma not only threatened humans directly, but also competed with them for the same wild game. The cougar's success as a lone hunter depended on the element of surprise, yet they stalked from ground level, rather than from treetop as myth suggests. A quick bite to the base of the neck coupled with agility and strength often spelled death for a puma's unsuspecting prey. Natives, unlike future European settlers, did not keep domesticated herds, so large cats could not threaten a community's livelihood directly; they could only endanger personal safety and compete for the same game. Despite the potential threat, Native Americans not only respected but also protected these predators.

Different tribes in North America told different stories about these elegant felines. In the Great Lakes region, they were known to stir waves in the lake waters and whip up storms with their tails. The Cherokee considered them the "lords of the forest," or *klandagi*. The Chickasaws called them a "cat of god," or *ko-icto*. In the Pacific Northwest, mountain lions were more treacherous than they were godly; there is, for example, the role they played in Salish folklore, according to which the slits that reach from chin to breastbone in the whale were caused by a cougar's wound. In North America, puma symbols can be traced back as far as the Anasazi, who scratched the feline's likeness into cave walls. The Hopi believed the cat to be a protector of the people, a god-like creature often consulted for guidance. Those who found the cougar as their totem were considered strong, in a silent, detached way. Cougar people could be counted on for solid, effective leadership, and they would never bask in the spotlight or let the power go to their heads. Wisdom, solitude, and stealth were on their side.

Cougar jaws, skins, and nails were often used in making heirloom ceremonial clothing and jewelry as a reflection of their qualities. In appreciation of the puma's power and presence in their lives, the image of the great cat appeared in many forms in Native American culture and society.

Another predatory presence in prehistoric life was the bear. Their images are found throughout Native American culture, especially in those from the bear's woodland and mountainous native habitats. Some of the bear's symbolic characteristics include strength, teaching, healing, humility, and dreaming, all very humanlike qualities. Grizzly and Black bears are the most common species in North America, and both play prominent roles in Native American belief systems. Regarded as forest masters, they were also considered part of the land itself. Whatever respect or disrespect paid to the bear would produce negative consequences not only in people's relationships with the bear, but also in the ecosystem itself. Although fearsome and often dangerous, the bear held a special, sacred place in Native American life and spirituality. Take, for example, the following legend from the Ojibwa or Chippewa tribes of the Great Lakes

According to the tales of the Midewiwin, the first council of the Mide spirits was held at the Center of the Earth and it was called by the upper air spirits to ask the help of the under earth spirits in saving a strange, unfurred animal named mankind.

Otter and Bear were chosen to push the first Tree of Life pole (Grandmother Cedar) from the Earth's Center through the surface, forming the first channel of communications between Above and Below.

"Hurry Up!" called Otter down the crack in the earth where the top of the pole had first appeared. "My fur is drying out in the warm winds Above. Give your best effort." So Bear gave one last mighty heave with his giant muscles. The earth trembled, and the first Tree of life emerged in the sunlight, quickly followed by Bear himself.

"Come on," urged Otter, "we have done as they told us. I am anxious to return Below."

"Not so fast there," growled Bear. He lifted his great head and curiously sniffed the warm smells of Above. "I would see this unfurred creature for whom the whole council was concerned."

"Very well," bobbed the agreeable Otter, "but make it snappy." The two totem animals did not have far to look. They came upon a cluster of the unfurred creatures pounding bark. Seeing the totemog, they howled, dropped the bark, and fled—all but one small manchild who could not even stand on his hind legs. Bear stared at the naked infant.

"No wonder they needed help. No claws, no teeth, no fur. Not even a Berry."

"Not even a WHAT?"

"Not even a berry." Bear pointed down an opening in the manchild's head out of which came wails of people sound.

"No safety berry. Like mine, see?" Bear leaned back his huge head, parting his gleaming jaws, and Otter obligingly peered into the cavern. There, hanging from the back of Bear's throat, was a round, ripe miskomin! (rose-colored berry)

"Sure enough," said Otter. "What do you do with it?"

"What do I do with it?" That's the Last Berry. It holds all the other berries I've eaten before down inside. And I never starve because the Last Berry is always there."

Otter slid impatiently into the water. "I don't really understand why anyone would eat berries." he called, "but if you think that manchild needs one—give him one and hurry up."

Bear crunched down on his great buttocks and slid down to the dune to the beach. Behind him, where his rump had opened up the sand, there grew a long vine with shinning leaves and little round berries just like the one in Bear's mouth. Bear reached over, yanked off a berry, and bopped it into the wailing manchild's mouth.

"There now," he rumbled in tender bear tones, "you shall not starve. You have a bear berry too."

The astonished infant was still, trying to keep his bear berry down. (That is what babies are doing when you see them silently swallowing. In swallowing, trying to keep their bear berries down.) The warm sunlight of Above shone upon the new bearberry vine and upon the plunge circles in the water as Otter and Bear returned to Below.

Bahmbtah-benahsee, (Tom-Tom Bird), who had seen everything that happened, flew to the Tree of Life. Carefully he positioned his grabbing toes into the oil bard. Then he threw back his handsome hammer head and beat out the first rhythm ever sounded on cedar. It said:

Behree
Bare Bear Behree
Papoose gotta
Bare Bear Behree
Gift of the Bear
(In Honor of Grandmother Keewaykinoway, Woman of the North West Wind)[1]

Because of the bear's honorable stature, bear hunting was accompanied by great ceremony and ritual in order to give the proper thanks and respect to the bear's spirit. A young man could prove his bravery and worthiness as an adult in mountain and woodland tribes with a successful bear hunt. When hunted, bears were either shot or trapped. After the kill, the head and hide of the bear were spread out along with foods the bear enjoyed, such as berries and maple sugar. Hunters skinned and dismembered the animal with a fine knife rather than carelessly butcher-chopping the carcass to show respect for the animal's spirit and the body it used to inhabit. At the village feast, a speaker would talk of the great reverence shown, so that other bears would know they were respected, welcomed, and valued in the society. Even the bones were gathered after the feast, lest other animals scatter them.

In northwest traditions, a killed bear was taken to the chief's house and treated as an honored guest. Dances and prayers were performed to show the bear's soul to show respect and protect future bear hunters. The identity of the Bear Clan of the American Northwest comes from a tale of a chief's daughter who fell in love with and married the son of a great bear chief. She had twin sons, and when the bear father was killed in a hunt, the tribe decided to use the bear symbol as their own. Legend tells that the twins had the ability to change between human and bear form at will and became the guardians of their people. By becoming the "Bear Clan" of the northwest, the clan was responsible for protection and defense of allied communities and their natural environments. In looking at native traditions, beliefs, and stories surrounding the bear, it is easy to see how American Indians incorporated a formidable foe into their worldview based on its characteristics and the role it played in the ecosystem, thus once again shaping their societies around their environments.

In some traditions, the bear held great potential for evil as well. The Navajo relationship was especially colored by a duality of symbolism. His name was never spoken, lest he might feel summoned to the community, but legend also featured the bear playing a role as a caring sister to the first human. Navajos developed ceremonial hunting practices similar to other Native American tribes, always respecting the object of the hunt; in this case, the bear. Showing their more mischievous side, bears often

An 1833 artistic rendering of the Mandan Buffalo Dance, a ceremonial preparation for buffalo hunts, by Karl Bodmer. National Archive Image number AISL 41.

"stole" fields from the Navajos. They seemed very attracted to Navajo cornfields, although the reason for this is unknown. Once a bear walked the fields, it was considered his (or hers), and tribes could never again use it for themselves. In a never-ending circle of connection and kinship, fear and respect often combined, producing a complex relationship wherein Native Americans never separated themselves from their spiritual brothers and sisters of the animal kingdom.

Smaller animals could be just as dangerous as large ones, especially in desert environments, and these communities incorporated them into their belief systems much like the woodland and mountain tribes did with their predatory neighbors. Scorpions and snakes of all kinds inhabited desert lands alongside native tribes. The Huichol people (pronounced "Wettchol") provide one example of this coexistence. They lived relatively isolated in the Sierra Madre Mountains until the arrival of the Spanish in the 1530s. Most Huichol religious beliefs aimed to balance and heal the earth and its environment. In their belief system, all spirits sprang from the same source, so the life forces of animals, people, and plants were not only connected, but ultimately one and the same. In this connected universe, certain animals symbolized certain things. Snakes represented rain and the dark clouds of a storm. This could be taken as foreboding, but more often it stood for the cleansing, replenishing power of rainfall, a natural event considered nothing short of miraculous in desert environments. Stories portrayed the scorpion as both fearsome and inspiring. Often seen as a protector worthy of great respect in spite of its deadly stings, it also brought good luck. As the living embodiment of the contradiction between life and death, the scorpion personified the life that the desert provided and the death that inevitably followed, often at the hands of that very same desert.

Spiders held positions of power in Native American belief as well. Although not all spiders were dangerous, the ones that were, along with their poisonous properties, were well known by native societies. One of the most common spiritual associations for the spider was as "grandmother spider," the weaver of the world who possessed a great maternal instinct. To the Hopi, she brought the gift of fire and wove the past as well as the future.

In the beginning, there was the dark purple light at the dawn of being. Spider Woman spun a line to form the east, west, north, and south. Breath entered man at the time of the yellow light. At the time of the red light, man proudly faced his creator. Spider Woman used the clay of the earth, red, yellow, white, and black, to create people. To each she attached a thread of her web which came from the doorway at the top of her head. This thread was the gift of creative wisdom.[2]

Ultimately, this story expresses the idea that all life and knowledge is connected—in this case, through the strands of the Spider Woman's web. If one strand is plucked, it can be felt on the other side of the net. If a strand breaks, the strength of the web suffers. To Native Americans, these analogies expressed their beliefs concerning the interconnectedness of life, not just in their own societies, but on the planet earth as a whole.

TOTEM AND FETISH SPIRITS: THE CLOSEST CONNECTION POSSIBLE

Most Native American societies believed that every human was born with guardian animal spirits for guidance, protection, and inspiration. Either a tribal shaman or a vision quest would often reveal which animal or animals had chosen a person as their protected charge. Some religions believed a person had three totems, one each for his or her past, present, and future. Other faiths suggested there were four, corresponding to either the four directions or the four elements. As many as seven totems could rotate in strength around a person's life wheel. The idea of totems should be familiar to anyone who follows the popular culture surrounding Native American society. Portrayals in movies and books often make totem animals and beliefs look much more spiritual and ethereal than they actually were—almost superstitious. Totems actually functioned like guides or teachers in Native American practice, and American Indians considered them a real presence in everyday life. A guardian angel of sorts, totems and their symbolism appeared in many native religions throughout the precontact time period. Some scholars suggest that totems represented physical, ideological, and sociological connections between tribes and their cultures, bridging gaps between cultural differences. On a more simplistic level, totem symbolism offers one method of examining Native American cultures' observations of and interactions with their environment. Animal guides usually represented the forces in nature that the animals' behavior most closely tied them to: for example, the eagle was in charge of soul transportation to the afterlife, soaring high into the sky with its charge. Totem animals and the beliefs surrounding them provide a perfect opportunity for analysis of human interpretation of natural environment. Because of their importance in American Indian beliefs, scholars can study individual totem representations to figure out what issues in day-to-day life stood out to natives as most important, to successful environmental interaction.

There is no general system of totem interpretation to which most religions subscribed. The most general assumption that could be made was that people could not choose their own totem; the totem chose them. They were not always animals of majesty and strength. Some animals were spirit guides only for certain regions, and the same animal might not symbolize the same traits in different societies. In some traditions, people saw signs or appearances of the animal, which might normally be considered coincidences, but were too frequent to discount. In other cultures, vision quests were the preferred mode of discovery; people undergoing their totem quest would isolate themselves, fast, and sometimes take psychoaffective substances such as peyote to achieve awareness and communion with their totem animal. Although the animal may possess qualities the person already had, more often than not, the totem symbolized that which the person needed to learn. By examining the use of totems, it is possible to learn much about native society and how people interpreted the world they lived in, where they saw themselves in it, and how closely tied they felt to their environment.

Animals also played a role in native spirituality as fetishes or talismans. Southwestern tribes are the source of this unique practice. The original Zuni name was *Ahlashiwe*. Fetishes from hundreds of years ago were stones shaped like animals or humans by the forces of nature. Native Southwestern legend suggests that the *Ahlashiwe* were humans or animals that the twin sons of the Sun Father turned to stone. The life force was then transferred to the stone, giving the person and tribe possessing the fetish a source of power and protection. Unlike totems, which attached themselves to particular people, the spirit in a stone fetish would benefit anyone who possessed it and gave it the proper respect. Fetishes are one more expression of the native belief that everything in the material and spiritual worlds is spiritually connected. By looking at all life and forms of nature as tied together, Native Americans gave an entirely different meaning and interpretation to their natural environment, providing sources of power, strength, and guidance that reached beyond their observable reality. This connection helped individuals and tribes live in harmony with their natural environment. If there was honor and respect for the fetish's spirit, the energy directed toward the figure would be returned to the owner by the spirit within the stone. More recent fetish carvings often do not serve this spiritual purpose; instead they are carved and marketed as souvenir trinkets. In order to function as a true fetish, the carving must be blessed by a shaman. These objects have become collector's items in modern times, and as such, most of today's fetishes generally have no spiritual influence or power without a religious blessing. There is no evidence to suggest, however, that Native Americans considered these objects decorator items historically. It is only modern-day society that has put fetishes to this use. Prehistoric southwestern societies would have held these objects in high respect and reverence, and the pride suggested in the display and collection of these objects could be considered a great disrespect.

The basis of the fetish structure and symbolism is as follows: Six animals were connected to six directions and imbued with certain powers. The north was the realm of the mountain lion, who served as a protector on long journeys and vision quests. Wolves guarded the east and lent their abilities to hunts and quests. Badgers aided in finding herbs for healing and protected the south. The bear stood in the west and had special curative powers. The earth was the province of the mole, who protected the growth of crops and the "seeds" of human goals and intentions. And finally, the eagle carried spirits to the invisible world and delivered prayers or requests when a person sought answers to questions. Zuni fetishes were often suspended from *heishi* necklaces as far back as archaeology can trace. Prehistoric fetish relics have holes drilled in many of them, suggesting they were worn as pendants or beads. Traditionally, fetishes were very prized, private objects. Part of the care of a fetish included keeping it in a special container and making offerings to it to nourish the animal spirit. Amulets were even attached to the fetish to give the animal spirits good fortune and protection of their own. Initially, the only real fetishes were stones found in nature that had been shaped by the elements into animal form. Once the practice of carving them began, many materials were used to make fetishes, including ironwood, mother of pearl, and sandstone, which the southwest natives valued. Smaller carvings were highly valued because of the patience and skill required to produce the object. The time and value invested in fetishes demonstrate the important place they held in Zuni religion and belief.

DOMESTIC ANIMALS: PETS OR CONVENIENCE?

The only relationship left to explore is that of pet and master. History provides little evidential remains suggesting that prehistoric Native Americans kept any kind of domesticated animals except dogs. There is some oral evidence that hints at more exotic, tame animal companions, such as squirrels, monkeys, and reptiles, but anthropologists have found it simply impossible to decide whether there is any truth to these stories. Even the prehistoric relationships to dogs, which do not much resemble today's definition of *relationship*, were vastly different than modern Rover and Spot experiences. It seems that these differences arose from Native American beliefs concerning the nature of spirits and the human relationship to the natural world. "Ownership," as the Western world thinks of it, did not exist in American Indian society, especially not when it came to things with a spirit. Plants, animals, and humans all possessed a life force, an intelligence and presence that would not allow natives to "own" another being no matter what its form. Plant and animal essences were not considered higher or lower than human spirits, just different. Respect and understanding colored every relationship in the natural world. Ultimately the result was a coexistence of equals engaged in a give-and-take that served every one and thing involved.

The Archaic era in North America spanned from just after Paleo-Indian civilization through the Woodland periods and offers evidence of domestic animal-human relationships. Basically, no matter when a people reached their Archaic period, it meant they lived without agriculture or technical developments such as pottery. One of the oldest sites offering evidence of animal domestication is an early Archaic period dig at Koster, Illinois. Dated at least 8,000 years old, four shallow graves hold four canines that were laid on their sides. Although none of the graves were marked, the village buried them in the same area as adults and children and much in the same manner. Archaeological evidence suggests that Archaic people in North America developed close relationships with the dogs of their time. This, however, was a relatively recent development, in historical terms, and another source of evidence suggests a slightly different and older story. In 1997 genetic research out of UCLA suggested that the first canines in the world were domesticated as long as 100,000 years ago and descended directly from Old World wolves with no genetic influences from the coyote or jackal. More research results showed that human migrants from Siberia brought domesticated dogs with them over 12,000 years ago. The basis of this genetic science involves analyzing DNA from ancient canine bones in various areas of North America and around the world. The comparison results showed that ancient American dogs were more similar to animals from the Old World than to the gray wolves of North America. The assumption is that because dogs were rather expensive to maintain, requiring regular food and care, they must have been important to ancient societies for those people to bring dogs along on such a long and permanent migration. Furthermore, they must have been domesticated in order not to wander off from their human companions. To the best of academic knowledge, dogs are the only domesticated animal found in both the Old World and the New and it seems they have been here just as long as humans.

Out of all the animals to choose from, why domesticate the dog? How far back does the relationship between people and their "best friends" go? At best, scholars can make educated guesses regarding the depth and characteristics of the human–dog relationship of ancient times. Evidence shows that there was a genetic diversity among dogs both in North America and in Eurasia. Genetic analysis suggests that these dog populations separated by thousands of miles were actually related. It is possible that this relationship could have existed for tens of thousands of years, longer than with any other animal and even longer than the domestication of plants. Although North American and Eurasian dogs share common ancestors, the connection is thousands of years back, and modern-day dogs do not share a close

DNA link with their prehistoric ancestors. Furthermore, biologist Robert Wayne of UCLA conducted research that suggested that "DNA sequences from hundreds of dogs from dozens of modern breeds from throughout the world do not show traces of American ancestry . . . their absence from a large sample of modern dogs reinforces the dramatic impact that the arrival of Europeans had on native cultures." Not only were ancient dogs more closely related to Old World canines, but the arrival of modern Europeans also disrupted the line, eventually wiping out the genetic relationships that had come before.

Some of the best information on the dog-human relationship comes from Western observations at the dawn of contact. The Ottawas, for example, regarded their dogs as personal, valuable property. The Shoshone prized their animals so much that they would kill and bury the favorite dog of the recently deceased with them, so that the pair might travel as best friends in death as they did in life. The Hidatsa considered dog meat a highly respected healing food. In some areas, when game was in short supply, dogs often provided a good source of fat and protein. Although to modern society this may seem distasteful, even barbaric and in many ways contradictory to the "best friend" bond, ancient native societies often considered these honors the highest that could be paid. All beings participated in the circle of life, and sometimes that meant being consumed instead of being the consumer. Even in death, the spirit of the dog and its relationship to man commanded respect. Modern culture views dogs as companions and friends, yet the close spiritual connection between an ancient native and his dog exceeded anything today's dog owners would consider appropriate in both a positive and negative sense.

One role of dogs that has continued through the centuries is the role of hunting companion. Indians in the Pacific Northwest used their dogs to hunt elk, deer, sheep, bear, and waterfowl. Hunters trained some dogs to drive game into snares or traps. Inuit dogs hunted seals and polar bears. Within the villages, dogs often slept in the family dwellings and would be given charge of the children of the tribe when not assisting with hunting. In the very early 1500s, Spanish explorers witnessed large dogs functioning as beasts of burden. Some carried large packs on their backs or pulled *travois* or animal sleds. The dog travois was the most popular way to transport goods and belongings for migrating Native American people. Whether following bison herds or moving with the seasons, this unlikely pack animal made life easier and more mobile. Crossbar poles of the sled-like travois were attached to long poles with rawhide and then strapped to the dog with a rawhide harness. Dogs did not just ease tribal movement; they were what made it possible. Even if the saying "you can't teach an old dog new tricks" is true, Native Americans adopted new tricks of survival all the time based on experimentation and experience. One integral adaptation Indians made to their environment was the utilization of the dog as beast of burden, baby-sitter, hunter, food, and friend. No matter what animal is being examined, if it lived within the sphere of native existence, American Indians integrated them into their individual, communal, and spiritual lives.

NOTES

1. "Touch the Earth," *Kinnikinnik: Gift of the Bear.* The full text of this legend is currently available at http://www.ewebtribe.com/NACulture/articles/Kinnikinnik/.

2. This is a popular southwestern creation legend that is reproduced in many sources. It is available online through the Women's International Center at http://www.wic.org/misc/writers.htm.

3

Agriculture: Cultivating a Living out of the Environment

The American Indian is of the soil, whether it be the region of forests, plains, pueblos, or mesas. He fits into the landscape, for the hand that fashioned the continent also fashioned the man for his surroundings. He once grew as naturally as the wild sunflowers, he belongs just as the buffalo belonged.

Luther Standing Bear, Oglala Sioux

In the Native American mind, the hand that fashioned the environment also fashioned humans to survive within the environment. This meant that the Creator gave humans certain talents, adaptive qualities, and survival skills to develop and use to the best of their ability. Agriculture was one of those skills. The first signs of agricultural practice in the Americas appeared in South America approximately 10,000 years ago with the farming of potatoes and other vegetables. Within one thousand years, Central America caught on to the benefits of cultivating crops and began growing squash, pumpkins, beans, and corn, also known as maize. This meant that natives could rely less on hunting and gathering and more on a process that was largely under their control: planned farming. Although Native Americans had greater direct control over the success or failure of their farming efforts than they did over hunting and gathering, they still believed the ability to grow and harvest crops was a gift from the gods. Many tribal religions incorporated rituals and ceremonies to help ensure the favor of the gods and success of the crops. In addition to affecting religious practices, agriculture also allowed tribes to settle down, giving up some, and occasionally all, of their nomadic ways. Health and longevity improved with the increased availability of food, and communal, interdependent tribal networks began to develop as agriculture spread. Food surpluses also provided the opportunity for specialization, leisure activities, and economic growth. Archaeological records show that as tribes adopted agriculture, participation in recreation activities such as art and sports grew. Individuals also began to specialize in trade skills, becoming masters of their crafts. Pot making, basket weaving, jewelry crafting, and tool manufacture are some examples of areas in which American Indians could excel. Many fundamental advancements in society, economics, culture, and politics began with the simple planting of a seed, resulting in the harvest of more than just an edible crop.

THE GROWTH OF EARLY AGRICULTURE: DEVELOPING PRACTICES AND BELIEFS ABOUT FARMING

Evidence regarding early North American agricultural practices suggests that around 7,000 years ago, people began to settle in the Mississippi River basin during the summer, a change that greatly affected their natural environment. Their presence and the effects of their gathering practices encouraged the growth of plants with edible seeds while simultaneously limiting the growth and spread of plants with little or no use to the natives. Sometime during the next 4,000 years (this is as close as scholars can get to an estimate), American Indians began to farm some of these edible plants, and by 1,000 B.C.E., there were distinct varieties of and differences between cultivated and wild vegetation. Around 300 C.E., maize made its first appearance in North America as the next significant agricultural change, but did not become a major crop until after 1000 C.E. Eastern Native Americans began planting maize as well as beans and squash, establishing a permanent agricultural tradition often called the Three Sisters because almost every society that grew these crops grew all three in an interesting interdependent system. Because of a significantly warmer climate, it was then easier to grow these crops further north than it is today, so crops covered more northern lands than today's North American society would expect. Other indigenous crops developed during this time as well, in keeping with regional environmental characteristics. Although some of the indigenous seed crops had to give way to transplanted beans, corn, and squash, other native crops, such as tobacco, peppers, and sunflowers, continued to flourish through the centuries. Planting only what they needed to survive and could use and at the same time respecting Mother Earth, natives sought a balance between sustenance and reverence. Native American religion played a large role in the plants and methods they utilized to maintain that balance.

Native American uses of plants for food and medicinal purposes interest many people today. Ancient Indians apparently enjoyed long, amazingly healthy lives, and many believe this was largely because of the plants used for food and medicine. One society, the Anishnabeg peoples of the Midwest, created the *Mide,* or the Great Medicine Lodge/Society, to preserve their knowledge and beliefs about plants and their uses. One of the major beliefs was that every plant on the earth had a use or purpose, even if it was not medicinal or nutritional for humans. In order to stay in the gods' good graces and observe the proper respect for nature, societies learned the purpose of *all* plants as intended by the gods. Those entrusted with botanical knowledge focused their learning in specialized areas, such as medicines for certain ailments or crops in a specific group. It was their job to understand the spirits that provided the tribe with the plants themselves and the knowledge of their proper uses, as well as to offer them honor and reverence for those gifts. Offerings of tobacco or precious minerals were often buried close to the "central" plant, which was thought to house or represent the spirit of all the plants of its type. These beliefs were fundamental in shaping Anishnabeg daily life and interaction with native vegetation. Eventually, when the Anishnabeg people began to explore agriculture as an established practice, these beliefs formed the foundation for all farming experiments and practices, putting respect and thankfulness for the gods' natural gifts at the center of their lives.

Many native societies held beliefs similar to those passed on by the *Mide.* The Odawa of central North America believed that every element on the earth, from rocks to humans, possessed two parts: the body and the *manitou,* or the "spirit." Although not every grain of sand or blade of grass possessed a manitou all the time, all had the potential to, so it was necessary to treat everything with the utmost respect. If disrespected, *manitou* would pass on bad health and other negative consequences to the individual guilty of the disrespect. Family and tribal members could suffer as well. Every interaction with plants was thus considered an opportunity for reverence. Also, body and spirit, according to Odawa belief, never formed a permanent link, and spirits could change form at will. With this unpredictable element thrown in, it was always better to play it safe and respect all things in the natural world because people could never be sure of the *manitou* presence. Again, when agriculture came to the Odawa people, their beliefs about the *manitou* guided their cultivation rituals, and they directed most of their practices toward honoring the *manitou* within everything.

No matter what the specific beliefs and practices were, three crops made up the core of most tribes' cultivation list: maize, beans, and squash. Many tribes grew, cooked, and consumed these three foods (the Three Sisters) together. Each tribe did have individual ideas about the origins of these plants, however. Eastern Woodland tribes considered maize and beans gifts from Cautantowwit, god of the southwestern direction, and they believed he sent crows to deliver kernels of corn and beans to the plant. As a result, crows were highly respected and would never be harmed, even if they destroyed the plants themselves. All tribes practiced some ceremony of thanksgiving as well. Harvesting and planting were

Adobe Zuni homes with pumpkin garden in front. National Archive Image AISL number 10.

so important to the health and survival of a tribe that rituals were held every sowing and reaping season. The Wampanoag of the Northeast Coast celebrated harvest with feasting, dancing, and games. The celebration was called Nikkomosachmiawene, and part of the thanksgiving rites included wealthier members of the tribe giving away possessions to the poor. Through these practices and other acts of celebration and thanksgiving, the Wampanoag expressed appreciation to the earth and its spirits for the bounty of its gifts, becoming part of the cycle of giving and receiving by giving to less fortunate members of the tribe. What at its basis was a simple interaction with nature grew into an understanding of the interdependence of all things that colored every festival and ritual in tribal society.

The Hopi celebrated a bean festival that featured male dancers dressed in animal costumes who performed intricate dances of reverence and spirit-calling in the hopes of ensuring a bountiful growing season. Along with the sounds of rattles and clapping tortoise shells, the dancers would make loud bird and animal calls during the ritual, appealing to various animal spirits they believed would help ensure fruitful crops. Some of the younger participants would leave the dance circle to call to the spirits from the outskirts of the ritual area and then come back again to continue the dance, spreading the call far and wide. Because of the understanding that everything on earth is connected, the Hopi believed that different animals and birds were important to agricultural success, much like the Wampanoag beliefs about the crow's role in agriculture. This dance was their way of honoring the animals' spirits and calling them to the planting site. After hours of dancing, the men would climb through the roof of a *kiva*, a Hopi ceremonial hut, and remain inside for over a week. The kiva functioned like a sweat lodge, and the beans were stored there with the men. The high humidity helped the beans sprout, preparing them for planting before the spring rains. While in the lodge, the men would pay respect to tribal ancestors as well, in order to obtain their protection and blessing from beyond the spirit realm.

An interesting sidenote is that in Hopi religious belief, there is an intermediate plane between the gods and humankind. *Kachinas* inhabited this realm, and sometimes the gods would request that the kachinas descend to the human plane to observe rituals and ceremonies, making sure that the tribes performed the proper rites and did it well in the process. It was the gods' way of checking up on humanity to make sure humans deserved nature's bounty, good health, and good fortune. Today this has evolved into participants called "whippers" who confront outsider observers as a test of who they are and their significance to the tribe and the ceremony. They try to scare away anyone not of the tribe through loud chanting and aggressive dancing. If the bystanders show no fear or annoyance, then the whipper treats them as kachinas and leaves them in peace. Although few natives today believe in the existence of kachinas, continuing these ancient tests serves another, more modern purpose. With the recent fascination with everything Native American, many tribes have become very protective of their celebrations. Outsiders who do not understand the significance or respect the sacredness of native religious practice can dishonor and disrupt something that is very holy to the participants. If potential observers do their homework, they will know that they should respond to whippers appropriately by quietly observing the rituals. If they do not, then the whippers will not leave them alone until they leave. Even today, adaptation plays a large role in the functioning of Native American society. In every aspect of Native American existence, it is easy to see the connections between humans and the natural environment around them—connections that colored every thought and move and that survive in today's native cultural expressions.

SPECIFIC CROPS: WHAT WAS GROWN, WHERE, AND WHY?

Most areas in North America focused on the Three Sisters as their crops of choice: maize, beans, and squash. Not only did these crops survive in a variety of environments, but they also provided almost a total spectrum of nutrients important to healthy living. The myth of the Three Sisters closely reflects a very real physical truth. According to most tribal beliefs, the Three Sisters represent three goddesses that could not be separated. Each sister goddess protected one of the three crops utilized by major farming cultures across North America. To ensure that the sisters' spirits were never separated, the story dictates, they must be planted, cooked, and eaten together—always. The details of the story varied across the continent, but at its basis, most natives believed that sisters symbolized unity and mutual support, and that became the basis for growing, harvesting, and consuming the crops together. This amazing trio of coexistence resulted from Native American belief and ingenuity, providing the perfect basis for personal health and crop success. Their connection, though, is much deeper and more significant than this story suggests.

Maize, beans, and squash were also known at the Indian Triad, or *Dyonheyko*, which means "ones that sustain our lives." They provide a perfect balance of nutrition, and interestingly, the Three Sisters are *much* more nutritionally effective when cooked and consumed together than when prepared and eaten separately. Their unique properties encourage the human body to create complete proteins chains normally provided by meat consumption, thus eliminating the need for meat altogether. Each plant contains certain amino acids that when combined produce the complete protein. The only thing missing for a healthy diet was vitamin C. Apparently, these three plants could sustain human life very successfully all on their own. When grown together, they even produce more harvest on smaller plots of land than when grown separately, and they require less water and fertilizer in the process. This is the first known example of symbiotic planting. The stalks of corn functioned as support for the beans to grow upon when planted beneath the corn. Bacteria from the beans turned nitrogen from the air into a usable form for the other plants, which strip nitrogen from the dirt. Once the beans released the nitrogen into the soil, the nitrogen acted as a natural fertilizer for the squash and corn. The bacteria needed for this process even became stronger because of the sugar released into the soil from the corn's root system. To top it all off, the broad squash leaves shaded the soil, helping prevent moisture evaporation and restricting weed growth. These crops really were optimally successful *only* when grown in concert. Planting them together could produce as much as a 20 percent higher yield per acre than could growing them alone.

A bonus to this reliance on the Three Sisters was that many tribes developed no dependence on herd animals for food. One positive side effect of less constant contact with animals was that the occurrence of animal-carried and animal-transmitted disease in Native American society was extremely low. Less meat also meant less fat, leading to a more fit and healthy life. Only in very northern areas was fat consumption a concern because in order to stay warm during colder months, a natural store of body fat was necessary. Keep in mind, though, that the climate was generally warmer then than it is today. Winters harsh enough to require "fatter" bodies for survival did not reach any farther south than central and southern Canada. The large majority of agricultural communities found the Three Sisters' nutrients more than sufficient. Because of the unique success of these crops, many communities turned away from hunting and foraging to the more permanent, predictable, and successful process of agriculture. In adopting the Three Sisters, many areas of the continent incorporated other beneficial crops more specific to their regions. In New Mexico natives incorporated a fourth sister, the rocky mountain bee plant, named for its sweet, bee-attracting flowers that greatly help the pollinating process. The seeds were edible as well, and natives used the plant to make the black coloring used in native Southwestern pottery. Even further south, around the Mexican border, chilies, cactus, maguey, and amaranth were added to create the seven warriors, contributing vitamin C and other nutrients to create the perfect holistic diet. In the Great Lakes region, wild rice provided a tasty complement to staple crops, and cotton emerged in the Southeast as a trade substance. No matter what the additions were, the Three Sister provided a basis for successful, healthy living on the North American continent. They were dried and stored as long-term supplies, freeing native societies from their dependence on the seasons for food. A perfect nutritional balance was available year-round, making life easier and immensely more flexible.

Examining the crops' individual strengths sheds light on why natives used these plants so extensively. Corn, for example, was probably the greatest agricultural development in human history. It produced three to six times more food per plant than any other crop. Corn produces anywhere from 500 to 1000 seeds per cob, and this ability exists nowhere else in the natural world. The closest relatives only produce about 50 seeds and the best assumption is that corn is either a natural or human-directed hybrid. The earliest useful varieties probably produced two-inch-long cobs with kernels that dried rock-hard on the core and was probably a popcorn-like corn. The kernels, based on archaeological analysis, would have been eaten right off the cob. The origins of beans and squash are much more straightforward. Wild, uncultivated cousins of both beans and squash are easy to find today, and a simple process of selective harvesting, seed-banking, and planting in prehistoric times produced the domestic varieties we have today. All around the North American continent, natives used processes of crossbreeding and selective cultivation of the Three Sisters in order to develop plants most suited to survival and sustenance.

Geographically, the woodlands, prairie, plains, Great Basin, and plateau native cultures all utilized the Three Sisters to some extent. Remember, because the climate 1,000 years ago was much warmer, farming areas reached much farther north than today's agricultural belts. As mentioned earlier, different regions added unique supplemental crops to their farming rosters. Red-seeded amaranth and black-seeded sunflowers used as dye in the Southwest complemented food crops. Corn that matured in only 60 days and drought-resistant tepary beans grown by the O'odham in Arizona, as well as sunflowers containing genes for resistance to a devastating sunflower rust, chia (an important source of protein, oil, and fiber for the O'odham), and red-seeded watermelons, all contributed to a rich genetic agricultural legacy. In prairie lands, natives cultivated small medicinal crops to help support community health. Even the highly migratory Plains Indians cultivated medicinal plots for short-term use and explored some Three Sisters farming efforts, because the benefits were simply too good to pass up. Overall, the Three Sisters and their "spiritual" bond enabled healthy, resilient, advanced societies to evolve based on innovative, intuitive agricultural developments.

NATIVE AGRICULTURAL SCIENCE: EXPERIMENTATION AND ADVANCEMENT IN PRECONTACT ENVIRONMENTS

Native societies could not have stumbled onto this wealth of nutritional knowledge blindly; they had to come to it through a process of experimentation, observation, and adaptation. Experience was the teacher natives learned from to develop advanced farming methods and successful crops. Nothing the natives did was easy. It took generations to weed out weaker plants and selectively crossbreed certain species for a higher, stronger yield. It took generations to learn from experiments with planting techniques in order to understand and utilize the most productive agricultural systems. In breeding plant varieties and developing farming methods, they had to keep in mind such concerns as available moisture, soil type, and climatic conditions and how those could change or might remain the same. In most areas, women were the primary agricultural specialists. The only exception to this was the Southwest, where men took the lead in shaping Southwestern agricultural efforts. The change from a foraging culture to a more stable, sedentary existence was not easy, and each tribe took different paths to get there with varying results, based on the available natural resources and the environment that supported them.

5,000 years ago, hunting and gathering societies were by far the predominant social structure. As social groups became larger, basic horticultural efforts evolved. Using small plots of land, tribes grew only enough food to provide for a family or a small, close-knit tribal group. These efforts, though, were very dependant on weather patterns and climate, and that dependence encouraged a seasonal migratory style of living. Advancements in tools, food storage, and crop systems all affected this lifestyle change. The agricultural methods adopted and advanced by Native Americans preceded similar European developments by centuries. Crop rotation was one system adopted by Native Americans that revolutionized the production level of harvests, and when combined with major advancements in irrigation methods, it offered tribes the opportunity to grow enough surplus food for storage and trade. Natives also pioneered food preservation techniques that helped support tribal stability and survival. Tool developments made planting and harvesting a much less labor-intensive process. All of these achievements helped propel native societies toward the development of successful, independent civilizations.

Anasazi development between 450 and 750 C.E. in the American Southwest offers an interesting and useful case study in prehistoric agricultural science. The southwestern environments inhabited by these tribes were not the most hospitable on the continent. The Anasazi faced unique challenges in the development of successful farming methods because of their desert environs. Around 450 C.E., the Anasazi began to plant small plots of vegetables and weave baskets made specifically for storage, beginning the move away from foraging. They observed the fertility or producing ability of different soils and, based on their observations, moved their crops to areas where they could be more successful. Larger plots of cropland and bigger baskets helped them better use their gains in produce. They also began building their houses close to the fields for convenience, and this development signaled the beginning of the Anasazi shift to a more sedentary society. Hunting and gathering were still important, but development of tools and storage techniques gave them backup resources when hunting and gathering results fell short. By 750 C.E., the Anasazi society could be considered a settled, agricultural people. They built long-term storage facilities made of clay and stone, fashioned pottery for transporting water, and planted large fields of beans, corn, and squash (the Three Sisters' first appearance in this region) watered by amazingly advanced irrigation systems. The Anasazi continued growing and expanding along these lines for almost 600 years, despite the difficult, aggressive climate of the desert Southwest. They developed large cliff dwellings that continue to inspire and awe modern society. They cultivated every piece of arable land available to them. Despite their pioneering spirit and amazing success rate, droughts and game shortages took their toll. They were eventually forced to abandon their cliff dwellings and migrate in smaller groups to different areas of the Southwest. Their populations had simply grown too large for their environment to sustain, even with their advanced technology. Although they were forced to disperse, the Anasazi did not disappear; they simply evolved. Even though their old way of life vanished, it could be said that in letting go of what was not working and moving on to a different societal structure, the Anasazi adapted to the natural challenges they faced and overcame them.

Another type of agriculture in a different part of the American continent suggests advanced development of agricultural techniques long before the Anasazi. The Fort Ancient area of Ohio has provided interesting evidence concerning prehistoric agriculture in North America, discounting the suggestion that agriculture made its way up to North America from more advanced neighbors in Mesoamerica (2000–1500 B.C.E.). Fossils of seed coats or shells and pollen concentration in rocks helped researchers design maps of seed characteristics based on their locations. The arrangement and location of the pollen residue and fossils suggest that natives cultivated certain plants in certain areas, in configurations simply not possible by natural processes. The field work done by Kendra McLaughlan with the University of Minnesota resulted in the assessment that the "pollen record reveals that prehistoric agriculture in North America was more extensive than previously assumed." Ultimately, considering these recent finds, scientists must reconsider the "nature, extent and geographical distribution of prehistoric human impacts on the North American landscape."[1] How cultivation began and how the plants arrived simply cannot be taken for granted when so much evidence remains to be discovered.

Native farmers often focused on the rich soil of river valleys and flood plains for cultivation, when those lands were available. Tools made of wood, stone, and bone proved useful for easy planting. In lands composed of heavy clay soil or areas covered with grasses, tilling was not so easy. To cut through the soil, sharper, more solid tools were used to force the ground open. No matter what the tools were made of, all native societies took care to till only as deep as necessary for planting, in order to respect the body of Mother Earth. Preparing the soil for the tilling process took many forms as well. East of the Mississippi River, in woodland areas, native farmers girdled trees, a process of slowly killing a tree by making one-inch or deeper parallel cuts around the entire width. This cut off the water and nutrient supply to the rest of the tree, killing the top portion. In heavy woodlands, this was the most effective and time-efficient way of thinning forests to allow in more sunlight. These "clearings" were carefully managed, and the spirits of the forest and woodlands were consulted so that natives would not offend or overstep their boundaries. Another method of preparing farmland was to burn underbrush and old crops to rid the land of ground cover, while simultaneously adding valuable nutrients to the soil. Some tribes, especially in the plains areas, developed an early practice of crop rotation, allowing fields to lie fallow or unplanted to replenish the soil of its growing ability. These methods today are based on an understanding of plant growth and nourishment processes and are often employed on today's farms. The natives using these methods did not necessarily have the same scientific understanding of plant biology, but still, through experimentation and observation, they developed methods reflected in today's more "advanced" scientific farming practices.

To further protect crops, early pesticides were used. The Mohawk tribes soaked their seeds in a hellebore herbal liquid to poison crows, keeping them from destroying their crops. The Navajos coated the plant part of squash with urine and goat's milk to protect against damage by hungry insects. Many native tribes spent hours and hours picking insects and worms off of crops by hand when they had no other defense. Because of the lack of what is considered "modern" technology, everything was done by hand until tools could be developed to facilitate the planting and harvesting processes. To help with harvesting, Native American farmers could use peg-like tools to remove the husks from corn and shells or other scooping-shaped tools to shear the kernels off the cob. Gathering sticks and knives helped reap in the rice crops. Tools helped store as well. Mortars, pestles, and baskets were used to thresh or pound the harvest into usable form, and special baskets helped winnow or sort the storable food. Native Americans used everything from baskets to in-ground caches to store food in the effort to protect it from weather, pests, rodents, scavengers, and thieves. Any natural resource that could be used or adapted for use found its way into Native American agricultural practices.

Over thousands of years, many different varieties of plant species were bred using the same innovative and observatory skills necessary to develop advanced planting and harvesting techniques. Some crossbreeds were accidents and some not, but all mutations served to advance understanding of farming science. One common method of encouraging the survival of the strongest plants was to plant more than necessary and then pull the weaker, smaller plants, leaving the better specimens to mature. By using the seeds from this weaning method, over the centuries native

Stone and clay curios and small grinding and cutting tools created and used by prehistoric southwestern agricultural societies. Denver Public Library, Western History Collection, Call Number P-361.

farmers learned that the best crops came from the fattest and most uniform seeds. Farmers cleaned and sun-dried seeds for future use only after choosing the best specimens for the next year's planting. This process of selection, over time, bred plants that produced better seeds than the ones before it. Often, to protect the quality of the seeds and future crops, planters interspersed different crop varieties on single plots so as to minimize the possibility of unintentional cross-pollination. In Kentucky, for example, gourd or squash seeds that were native to Mexico were found in archaeological sites. They could not have gotten there on their own; they had to be transported there by someone. These seeds were ancient, over 3,000 years old. The most interesting part is that the records shows that as the years progressed, the seeds became larger and their protective coats thinner (as a result of human selection and protection), suggesting that through the process of weeding out apparently undesirable seeds, natives nurtured a more productive and successful species. And where there is success, there is surplus. Could this have been the beginning of early capitalism? Experimentation with the environment set many tribes on the path of spiritual, physical, and material success.

ECONOMICS AND AGRICULTURE: FARMING AND CAPITAL GROWTH

Prehistoric Native American economy looked and functioned rather differently than Western culture would expect. Because material wealth was not valued in most native societies, economic systems evolved, and tribes functioned on a barter basis. Different tribal groups needed a common frame of reference, a common economic language, when trading goods. As a result, tribes specialized in different commodities, ranging from clothing, tools, and accessories to crops, animal products, and raw materials, giving each society different commodities of value to barter with and trade. The term used to describe these economic systems is "subsistence economy." This meant that tribes engaged in the trade of wild animals, plants, and their products or of cultivated domestic equivalents in order to ensure the tribe had everything it needed. Most natives did not see a purpose in collecting more goods or wealth than they could use, and as such, luxury items and materialism held little significance in American Indian economy. Common prehistoric trade goods included agricultural and building tools, animal by-products for both food and manufacture purposes, nonedible crops such as tobacco and cotton, food stuffs (both plant and animal), clothing and ritual goods, jewelry, and medicines. Had one tribe tried to provide all of these necessary goods for themselves, it would have taken all of their efforts, and most likely, they still would not have succeeded. By developing a trade-based subsistence economy, natives could specialize in their area of choice and benefit from the expertise of others.

The "local" environments (local generally meant a much larger area in prehistoric times than it would today) of each tribe entirely determined the basis of economy. The economic structure, for example, of the Lower Pecos area in present-day Texas was based largely on hunting and gathering. Different sites throughout Texas offer detailed evidence for analysis of the regional economic system. The dating stretches back all the way to 7000 B.C.E. and examination of archeological hearth remains. At a site called Baker Cave, the remains of 16 different kinds of plants, 6 different fish, 18 species of reptile, and 11 other assorted animals suggests that the tribes kept their foraging areas wide while trading when necessary. Some of the remains at Baker Cave were either nonnative or lightly represented in the region, suggesting that they were imported, offering suggestions as to what areas of specialization tribes focused on and defining not only what the Baker Cave residents utilized, but also what their neighbors provided.

Another example is the Headwater area of the Colorado River. People first arrived there approximately 10,000 years ago when the area was undergoing the transformation from an Ice Age to a more seasonal climate similar to today's. Larger mammals died off, and forests expanded. The piñon pine was particularly successful in this region. This tree was extremely important from an economic perspective. The nuts of the tree were delicious, nutritious, and perfect for long-term storage. Individual trees produced the nuts in abundance, and tribes in the area made good use of them until these forests began other natural changes a few thousand years later. Bison were also extremely important to regional natives, but even this resource fluctuated in availability, virtually disappearing between 5000 and 3000 B.C.E.. The prehistoric record of this region, based on artifacts like pottery and obsidian, suggests that when goods were not available, tribes expanded their network of contacts and definition of "local" to provide what the tribe needed to survive. At each point of change, natives had to adapt their economic trade systems to deal with environmental fluctuations.

One development important to the Headwaters people (scholars are still undecided as to who they actually were) was contact with farming cultures to the south. Being in an area that was too cold for reliable successful farming, these natives needed agricultural support. But they also had something to offer. The farmers benefited from the Headwaters' wealth of hunting resources, and ultimately, it benefited both communities to base their economic relationship on a trade of goods and land access. The most challenging and impacting environmental adaptation for the Headwaters economy was the introduction of other people, specifically the Spanish. With the introduction of the Spanish in the 18th century came domesticated animals, such as horses, sheep, and goats. These animals were so important that their effects spread much faster than Western documentation of those changes could. Basically, scholars know, only according to archaeological record, when these animals were introduced. However, by the time Western observers showed up to record native use of these animals, they were well ingrained into American Indian society, suggesting that the tribes embraced the changes this new environmental factor brought.

Prior to the arrival of Europeans though, the Headwaters region in Colorado based its economy largely on hunting and gathering. Until the piñon pine disappeared around 3,000 years ago, natives spent much of their time moving around, gathering foods for storage in preparation for a settled winter. The relatively quick environmental climatic change that resulted in the disappearance of the piñon pine had wide societal ramifications. People no longer settled down for the winter, traveling outside of the Gunnison Basin area to obtain their needed food sources. Hunting persisted, and corn made its first appearance in the region, but each tribe continued to specialize in its own areas, adapting to the changes but also continuing their basic economic way of life. Even if experts have few, if any, clues about the identity of the natives in the Gunnison Basin Headwaters area, the archaeological record preserved enough evidence for scholars to analyze and come to conclusions about society patterns.

Even individual land-use rights and patterns varied, depending on environmental factors. No one really "owned" the land; they simply were allowed use of it from the gods in what could be called "tenure." On the East Coast and in the Great Plains, tribes practiced a combination of communal and land tenure, which directly affected agricultural economic systems. A village or tribe claimed land-use rights, but within that community, the women usually controlled the actual fields. The only requirement was that the women should use an appropriate amount of the land she controlled for farming given the size of the group for which her farming would provide food. If she failed in that task, then another individual or the community could take the land from her for someone else to use. Tribal leaders usually portioned out plots of land, but there was no set pattern across tribal lines for who received what land and how much. A woman could farm as much land as she felt was necessary. Although croplands could pass down through families (through the mother's side), no one person could claim *absolute* right to ownership. It was not possible, for example, to *sell* land, like the Western world would think of it. Natives believed the land did not belong to this generation alone; they were simply protectors for future societies, and the gods had given them use of the land to prepare for the generations to come. The Southwest, however, offers one example of land-use rules that functioned a little differently than they did across much of the continent. Individual men, rather than the women, controlled the land, and when land was handed down through families, it passed through the father's line. Among the southwestern peoples, the Papago and Yuma tribes were good examples of this practice. The Pueblo Indians operated much more like the East Coast tribes, putting their women in charge. The Navajos often split the gender rights and responsibilities and employed both communal and individual land-use rights. Depending on the roles adopted by the two sexes in response to natural environment resources and challenges, access to the land varied. Basically, tribes recognized a collective right to large tracks of land and the individual right to cultivate smaller plots within that large area, working in unison with their surroundings to carve a happy coexistence from the soil. Ultimately, environmental factors determined responsibilities and style of native economic life. As a result, land use and agriculture sat squarely in the center of day-to-day economic activity.

NOTE

1. Both quotes in this paragraph are taken from Kendra McLauchlan's study titled "Plant Cultivation and Forest Clearance by Prehistoric North Americans," available from http://www.dartmouth.edu/~kmclauchlan/McLauchan%2003. pdf.

4

HUMAN HABITATION IN THE ENVIRONMENT: LIVE AND LET LIVE

May the warm winds of heaven blow softly on your home, and the
Great Spirit bless all who enter there.

Cherokee blessing

When *Usen* created the Apaches, he also gave them their homes in the
West. He gave them such grain, fruits, and game as they needed to eat . . .
and all they needed for clothing and shelter was at hand. Thus it was in
the beginning; the Apaches and their homes, each created for the other.
When they are taken from these homes, they sicken and die.

Geronimo, Chiricahua Apache

Why did prehistoric Native Americans choose to live where they did?
Would they have even considered it a choice? It is easy to understand
how environmental and climatic factors could force a people to move,
but where is the line between "stay" and "leave"? Throughout history,
humans have adapted to the environment, changing as needed to survive.
Sometimes, however, humans also migrated out of necessity and hardship. The ability to sustain the tribe determined whether a people would
stay in an area or desert it for greener horizons. Some peoples kept their
local area small, building large structures that served as a home base for
farming, hunting, and foraging. Other cultures embraced larger areas,
migrating with the seasons and availability of resources. Depending on
their surroundings, the climate, and natural materials, shelter took many
forms. When thinking of a Native American house or dwelling, most
people think of the stereotypical tepee made of logs or poles and tanned
animal skins. Although some prairie and plains tribes lived in these types

of shelters, most North American Indians developed other structures
very different and more appropriate to their environments and lifestyles.
Home is where the heart is and a native tribe's heart beat in and around
the structures that housed the people. One of the most important elements in the health and success of native society was the house.

THE PEOPLE AND THEIR CLIMATE: SEASONAL
EFFECTS ON NATIVE LIFE

Everything known about prehistoric societies is based on oral tradition and physical evidence passed on and preserved over thousands of
years. In examining the prehistoric North American climate, geological
evidence comes into play. Out of all animals, humans are the only ones
to use intellect and culture to adapt to their environment. The earliest of
these adaptations would have taken place during the Pleistocene Epoch,
which started 1.65 million years ago and ended around 8,000 B.C.E. This
was the geological period that just preceded the time when many believe
humans arrived in North America. It is known as the Glacial Epoch or Ice
Age, and it experienced regular climatic changes; major shifts in temperature that occurred every few thousand years. The sea level was lower, as
much as 300 feet lower, because of the large amount of ocean water frozen
as glaciers. Temperature drops and the subsequent refreezing of oceans
exposed the Beringia Bridge at various times by tying up even more ocean
water in glacier form, allowing for the early migration of humans into
North America. The exact cause of ice ages is unknown, although there
have been several during Earth's history. One theory suggests that in past
ice ages a solar shift in the sun's position reduced the heat that reached
Earth, causing the climate to cool drastically. Another suggestion is that
atmospheric changes somehow blocked or reflected the heat trying to
reach the planet, causing a major cooling trend. The Pleistocene also saw
much volcanic activity and volcanic ash could have saturated the atmosphere, affecting global temperatures. Scholars may never know what
caused the ice ages. A deeper understanding of these past events might
be helpful today; some scientists today think that air pollution may bring
about another. Only time will tell.

Different areas of the planet experienced the Glacial Epoch at different times, and for North America, the Pleistocene extended from about
1 million to 10,000 B.C.E. The ice sheets alternately advanced and receded,
creating cold and warm temperature fluctuations. With these conditions,
North America would have looked and felt much like the Greenland of
today. The most recent American ice sheet reached as far south as the Ohio
River and eastward to Long Island. In many places, it would have been
over one mile thick. As the ice sheet advanced southward, animals were
driven in front of it. This often created strange herds made up of large
and small mammals as the ice pushed on. Now-extinct beasts mingled

with smaller creatures who survived to today. In these herds there were mastodons and bears, wooly mammoths and deer, and saber-toothed cats and rabbits, creating a motley crew of migrants. Paleontologists can re-create the composition of these herds based on mass graves that have been excavated and analyzed. The presence of that much ice created unique conditions and challenges for life on the continent, while often preserving evidence for future analysis. The lands to the south were much cooler and wetter than today, as well as greener and more populated by wildlife. Deserts were virtually nonexistent. All that remains today of this chilly past is one bastion of salt water in the middle of Utah: the Great Salt Lake. During the Pleistocene, it would have covered much of Utah, Nevada, and Idaho. This is the environment ancient immigrants would have found upon their arrival to North America.

Or perhaps it was not. There is a theory supported by some hard evidence that humans arrived in North America approximately 40,000 years ago; 25,000 years earlier than most scholars commonly accept. Footprints made in volcanic ash found 80 miles southeast of Mexico City have been dated twice, using two different reliable dating techniques. The results prove that the footprints are 38,000 to 39,000 years old. Because of the location of the find (deep in Mexico), humans, if they came to this continent by way of the Beringia Bridge, must have arrived on the continent at least 50,000 years ago in order to reach that far south. Considering also the existing knowledge on prehistoric climates, a much warmer phase of the last ice age becomes the contender for the earliest known human habitation in North America. Not only does this discovery affect commonly accepted dates, but it also coincides with early Aboriginal migration to Australia, leading some scholars to believe that the first Americans could have been part of the same group of migrants. It also brings into question the method of migration; could early humans have traveled to North America by boat? The North American prehistoric climate also experienced a warmer phase approximately 70,000 years ago, and although there are no human-remains sites that date that old, there is a Brazilian site dated to 50,000 years ago, keeping speculation alive and well. This new evidence suggests it is possible that humans arrived during the earlier warm spell, opening the door for entirely new areas of analysis and understanding of human presence in North America. To fully comprehend how people adapted to their environments, it is necessary to know in which environment and time period humans first arrived. Although archaeological certainties are difficult to come by, discoveries such as the footprints near Mexico City get the world closer to knowing where early humans came from and how they lived. Scholars analyzing the prints, professors Dave Huddart and Matthew Bennett, and Dr. Sylvia Gonzalez point out that this discovery "shows our ancestors adapted to new environments much quicker and more easily than we had imagined."[1] Dr. Gonzalez is one of a growing number of experts who believe humans might have arrived here by boat rather than by foot. Although both explanations provide food for thought and argument, one thing is certain: again it seems that adaptation is the rule, rather than the exception.

In the long run, science can look at these climatic patterns in detail, but large patterns and time spans really have little relevance to daily life. The Earth is currently experiencing a period of global warming, and every year, people across North America are affected by the side effects. In this sense, individuals are directly connected to their environment and the climate in which they live. Scientists, however, often look at climate on a much larger scale than one generation's life span, and in the example of the Pleistocene, which lasted almost 900,000 years, how relevant is that kind of epoch designation to people's daily lives? When climate specialists look back 100, 500, or 1,000 years from now, chances are their data and conclusions will be so large as to have little significance to life today. It is necessary to use a different frame of reference when trying to learn about a specific people, and it is absolutely important to understand more detailed analysis than broader climate generalizations can sometimes offer. For an understanding of a people and how they lived, their daily environment must be understood, and it is here that the challenge for anthropologists is often the greatest.

Taking into consideration these detailed climatic factors, the question still remains: why did natives choose to live where they did? An example of a tribe whose members chose to live in a difficult environment is the Sinagua. Nine hundred years ago, these natives picked the desert as their home. Close to present-day Flagstaff, Arizona, in Walnut Canyon, the Sinagua built large stone dwellings on cliff ridges, often situated under craggy overhangs that hovered over 300 feet above the canyon floor. Using stone, mud, and plaster, they built pueblo-like buildings with rooms sitting adjacent to each other, much like an apartment building. They positioned their homes strategically, facing the sun, so that when darkness came, the masonry would have saved up warmth to help the inhabitants weather the colder nights. The relatively small size of the rooms suggests that the Sinagua spent little time inside, functioning as a hardy, outdoors people.

The name of the tribe, given to them by archaeologist Harry Colton, means "without water," suggesting further environmental hardships. In addition to tackling difficult building logistics, these ancient people were dry-land farmers with a growing season of only four months and a yearly rainfall of less than 20 inches, which complicated their quest for survival. "Many today see this arid and rocky land as inhospitable, but it remains that prehistoric people used what it had to offer to their advantage to survive and leave behind an amazing legacy."[2] In order for the people to reach their farmlands, trails had to be blazed from their cliff-side homes down to the farmlands, making pathways dangerous to carve and traverse. Treacherous lands and little water do not create a picture of desirable prehistoric living environment. Why would they stay? Some scholars suggest that because of a huge population growth during the 12th century when the Sinagua would have settled in the canyons, more choice locations were already taken, leaving the tribe to fend with what was available. Their location could have been a measure of protection against invaders as well, although there is no evidence to suggest major conflicts during this time. The hardships, though, helped created a life of unique and enduring beauty for the Sinagua.

For over 100 years, the Sinagua ruled the region, and then, for reasons still unknown, it seems they just picked up and left. The archaeological record suggests that they simply walked away, probably in family groups of just a handful of people at a time rather than as a tribal migration. Many believe they may have fallen victim to their own success. Despite the deep reliable water sources and relatively arable land (for the area), it seems they eventually grew too large for the canyon to sustain. They thinned forests for farming land and firewood, hunted extensively, and planted heavily in fields that may not have been able to handle the nutrient demand. Once their population grew too large for the environment to sustain, it is possible that they decided to leave for greener pastures. Other reasons could have played a role as well, included bad religious omens, disease, or drought, but no one knows for sure. The most feasible scenario has the people integrating themselves into the Hopi tribe, adapting as needed to continue their survival. To the Hopi, they are the *Hisatsinom,* the "People of Long Ago," and although they disappeared as an independent unit, their knowledge and legacy continued through their joining with other tribes, a necessary adaptation for the Sinagua to survive.

Many other microclimates existed across North America, and every one of them hosted Native Americans. For as many tribes as there were, there were just as many reasons for staying in their native environments. There were also just as many reasons for leaving when the time came. Although climate played a major role in *how* Indians lived, it rarely was their sole reason for choosing to stay where they did. Natives did an amazing job adapting themselves and altering their environments to make survival easier. The earliest ancestral humans needed protection from predators and the elements and took shelter in caves and under rock overhangs. Eventually, they improved upon these early shelters by adding floors, walls, entrances, and fireplaces. The next step was to build dwellings in areas where no natural shelter existed. As independent houses emerged, other changes in lifestyle followed suit. Natives developed and perfected tools and other accessories as needed and desired. This process took place over tens of thousands of years. No matter how advanced a civilization became, however, the foundation of life was always the home, built to shelter, protect, and nurture. Climate and environment provided the means to survive, whereas ingenuity and flexibility provided the way.

THE SHAPE OF THINGS: STRUCTURE OF SHELTER DETERMINED BY ENVIRONMENT AND CLIMATE

Through the centuries of changing natural habitats, shape and form of native housing was a direct reflection of the environment in which the people lived and once perfected, housing styles remained relatively constant, evolving only in response to variations in natural environment. Each region in North America experienced different climate patterns, natural forces, and animal threats, all of which shaped the structure of human dwellings. Beginning in the East, the first region to look at is the woodland area, which spanned the entire coast, from southern Canada down into Florida and offered several different microclimates of habitation. Coastal woodlands varied drastically and consequently, so did native dwellings. The most common was the *wigwam*, the Algonquian name for a house with a wagon-shaped top, rounded roof, and straight sides. Wigwams were perfectly adapted to a semi-nomadic style, being both easy to set up and tear down. Natives drove strong poles into the ground and bound them together at the tops to form arches; then they covered them with woven mats. There were doorways on each end of the structure and a hole in the top for ventilation and smoke release. At the arch, the houses would stand over 14 feet high and run up to 20 feet long. In some areas, the houses held only one family. But some tribes, like the Iroquois, extended these buildings to over one hundred feet in length and divided them into rooms, housing two to three families who shared communal fires in one of the central areas. Natives used wigwams for sleeping, storage, and weather protection. During migration, the only things left behind were the poles driven into the ground. With small variations, the wigwam served the Woodland people as a major form of housing that was both adaptable and appropriate for their forest surroundings.

Another form of housing found in the eastern woodlands was the longhouse. Rather similar in structure and construction to wigwams, the longhouses functioned somewhat differently. They were long, narrow buildings usually covered with bark. The inhabitants were part of one large extended family, the connection being that all women and children in the house came from the same clan. Several longhouses built in one local area constituted a village. The Iroquois often protected their longhouse villages by building tall wooden fences as an enclosure. They planted their gardens close to their homes because daily life revolved around these structures. Built very much like the wigwam, poles were set vertically into the ground with "Y" shapes cut into the tops of the poles. Then other poles were latched horizontally onto the vertical ones, resting inside the "Y" cuts, to make strong, rectangular divisions in the walls. The people constructed roofs by lashing saplings together and arching them over the top with horizontal crossbeams added for strength. These buildings reached as high as 20 feet tall and were anywhere from

40 to 200 feet long. The Iroquois used three-by-six-foot sheets of bark to construct the walls and roof, and when builders combined this with reinforced roof architecture, these homes functioned well to keep the winter snows out. To finish off the structure, more poles were attached to the outside, strengthening the walls and securing the bark in place. On the inside, storage spaces and beds lined the walls on upper and lower platforms. Fire pits sat in the middle of the floor, with smoke holes over each one. The Smoke Dance of the Iroquois developed, it is believed, to help fan the smoke toward the holes in the ceiling. Finally, an image of the clan who lived in the house would be painted over the door, letting all know which family lived in the longhouse. Clanship, which passed down through the mother, was very important, and it functioned as the organizational structure of the extended family. So important was the longhouse to woodland native society that today symbolic drawings of the longhouse include five smoke holes to represent each of the tribes of the Iroquois Confederacy of Five Nations. In 1140 C.E., the "Peacemaker" of the Iroquois, one of the foremost leaders of the time, told each of the five tribes that they would come together in friendship and peace, as one long house, and so the symbolism was born and survives to today, stressing the importance of family, friendship, and community.

Moving westward into the prairies, housing evolved differently as a result of the environment. Several types of houses dominated prairie culture, and the various styles were often mixed throughout the region. The Dakota tribes, for example, lived most of the time in hide-covered tepees, which were very similar to Plains tribe tepees. This practice of "house borrowing" is partially responsible for the erroneous impression that most American Indians lived in tepee structures. More common was the earth lodge, and it was most functional for the Missouri River area. It consisted of a cylinder-like base with a cone-shaped roof and extended tunnel entrance. The entire house was covered with dirt and measured from 30 to 40feet in diameter and five to seven feet high. Prairie Indians would dig down in the floor dirt to expose more compact earth and dig a hole in the middle of that floor for a fire pit. Platforms of poles served as beds and seating. Most earth lodges were home to extended families of tribes such as the Pawnee, Missouri, and Mandan. Moving south, grass-thatched houses were more common, used by the Caddo and Wichita Indians. The fireplace, as usual, was in the center, except these structures needed no smoke holes; the thatch walls provided natural ventilation. Bed platforms lined the walls of these buildings that were home to a number of individual families functioning as an extended unit. Standing 15 feet tall and up to 20 feet in diameter, the home's size made for close quarters by today's standards but was perfect for native southern prairie purposes. They spent very little time inside their homes and so needed much less space. Combine this with the fact that materialistic society simply had not evolved yet, and the result is that prehistoric natives needed much less space either for living or for storage. In the area around the Great Lakes, the domed houses natives such as the Ojibwa built were closely related to woodland wigwams. Woven or sewn mats, pieces of bark, and sometimes tanned hides covered these Great Lakes dwellings. Single families occupied small houses that were generally circular in shape and larger families lived in elongated, more oval-shaped houses. The environment supplied the resources and Prairie Indians created the culture, while providing the choice of several different styles.

Farther west into the plains, the tepee was by far the most popular housing choice. Carefully constructed, made of sturdy poles latched together at the top covered with a tanned buffalo hide, the structure offered easy assembly, teardown, and portability. Rather than standing upright like a cone, which is most people's mental image, the tepee of the Prairie Native Americans sloped asymmetrically, with the longest side facing the prevailing wind direction, strengthening the tepee against the often-dangerous prairie winds. Smoke flaps and control ropes provided intricate systems of both ventilation and insulation that helped make extreme winters and summers more bearable. The tepee was set up by bracing three poles against each other and then pulling the poles up using a rope hoist. Then other supportive poles were latched on and the hide cover was pulled down over the top. The fire pit sat in the center with beds placed around it on the ground. With the house reaching as high as 12 feet and being even larger in diameter, the covering of the structure required anywhere from 15 to 20 buffalo hides. The building and dismantling was the job of the women in the family, as was tanning the hides and making the cover.

Reproduction of a book illustration showing a Mandan village in a traditional layout. The image was drawn sometime around the turn of the 20th century. Denver Public Library, Western History Collection, Call Number X-32543.

At most, men contributed the poles for the houses, and as a result of this unequal contribution, the women owned and controlled the tepees entirely. Once the women had them torn down and stored for transportation, dog-pulled travois made migration immeasurably easier. The structure of the tepee would often have symbolic meaning as well. Poles could serve as a method of teaching important values; each of them represented different morals in native society, so the people living in the tepees felt surrounded by what they considered the central elements of their society. Even with the weather and temperature challenges of prairie expanses, natives found ways to utilize available resources, express meaning in their lives, and live in comfort.

Looking on to the Great Basin and using the Shoshone as an example, two common structures stand out. This arid region also utilized the tepee, but as a more upright, conical home than the Prairie Indians' version. Roughly 20 to 25 poles were erected as the backbone of the structure. The tepee was usually covered with thatch held down by pole bindings, but sometimes hide or bark was used as well. This structure was smaller than its plains equivalent, but otherwise used most of the same structural details and functional adaptations. On the inside, the two different variations looked very similar. Sometimes the dwellings would be painted, telling the stories of the family that lived within. Spiritual leaders always blessed the new buildings before they covered the poles, praying that the family would have a happy life, the doorways would be protected from evil, and that the house would always be open to the hungry, orphaned, and elderly. The second most popular house of the Great Basin was a domed unit covered with thatch or brush. In the summer, natives often made dwellings from green, leafy branches instead of the dried materials used in the fall and winter. These dwellings were temporary and often left behind when the tribe moved on. Most of the archaeological record suggests that Basin housing was usually rather crude, easily assembled, and soon abandoned or moved because of quickly depleted local resources. Whether taken with them or left while in the pursuit of sustenance, native housing in this region represents the highly mobile, challenging, and fluctuating nature of the Great Basin.

The plateau environs offer yet another opportunity to examine how climate and environment affected a society's life. The plateau natives, such as the Spokane, Nez Perce', Yakima, and Kootenai tribes, lived in pit houses, one of the oldest Native American building types. It used earth berming, a technique of either digging the house partially into the ground or building up earth around the walls. Even digging just a few feet into the ground helped regulate temperature because at about five or six feet deep, temperatures are much more constant than on the surface. Building up earth ledges around a structure is not quite as effective, but still does a great job as insulation. Although the temperatures did not vary as much in plateau areas as they did in the prairies, hot summers and cold winters were generally the rule, and the protective earth made for a cooler summer and a warmer winter inside the houses. The plateau region was home to many microenvironments as well, ranging from high mountains and dense forests to arid plains and lush valleys. These differences in local environment affected the shape, structure, and materials used in pit houses, but pit houses remained the basic plateau home structure. After digging the hole for the house, natives used a framework of wood poles above the ground walled by mats and roofed with sod. The entrance was usually the smoke hole in the roof, a rather unique feature. During the summers, some tribes made more portable houses shored up with dirt on the sides and these structures were easier to take down and move when necessary. The combination of these materials with earth insulation shows intelligence and ingenuity in utilizing readily available resources.

Over on the West Coast of North America, history shows yet another variation on a common theme. Just prior to contact in the late 1700s and early 1800s (Meriwether Lewis and William Clark were the first white faces many in the West had seen), West Coast houses were made of massive cedar posts and beams with removable vertical wall boards that were set into grooves at the top and bottom of each section, making the houses square. The people of the West Coast thought of the world as a huge box that contained all of the souls in creation either in animal or human form. Boxes played a major role in almost every facet of coastal native life from birth, through adulthood, and into death. The family group, a smaller collection of souls, was kept in a box, the house, and based on their belief of the world being one large box of spirits, the house represented all of creation in miniature. Each house had three doorways or openings—one each for living people, the deceased, and spirits—as they believed the earth to have. They also considered their home a living being with skin and bones (the framework and planks), and it protected its inhabitants from danger and evil influence. Because of the highly symbolic nature of West Coast houses and the fact that they were made out of wood, the homes were usually decorated with beautiful, intricate carvings to show honor and respect to the universe it represented and the spirits within.

Housing on the West Coast varied within regions just as housing did across the rest of the continent. The principal type of housing in southern California, for example, was "wattle-and-daub." Natives first built a round, dome-shaped pole framework and then walled the frame with wattle (bundles of woven sticks and reeds). Packed with daub (clay or mud), the structure proved to be very weatherproof. A feature of this building technique that makes it useful to archaeologists is the fact that when the buildings burned, the daub cured or fired much like pottery would. Through a system of tests, it is possible for scientists to distinguish between structural daub and pottery clay, and often these remnants contain many clues to southern California native life. Fingerprints and handprints have been found in fire-cured daub, telling the story of construction. Vegetation imprints tell

Laguna Pueblo in New Mexico shown from the back with wooden ladders, wood-framed windows and doors, and additional mesas in the background. Denver Public Library, Western History Collection, Call Number N-75.

what kind of plants were either used or grown in the area. Pole impressions can often help determine size, shape, and construction methods. A wealth of evidence is often present in the most unsuspecting of places.

Ending this tour of North American housing in the Southwest, several different kinds of houses must be examined. The Pueblo peoples such as the Hopi and Zuni peoples lived in rectangular, flat-roofed rooms built flush against each other to form a continuous large village similar to apartment complexes. Built either from stone or adobe (clay), the appearance varied little across the region because of the plaster used to cover the walls. The lower rooms had no doorways or windows, and residents entered by climbing down log ladders through openings in the roof. The rooms were about twelve feet square and grouped together to house several hundred people. Each family lived in one room, although many had other rooms for storage and ritual purposes. Lightly furnished, only one or two benches and niches in the walls served as places to sit and store goods. Another type of house found along the Colorado River used by the Pueblo-related Yumans is the Mohave structure. It had a frame of logs and poles, walled by thatched arrow weeds and finished with a covering of sand. The structures were nearly square at 20-by-25 feet, with one door in the middle of the wall facing the south. Sand covered the roof and three sides of the house, making it only visible from the front. Small fireplaces sat near the door, but in the warm climate, these were probably rather unnecessary. Nature provided the resources to comfortably house the extended families of the Yumans.

For most of these peoples, decorations were scarce, although some simple art created by mixing paint with masonry remains on the walls. The meaning of these frescoes is unclear; they may have been ceremonial drawings, family histories, or even graffiti, but there is simply not enough evidence or information to assign a specific meaning to them except to say that they must have played a symbolic role in the lives of the clans that used them. Scholars know something about the furnishings as well. They used looms to weave cloth, and apparently, this was the realm of men. Inside their homes, women fashioned pottery for family use, as evidenced by tools found inside the houses. The only other furnishings were bed platforms and sometimes chair or stool-like pieces, testifying to the simplicity and utility of native furniture.

Non-Pueblo people, like the Opata, occupied the northern and eastern part of the Southwest and lived in crude conical tepees made of poles

These hogans are representative of the style constructed by Navajo Indians. They are hollow mounds of earth covered with a layer of dirt, and they have one entryway with an animal hide door cover and vent hole for fire smoke at the peak. Denver Public Library, Western History Collection, Call Number GB-5481.

leaned together and covered with thatch, brush, wood, or bark. The Navajo hogan was originally such a structure, but evolved into a hexagonal building with walls constructed of horizontal logs. As in many belief systems, the Navajo incorporated their ideas about the universe into the shape and function of their homes. The hogan was supposed to be a smaller version of the universe with a balance of both male and female. Many Navajo utilized two different kinds of hogans, separating male and female entirely, with the male hogan the focus of ceremony and healing and the female hogan the family home. Hogan construction followed a very specific, ritualistic path of ceremony and dedication. Once completed, the hogan would host everyday rituals meant to ensure harmony within the individual, the family unit, and the tribe. Some semblance of this significance can be found in the beliefs about the connections between housing and daily life. Other people in the Southwest lived in domed huts covered most often with thatch, and depending on the area, they might have been round or more rectangular. There were also rectangular houses with flat roofs in the more southern areas of the Southwest, but they tended to be set apart from each other, not clustered together in the Pueblo style. Peoples living close to Meso-America lived in houses with four rectangular walls and a roof that was triangular on two sides and more rectangular on the other two, looking a bit pyramidal. The most well-known tribes of this area would have been the Yaqui and the Tarahumara. These cultures inhabited the physical and cultural space between the fully Pueblo people to the north and the people of Meso-America to the south.

As this discussion shows, housing took a wide variety of forms based on local resources and climate factors. Different cultures ascribed different symbolism to their homes, and that affected shape, form, and function. Many tribes used more than one kind of dwelling, depending on the available building materials, season, and wealth of the family unit or clan. For example, many tribes in the Midwest lived in large, multifamily houses during farming season, but during the buffalo hunts, utilized smaller conical tepees they could tear down and transport easily. In another example, wickiups were temporary houses used by nomadic Native Americans in Arizona, New Mexico, Utah, Idaho, and California, making this structure a multiregional entity. It used a framework of arched poles covered by brush, bark, rushes, or mats. The problem with so many varied environments and cultures is that things such as housing took on many forms, making definite, concise conclusions difficult. The previous discussions on housing describe dwellings used by the largest part of a regional population or for the longest period in a year. To discuss in detail the form all housing took would be impractical. And ultimately, no matter what the style or shape, the home represented the heart and culture of the group it housed. The centrality of the structure, its permanence, aesthetic appeal, internal furnishings and more give modern scholars a wealth of opportunities to look into the daily lives of ancient Americans and re-create the reality of their experience.

IN A HARSH LANDSCAPE: SPECIAL SHELTER CONCERNS IN THE FACE OF EXTREME CLIMATE AND ENVIRONMENT

Certain areas of the North American continent offered more environmental and climatic challenges than others, creating special obstacles for natives living in those areas. Tropical, swampy lands, high-altitude mountains, and arid deserts offered unique challenges to Native American shelter. Using tropical, marshy lands as the first example, the best adaptation is the chickee structure of the Everglade Seminole Indians in present-day Florida. *Chickee* quite simply means "house" in the Seminole and Miccosukee native languages. The Seminoles built their houses on higher ground because of the flooding and animal dangers of the swamp. Brent Weisman, associate professor and specialist in Seminole culture, says that "there would [have been] at least two different types . . . one without a raised wooden platform floor (only a dirt floor) for cooking, with the cook fire in the middle, and a sleeping chickee with a raised wooden split-log floor."[3] These wall-less buildings formed around structural poles were driven into the ground, and then the floors were constructed of long poles covered with cypress bark and leaves. The roofs were made of poles covered with bark and leaves and sloped down on each side from the center peak. The buildings stood so high off of the ground that the natives used ladders to climb up to the floor. The environmental advantages of the buildings included shelter from rain and falling objects blown about by high winds (the wide, sloping roofs) and ventilation in the middle of the stifling heat and humidity of the Florida panhandle (the absence of walls). Although these homes were taken down and moved easily, the construction of a new chickee was complicated. Cypress trees had to be cut down and they could be as large as four feet in diameter. Moving them was difficult, also; often the Seminoles waited for storms to flood the area, and then the logs could be floated to their destination. Cutting the palms for roofing took time and effort, but ultimately the work was worth it; it produced a house that would see them through their unique environmental challenges. Although the basic structural design is apparently thousands of years old and documented by western sources on first contact in the mid-1500s, the chickee saw a major rise in use and prominence during the early 1800s as Seminoles discovered the value of housing that was quick to assemble and disassemble in the face of American pursuit and aggression. Once again, native North Americans adapt within an ever-changing environment.

High in the mountains, natives faced different, but just as difficult, challenges to overcome—so much so that according to current understanding, few, if any tribes made high altitudes their home. For example, the Yumans, or Quechans (pronounced "kwuh-TSANS") can be found now at the meeting of the lower Colorado and Gila Rivers and probably have lived there for several centuries. They trace their origins, however, to a sacred mountain called Avikwame', near Needles, California. Their creation story suggests that the creator's son taught them vital survival skills before they moved down the mountain and south to their present-day location. In North America when tribes were considered mountain people, it was because their locale was the lower reaches and foothills of mountain chains. In many ways, this living at the foot of the mountains rather than in higher altitudes would make sense. Even during the summers, mountain environments would have been colder, offering fewer resources for building and sustenance. But mountain reaches held a fascination for tribes and often ended up being destinations in spiritual pilgrimages and exploration journeys. Although some tribes moved into the lower reaches of mountain ranges, the higher elevations were most often the realm of spiritual belief and practice. As such, most of the evidence found suggests that any lodgings built toward the heavens were temporary in order to serve those spiritual purposes. The adaptation to higher elevations apparently resulted in moving down the mountain to more hospitable, flexible habitats.

Cliff Palace, Mesa Verde National Park, Montezuma County, Colorado. Prehistoric Native American Anasazi cliff dwelling located at the top of Cliff Canyon. Buildings are made with masonry construction. In this image, kivas, storage rounds, and access ladders are all visible. Denver Public Library, Western History Collection, Call Number MCC-3060.

Deserts represent the third realm of challenging environment that natives faced in North America. Hot, dry days and much colder nights necessitated unique building structures and materials. Pueblos have been discussed, but here, the creation of cliff dwellings deserves attention. The basic structure was similar to pueblos; especially in the way the rooms were built flush with each other side by side and on top of each other like apartment complexes. The Native Americans of the Anasazi culture built the ancient dwellings found in canyons and mesas around the tributaries of the Rio Grande and Colorado Rivers in New Mexico, Arizona, Colorado, and Utah. These ancestors of the Pueblo people built cliff dwellings between the 11th and 14th centuries. Taking advantage of natural shelter, they built large communal structures situated on ledges in canyon walls and on the flats of mesas. The basic construction material was sandstone, which they shaped into blocks about the size of a loaf of bread. They mixed mud and water to make a mortar that held the blocks together. The living rooms in these structures were about six by eight feet in size, with smaller rooms in the back and on upper levels for storage of belongings and food. To get to these levels, ancient natives climbed the cliff faces using toe and hand holes, which would have been hard enough in itself, but they apparently had to carry game, crops, and other supplies up this way as well. Because access to cliff villages was difficult, they proved easily defendable against aggressive tribes like the Navajo. The villagers were settled farmers who planted their crops in the river valleys below their houses. Many of their daily activities would have taken place in courtyards that their houses surrounded. One bonus for archaeologists is that their living situation encouraged these people to keep their trash close to home. Everything they wanted to get rid of, they tossed down the slopes in front of their houses, leaving garbage piles of information for future discovery. Much of what scholars know of these people comes from their discarded garbage.

One extreme environmental event that could be considered accidently threatening or sometimes intentional and that affected many different cultures across North America was burning specifically of houses. Many reasons for burning have been tossed about by anthropologists, and the following are some of the most likely and most common explanations. Natural wildfires, human accident, intentional burning for both safety and religious reasons, and warfare could all explain the burning of houses. Remains and artifacts can help reconstruct a picture of events. Enemy attack, for example, is a likely culprit if there are bodies inside the structure. If there are personal possessions in the house, scholars might assume that the fire was an accident. If there are funeral accoutrements, then religious reasons take first place. The Upper Republican culture in southern Nebraska is one area that might have experienced regular intentional house burning. The large number of burned houses found in so many sites suggests that people intentionally burned old houses, perhaps to keep them from the hands of enemies or to protect unsuspecting future inhabitants from unsafe structures. Fire played many roles in every Native American society and must be addressed as both friend and foe when studying their ancient history.

One building technology that crossed regional boundaries was the practice of berming, and it often came in handy in the face of extreme temperatures. As mentioned before, berming is the oldest and most effective example of using natural resources to protect a house from the elements. For example, one of the older civilizations in North America, the Anasazi of the Southwest, lived in aboveground structures made of poles and thatch covered with mud, before moving to cliff dwellings almost 300 years later. They connected these houses in long rows, multiplying the insulating effects of the mud-covered thatch. When they finally abandoned these houses, the best guess is that the threat of invaders drove them to the cliff heights. Other examples include the Pawnee, who lived in multifamily earth lodges built on frames of wood that they covered with willow branches, sod, and earth. The Omaha, Osage, and Winnebago lived in more tepee-shaped homes covered with earth, whereas the Wichita chose grass instead. The insulating benefits were top-notch, but the longevity of the houses was not. Because of the weight and moisture content of the dirt, wood frames weakened over time, usually collapsing within 10 years. A less damaging method of utilizing this readily available resource was to dig down into the ground and start building the house there. Not only was there the benefit of dirt insulation, but additionally, the ground itself holds a lower constant temperature than the aboveground air. The early houses of the Mogollon and Hohokam were partially buried. Having a home that was cooler in the day and warmer at night was a major benefit for desert-dwelling people. A typical house sat in a square pit approximately three feet deep. They placed four posts in the corners to support the roof beams, and then poles on the ground leaned against the roof structure to create sloping sidewalls. Branches, grass, and a thick layer of adobe finished off the outside. Through ingenuity and experimentation, natives adapted to the best of their ability in difficult, challenging climates to survive and overcome.

ARTISTIC EXPRESSIONS: THE ADORNMENT OF EVERYDAY LIFE

As this chapter shows, "home" played a central role in the lives of North American natives, in many ways similar to today's society. Home represented the heart of the family, the soul of a clan, and the people who belonged to that clan. Just like an individual, maybe even more so, a family or clan developed a history and a personality. Some tribes took the opportunity to display these personalities through art in and on their homes. Among the Kiowa and the Cheyenne, painted tepees were valuable objects of prestige. Approximately 20 percent of all their tepees were painted, and unlike the ones that women owned, only men owned and controlled the painted tepees. The designs were often inspired by spiritual experiences of the men and therefore were their real property. In some tribes, painted tepees performed a service, such as assuring favorable weather or successful hunts. As representations of spiritual experiences, these artistic dwellings held great power in tribal culture. Another expression of family and history was artistic carving on wooden houses or cedar "totem poles" placed outside. These told the histories and adventures of those that lived within. In the study of artistic adornment on native housing, it is apparent that the images were more than eye-pleasing artwork; they were an expression of a family, clan, and tribe's personality, history, and spirituality. Art is universal among human cultures; the difference comes in the meaning. Archaeologically speaking, the oldest known human art, so far, is about 40,000 years old, so humans have been creating art for a while. For Native Americans, symbolic art and its techniques developed over time and were not generally open to the viewer's interpretation, like most art is today. To fully understand and appreciate Native North American art, it is necessary to stand in the shoes of the culture and individual who produced it, leaving present-day experiences and biases behind.

One interesting, unique, and familiar practice relating to the prehistoric home and family was the carving of totem poles. Six coastal tribes carved totems before the arrival of Europeans: the Nuxalt ("nu-halk"), the Kwakwaka'wakw ("kwak-wak-ya-wak"), the Haida ("hydah"), the Tlingit ("kling-kit"), the coast Salish ("say-lish"), and the Tsimshian ("sim-she-an") people. Although the assumption is that many more tribes carved totem poles, those people would have adopted the practice after contact with Europeans. Some archaeologists suggest that there were no tribes that carved poles before Europeans arrived. The evidence against this belief lies in tribal stories and oral tradition. The traditions, form, and designs of totem poles are so complex and distinctive that it would be difficult to believe totem carving to be only a recent development. The phrase "totem pole" is not the true name either: *gyaa'aang* is the Haida word for these creations. The translation is "man stands up straight." "Totem" is not an accurate word for the spirits and animals represented in the carvings either, which actually represent animals deserving of special treatment on the basis of their spiritual and religious significance. The beings carved into these poles represent deeds, ancestors, or story representations, but have less religious meaning than the word "totem" suggests. The biggest change following the arrival of Europeans besides spread of the practice, was the size of the poles; access to European wood-carving tools advanced the art in complexity and size.

Materials for construction, however, remained the same. Both before and after European contact, costal natives used cedar for housing because it is one of the most rot-resistant woods on earth. Natives knew this and used it for their carvings as well. The faces and decorations on the totem represented family and ancestors, along with their past achievements, adventures, and relationships. A person approaching an ancient village first would have seen single-story rectangular houses with towering totem poles at the corners. The specific types of poles were crest poles that portrayed the ancestries of specific families, history poles that recorded the histories of clans, legend poles displaying folklore and other societal stories, and memorial poles carved to honor an individual person. To read the poles and understand their stories, a person must start at the bottom and work to the top. Basically these tribes provided the present with carved history books, treasure troves of information preserved for future generations.

In the analysis of painted artistic expression on native homes, there are as many reasons and symbolisms as there are painted tepees in history. The following is taken from a Blackfoot Web site on tepees and their symbolism:

> The designs that are painted on our tipis are more than pretty images; they connect us with the Spirit Beings in the world around us . . . the right to use . . . designs is a privilege and must be formally transferred in a ceremony . . . [because] the paintings on our lodges were given to us by *Papai-tapiksi,* the Dream Beings.[4]

Each artistic creation served a specific purpose and underwent a special ceremony to be dedicated for that function. Some helped call buffalo for the hunt, some encouraged favorable weather, and some supported fruitful foraging. Even the different parts of the tepee had special symbolism according to the Blackfoot. The lowest part of the tepee symbolized Mother Earth, and often natives painted either rounded or pointed shapes along the bottom to represent important hills or mountains in their environment. The middle of the tepee covers stood for the realm of family and the animal spirits that helped them. The animals represented helped ensure prosperity, health, and long life. The one animal symbol that superseded the others was the *apa-nii,* which is a butterfly or moth. This symbolized the Dream Beings, the deliverers of the images and other messages to help direct daily life. Finally, the top third was the heavens adorned with stars (painted circles.) According to Blackfoot legend, children who were lost or neglected would go to live in the sky, out of the reach of sadness and loneliness. Circles were painted to remind the people to cherish and care for their children. Here the home represented not only those who lived in it, but also the environment, the community, the heavens, and the spirit world as well—nothing less than the totality of Blackfoot existence.

When the Dakota people stood on the ground and looked around at the land, the horizon, and the heavens, they saw their tribal home and re-created that in their family homes. The flat, circular base of the tepee was like the circular horizon, and over that hung the cover of the sky. A Pawnee priest put it this way: "If you go on a high hill and look around, you will see the sky touching the earth on every side, and within this circular enclosure, the people dwell."[5] In many tepee cultures, the woman was the owner, which meant if the man wanted to paint the tepee, he had to obtain the permission of the female. Even though women had the final say, the size of the tepee often depended on the man, given that he had to provide the materials. It was said that those with the fastest horses had the largest tepees. Those at the front of the hunt were in the best position for prime buffalo hide. Ultimately masculine and feminine influences were balanced on the tepee. Animals drawn on the north side of the tent were usually female, for example, whereas those drawn on the southern side were male. Although the visions emblazoned on the dwelling came from the man, it became a balance of opposites when painted on a basically female house. All designs appeared to Plains natives in dreams or visions. Often the dream visitors were spirits of an animal species wishing to reveal some of their power or influence to the dreamer. The use of this power was exercised through the painting of the lodge or tepee. Detailed instructions came with these dreams and had to be followed perfectly.

Once these paintings were complete, generally the original owner was the only one who had the right to utilize and call upon the spirits depicted on his family's dwelling. Certain rituals belonged to him and his family alone, and the trappings of those ceremonies hung in a medicine bundle at the back of the tepee for protection. When the hide covers wore out, special actions were necessary for disposal of tepees adorned with powerful images. Designs could not be copied either. If one man had not had his own vision or dream, the only hope he had of acquiring a tepee with images already painted on it would be to "purchase" it through elaborate ritual procedures. Whether purchased or dreamt about, however, the erection of a new dwelling called for a consecration.

Today is the day I put up my new home. I leave You to the care of the four winds. Today is the day You can see Yourself in my lodge where You can do as You please. We cannot tell You to do this or that; we are only men. You, our Maker, direct us whether it be bad or good; it is Your will. Help us to think of You every day we live in this lodge; guard us in our sleep and wake us in the morning with clean minds for the day. (Rock Thunder of the Plains Cree)[6]

Even when moving a painted tepee, special rituals and observances were important. Fires would be built in the tepees only after the cover was on and sacrificial goods, such as tobacco and sweet grass, had been brought in to conduct the ceremonies. As the sacrifices were made, the leader (owner of the tepee and the original vision) would sing for the gifts of the painted spirits. Women would bring in food, and the eating and singing would continue until the food was gone. Once the ceremony was over, the spirits' presences and protection were assumed. As long as the tepee stood and the family paid proper respect, the gifts of the animal spirits would not leave. Once the cover began to show signs of wear and tear, however, it was carefully taken down and sunk in the waters of a lake. In this way, it would return to the realm of dreams and visions, where it could be reborn to another.

A spirit animal has given me my lodge,
An animal who will be my ally,
Whose power will assist me to ride the wind.
It is my own view of God speaking,
It is my Teacher who gives me this center of power . . . this tipi,
Wherein I may realize the Great Mystery of life.[7]

Unfortunately, many forms of artistic expression have been lost to the ravages of time, mainly because of the impermanance of the materials used to create them. Evidence suggests, for example, that some southeastern natives created images on their walls using colored clay. American Indians definitely expressed themselves artistically on cave walls, using clay, paint, and chiseling. Although these designs did not always adorn the walls of the home, the stone surfaces that contain images are always found in or near habitation sites. Two types of cave or rock drawings exist. The first is a petroglyph, art that Native Americans chiseled, pecked, or carved into stone. The other is the pictograph or painted images on the walls' surfaces. These are the types of art that were most likely to suffer from the damages of time. Unfortunately, contact with Europeans changed many native practices, including art. Whether as a result of European cultural influences or of decimation of the population, by the 1700s, few tribes had many remnants of their past artistic traditions left.

MANY BUILDINGS FOR ONE TRIBE: OTHER STRUCTURES THAT MADE UP NATIVE COMMUNITIES

In addition to the various types of permanent dwellings across native North America, there were many structures used for purposes other than living. Goods storage, religious ceremony, political proceedings, healing ceremonies, and personal cleansing often warranted their own facilities. Combined, these structures constituted the totality of native society. Whenever a tribe needed to build villages or encampments, one of the first natural concerns was defendability. The site needed either to be protected by natural features or to offer a strategic advantage for human defense. The concern over availability of water, game, foraging, and building supplies came in a close second. Once they selected a site based on these necessities, then each culture planned its community based on many cultural and environmental factors. The village plan tells just as much about tribal life as do specific artifacts and structural ruins. In some areas, protection from invading humans was most important. In other regions, it might have been natural threats, such as aggressive animals or flooding rivers, that concerned people the most. A village set up without addressing these concerns was a recipe for failure. The blueprints of villages are major clues for analysis, leaving behind a detailed story about native response to challenges specific to each area.

The most common village setup put civic or community structures at the center, surrounded by family dwellings and individually used structures. Ceremonial or public buildings, sometimes called "townhouses," often faced inward toward a central plaza or community meeting area and sat on naturally raised or man-made elevated mounds. These areas hosted various activities such as ceremonies and games. Specialists are not sure what function some of the larger buildings served in many regions. Religious use is a possibility, but it is also feasible that important families occupied these buildings placed in apparent positions of honor. Regardless of structural purpose, most villages organized around this basic setup. The Creek culture, for example, set up its villages with a large, circular meetinghouse in the middle next to a square plaza surrounded by four buildings. This area was the community meeting spot. Another court provided space for games. Radiating out from the town center were individual homes and garden plots. Creek tribal chiefs had their own version of the town square as well, with four buildings bordering their meeting space. Many versions of this theme existed in most areas of North America. The only consistent deviations from this theme were the tribes of the Southwest. Their unique desert environment made this layout physically impossible. One other variation was the addition of man-made fortifications that were sometimes necessary when nature and location could not provide the needed protection. Regardless of obstacles and exceptions, communal needs and natural resources shaped the character and personality of native villages into a reality unique to each culture.

Although some structures, such as the border buildings surrounding central plazas, lack a definite explanation of purpose, many nonresidential buildings left behind excellent clues for analysis and interpretation. One of the most commonly occurring and best understood is the *kiva* of the Southwestern tribes. Because the kiva survives today in native culture, it is easier to trace the history of its use and importance. Evolving from the pits beneath pit houses, these buildings played a large and important role in many native cultures. The modern kiva closely resembled its ancient ancestor in that the ladder entrance through the roof survived, as do the smoke vents. Fires were still built in the center, there were no windows, and a hole in the floor, the *sipapu*, represented the entrance to the underworld and the symbolic origins of the tribe. Its function changed little as well. Pre-dance rituals still took place inside the kiva, men still conducted clan and village business inside, and some tribes retained the custom of having young men live inside the kiva until their coming of age. Women were rarely allowed inside. Originally kivas were built into the ground, but as their use spread, they were built above ground as well. Benches lined the walls, punctuated by structural support beams to hold up early domed-shaped roofs. Today many kivas are square, but the kiva still serves the same purposes as the historical kiva: it is a physical and spiritual center for the community.

The Anasazi were one community that heavily depended upon the kiva as a center of religious and social life. One type of structure they built that incorporated kivas and stands out as unique in Native American culture was the "Great House." Around 900 C.E., the Anasazi began building large village-like structures that contained hundreds of rooms and many kivas. The largest, located in Chaco Canyon, is shaped like the letter "D," stood five stories tall, housed 800 rooms, and included at least 37 kivas. It could have accommodated as many as 3,000 people, but there is little evidence to suggest such a large resident population. One theory suggests that Chaco culture spread over a larger region than previously assumed, something close to the size of Massachusetts and Maryland combined, and that Chaco Canyon was the political center of that expanse. Others suggest that it could have been a storage facility on a grand scale. Solar calendars in the complex suggest a religious connection as well, so perhaps it was a focus of ceremony and pilgrimage. As the Anasazi way of life began to wane and the people started to disperse, their descendants copied this "Great House" blueprint, but on a much smaller scale. Without future major discoveries like the massive Chaco Canyon complex, the present may never know the real function and purpose of these amazing "Great Houses."

Another common building that is better understood is the sweat lodge or bathhouse. It was often one of the largest structures in the village and sat near the center. Spiritual purification and preparation for important events and ceremonies always took place in the sweat lodge. Some variations upon the sweat lodge were "medicine lodges" that, rather than utilizing steam for purification, used the smoke of sacred herbs and other medical techniques to cleanse the body. Different cultures employed different construction methods, and the details of purpose varied, but some characteristics were common to all. Most lodge entrances faced east, the direction of the light of wisdom. Steam came from rocks heated in a fire that burned east of the structure along the path or "Good Road" that led to the entrance. Many cultures used hides or blankets to cover the lodge, which created total darkness inside. The darkness represented ignorance, and the glowing rocks brought in the light of wisdom to illuminate that darkness. The personal strength and communal unity engendered by the use of sweat lodges would eventually be seen as a major threat by Europeans, testifying to the power that the lodge represented to those that used it.

Although not really a "structure" in the modern sense of the word, storage pits played a major role in village life while often preserving artifacts for future study (the absence of a large number of these at the

Chaco Canyon complex is one factor giving investigators great difficulty in analysis). Most storage pits were bell-shaped, looking something like a Liberty Bell pushed into the ground. These pits were typical of many native societies in the Great Plains and were most often used for the long-term storage of crops. The pits were not large enough to hold enough food for more than two or three families, so these pits were often numerous and distributed around the village. The narrow opening to the pits was necessary so that they could be covered with a large rock, piece of wood, or even buffalo hide, which was then covered by smaller rocks or dirt to secure and protect it from human and animal raiders. The pits were also used for trash disposal, a function especially valuable to scholars today. One of the best ways to learn about a people is to study what they throw away. Another method of more temporary storage found close to homes was an arbor. Constructed of four poles and a rectangular roof, it often had only one or two walls and provided shelter for working people and a place to dry corn, meat, and other foods. Many deviations on the storage theme existed across the continent, as did other specialized buildings, but wherever Native American communities settled, they built and adapted their traditional structures to help provide an easier, more successful way of life specific to their environmental benifits or challenges.

NOTES

1. A summary of ancient footprint research conducted near Mexico City can be found at the online research center, Somos Primos. David Keys, "Walking with Ancestors: Discovery Rewrites American Prehistory," *Archaeology Correspondent* (July 2005).

2. James Abarr, "A Look Back," *Albuquerque Journal* (2000), available from http://www.abqjournal.com/venue/travel/tourism/heritage_walnut.htm.

3. Brent Richards Weisman, *Unconquered People: Florida's Seminole and Miccosukee Indians* (Gainesville: University of Florida, 1999), 48.

4. Glenbow Museum, "Tipi Designs," *Niitoy-yiss: The Blackfoot Tipi.* Available from http://www.glenbow.org/exhibitions/online/blackfoot/main_eng.htm.

5. Following in the Buddhist tradition, the Theosophy Trust follows a humanistic, natural path of respect for all of nature and meditation as a path to enlightenment. Of particular use to historians, part of the mission of the "Theosophy Trust" is to preserve indigenous interpretations of their own religious beliefs from many cultural areas around the world as based on oral and cultural traditions and this quote is taken from their collection.

6. From the Theosophy Trust's article on the Tipi as a religious, social, and cultural symbol of the Native American worldview.

7. Helen Valborg, "The Tipi," *Hermes Symbol Articles* (1984), available from http://theosophytrust.org/tlodocs/articlesSymbol.php?d=TipiThe-0482. htm&p=23.

5

SURVIVAL OF THE MOST RESOURCEFUL: HUNTING AND GATHERING

I was born where there were no enclosures, and where everything
drew a free breath . . . I know every stream and every wood between
the Rio Grande and the Arkansas. I have hunted over that country.
I lived like my fathers before me, and like them, I lived happily.
Ten Bears, Yamparethka Comanche

In 1634 William Wood wrote, "It is to be noted that, for hunting, [Native
Americans] have no swift-footed greyhounds to let slip at the sight of the
deer, no deep mouthed hounds, or scenting beagles, to find their desired
prey. They do all this themselves." In order to survive, Native American
hunters had to develop extraordinary skills. Depending on natural environment and prey, an American Indian hunter had to school himself
in many areas: climate, weather conditions, tracking, animal behavior,
species interaction, and geography, just to name a few. And whenever
a society relied on hunting as a method of sustenance, gathering often
came along with it. Frequently the boundary between hunting and gathering proved to be a blurry one because the two were so interconnected.
Natives, for example, consider the pursuit of smaller animals a process
of gathering rather than hunting, although the modern mind might see it
differently. Great knowledge and skill were required for both, but the term
"hunting" in an ancient context involved the chase and kill of medium- to
large-sized animals, which differed greatly from the pursuit and capture
of smaller creatures. The purpose of most Native American hunting was
to provide food for the family or tribe, but ceremonial, ritualistic hunting took place as well. Religious beliefs played various roles, such as
placing restrictions on prey and hunting techniques. Proper respect for
animal spirits was absolutely necessary to ensure successful ventures.

As part of North American native society, hunting evolved into an elaborate cultural practice filled with significance and characterized by great accomplishment.

THE SCIENCE OF HUNTING: SKILLS, KNOWLEDGE, AND WEAPONS

Today people spend years learning and perfecting skills and trades in order to provide for themselves and their families. If they are not successful, then their families suffer, but modern society often provides various safety networks for both temporary and long-term relief. For prehistoric natives, their contributions to the family and community were even more important. With no larger social security network to fall back on, if a community did not have good hunters, it did not eat. If a drought hit the area, the community did not eat. If they did not coordinate their efforts and plan for difficulties, again, they did not eat. Because they were so heavily dependant on themselves, each other, and the environment around them, without a larger governmental structure as backup, there was little room for error. As a result, people became experts in what they contributed to their society and how they did it. This required a significant degree of flexibility, creativity, and adaptability. By analyzing the world around them in order to survive as best they could, Native American cultures amassed a great deal of knowledge and experience. One area that demonstrates these accomplishments best is hunting.

Hunting could be considered one of the most necessary and complex activities in native culture. A native hunter had to acquire and perfect many skills to be successful. The three most important areas were weapons manufacture and use, detailed understanding of the prey, and knowledge of the natural environment. Weapons manufacture and function depended on available resources, craftsman skill, and the nature of the prey. There is a general chronology of weapons development that stretches across ancient North American history, but cultures progressed along that line at different rates. As cultures became more distinct and technologically advanced, weapons specialization occurred. Prehistoric hunters often considered their weapons their most prized possessions. They held a much higher personal significance than would weapons of today. For example, in most cultures, hunters would never consider using another's weapon. Part of the weapon's success was a result of the respect and treatment its owner provided. It was possible that using another's weapon might even be dangerous to the intruding user. Owners illustrated the personal value of their weapons through nonfunctional embellishment, much like the polishing and decoration found on some present-day weaponry. Hunters knew that meticulous construction and regular maintenance was absolutely necessary in order to ensure that a perfect chase would not be wasted when the weapon did

"Indian Hunting Buffalo" after the arrival of Europeans changed the Native Americans' mode of transportation and hunting from foot to horse. Richard Dodge Irving. *The Hunting Grounds of the Great West; a Despiration of the Plains Game, and Indians of the Great North American Desert.* London, Chatto and Windus, 1877. Courtesy of The Bancroft Library, University of California, Berkeley.

not perform correctly. A subtle flaw could spell disaster in the field, so weapons required frequent, detailed attention. Weapons were a hunter's best friend in many ways.

Traditional weaponry fell into three basic categories: thrusting or throwing spears, the throwing stick or atlatl and dart, and the bow and arrow. The spear was the simplest of the three and was basically a long, sturdy shaft with a point either carved onto or attached at one end. The spear could only be thrown over a short distance, so the effectiveness relied largely on proximity and strength. The best-case scenario for spear hunting involved a pinned or trapped animal, so that the hunters could get close without risking injury while ensuring a successful kill. The atlatl (pronounced "atul-atul" and taken from the Aztec language) and dart was the next most advanced weapon, which scholars assume came to North America with ancient migrants. Evidence suggests that ancient hunters used the atlatl in the Old World as long as 20,000 years ago, although it probably arrived in North America only 10,000 to 12,000 years ago. The atlatl was basically a throwing device that made darts very accurate and very deadly. As a more flexible and powerful weapon, the atlatl and dart greatly increased a hunting party's choices for prey and chances for success. It was thrown using an arm motion much like the one used for a tennis serve. Everything about this weapon was a great improvement upon the older, simpler spears. The final and most advanced traditional weapon class then was the bow and arrow. Scientists believe it either came to or was invented in North America approximately 2,000 years ago and it quickly began to replace the atlatl and dart. The bow propelled a light shaft with a smaller point, which utilized a much higher potential energy than the enhanced kinetic energy of the atlatl. There was also the added advantage of stealth. In order to use an atlatl properly, the hunter had to stand upright, giving away his position. The flexibility of the bow and arrow allowed him to crouch and hide, giving him the advantage of surprise. This weapon system represented the longest distance range and most deadly accuracy available to prehistoric hunters.

Sometimes special damage considerations were important, such as when hunting small animals, so the nature of the prey often determined the appropriate weapon. Although the meat was a useful part of the kill, the skins or furs were also important, and in the smaller creatures, rips in the skin could render the entire pelt useless. Darts or arrows cut into the skin and sometimes tore the pelt irreparably. Rabbit sticks, blunts, traps, and snares circumvented this risk. Each culture had its own variations on these skin-preserving weapons, choosing different ones based on local resources and the nature of their prey. The rabbit stick, for example, was a two-foot curved throwing stick made of wood that could be hurled at an animal or used as a club. Nets made of plant fibers could be used to trap or snare small animals, for example, by stretching them across narrow expanses in preparation for the gathering parties to drive their prey into the traps. In another weapon system, carved stones called bolas were tied to the ends of long cords, whirled overhead and then released towards the animal to hit or entangle it. They also latched blunts to the ends of arrow and dart shafts that were literally blunt instead of sharpened so that they could stun their prey without piercing the skin. Natives used various styles of snares to catch smaller animals by the leg or neck. Ingenuity and flexibility was the key to the successful pursuit of smaller, yet still tricky, prey.

Understanding and predicting the behavior of prey also constituted a large amount of hunters' studies and attention. Every species had unique patterns of behavior that changed depending on the presence of other animals and environmental factors. Age, sex, and body condition of the prey played a roll as well. In order to even scratch the surface of this kind of knowledge, hunters had to begin their education at an early age. They also needed to understand the behavior of other animals in the area. The actions and reactions of other species provided clues during pursuit that could turn the tide of a hunt. Calls and movement of other animals, when read correctly, told a story of prey behavior only a trained hunter could read. Take the buffalo, for example. One preferred hunting method involved a communal effort at driving herds of buffalo or bison over the edge of a drop. Although this may sound pretty straightforward, it required many days of preparation, a large group of hunters, and special geographical features. The presence of other animals could change the hunter's herding success. It was not until the reintroduction of the horse through European contact that buffalo hunts on foot gave way to more advanced, flexible techniques.

The methods used in hunting buffalo also varied according to season, landscape, and available tools. Hunters often covered themselves with coyote or wolf hides to approach the buffalo without alarming the herd. When they got close enough, they could either drive the buffalo over a cliff or use weapons such as the atlatl or spear. Native hunters also built pens to corral the animals. Dogs helped drive the animals into the pens for the kill. In winter, the hunters wore snowshoes, while dogs chased the animals into deep snow to slow them down. In order to execute a successful drive, natives had to know what would drive the buffalos, how they would react, and any possible elements that could affect the herding, including sudden weather changes and the presence of other animals. Additionally, natives timed the hunt to their best advantage. Harvest schedules, bison herding cycles, local resources, and seasonal timing all played a role in the execution of a buffalo hunt. If the bison groups were not herding, or moving together, which they only did at certain times of the year, the hunt would be less fruitful. If the weather did not turn colder soon enough after the hunt, preservation of meat became difficult. Many factors had to be considered to ensure a productive drive and storage so that a tribe could make the best use of its newly gained resources.

Other hunting methods involved only individual or small groups of hunters. A common misperception is that one or two hunting techniques could be used in every situation. Every hunt required a different plan, different tools, and different knowledge. Seemingly small details such as the time of day and distance from water were important in putting together a successful hunting strategy. Even though several species might be in the same place at the same time, the complexities of a successful hunt required parties to pursue only one. The effects of this lifelong training reached beyond the realm of hunting as well. Territory and prey specialty affected family structure and personal relationships. Because of the high level of knowledge and training required to master hunting, the hunter was very reluctant to change territories or hunting specialties. Men began training their sons at a young age, and if men had been expected to move upon marriage into a new clan, that training would have been lost. As a result of this, these cultures functioned patrilineally, with the male as the central focus, so that upon marriage, the wife relocated and adopted the new tribe as her own. Because different animals used and reacted to their environment in different ways, it was important to know their behavior and be able to predict what they were doing and would do even when they could not be seen. The detailed knowledge and necessary territory familiarity directed hunting societies to evolve into male-dominated cultures in order to successfully pass on hunting traditions. When combined with mental and physical conditioning, the result was a highly trained, intelligent hunter with strength, agility, and stamina—a natural adaptation to the environmental challenges and necessities of the hunting profession.

THE SCIENCE OF GATHERING: SKILLS, KNOWLEDGE, AND TOOLS

Whereas men were generally the hunters in hunter-gatherer societies, women were usually the chief gatherers. When game was scarce, it was the gatherers who often saved the society from starvation. Gathering involved the collection of roots, greens, berries, nuts, or small animals, and as in hunting, each species required specialized knowledge and skills. Hunting and gathering is the most ancient method of providing food for a society. It was only about 10,000 years ago that agriculture began to work its way into civilization on a permanent basis, but some societies, because of their environment, continued hunting and gathering well into the 20th century. When a society relied on gathering for sustenance, it was a passive or nonhuman-directed method of subsistence, the complete opposite of agriculture. Although many of these societies employed methods such as burning or selective harvesting in order to increase the abundance of useful plants, if they intentionally put seeds in the ground to make them grow, then they were no longer primarily a gathering people. Because of the seasonal nature of foraging, most gathering peoples did not establish permanent settlements because they moved when the local plant life and game could no longer support the community. Almost everything about the community depended on the amount of food available, and because this was often a limited resource, population densities in hunter-gatherer societies were lower than in other cultures. Social fractioning or disagreements also contributed to lower population counts, helping create a workable balance between populace numbers and available resources. The environment of a hunter-gatherer society determined every facet of their lives from size of the tribe, which stayed small, to length of residence, which was often short.

The most common form of gathering or foraging was the pedestrian pattern. These were the smallest of societies that moved around hunting and gathering on foot, and the number of people in an individual camp often varied through the seasons. They moved several times a year and so had a few lighter possessions and simpler, mobile houses. The tools they used for gathering were digging sticks for root plants, baskets for carrying and storage, and lightweight weapons for defense and small-animal gathering. The problem with studying societies such as these is that most gathering tools, such as leather snares or traps, plant fiber baskets, and wooden digging sticks, did not fare well against the natural elements. Basically, this means that the understanding of gathering techniques is at best murky, largely because of a lack of surviving evidence. Another problem for archaeologists is the identification of objects and the placement of them in a cultural context. Migration patterns and function might be easier to discern based on examination and analysis of the tool, but human motivation in creating or discarding it is elusive. One thing the archaeological record can tell scientists is that in order to survive, these native societies needed to be as flexible as possible to deal with the almost constant changes and challenges a highly mobile society faced.

Another interesting prehistoric category of native gathering people was aquatic foragers. They focused their efforts on gathering fish, mollusks, shellfish, and other water creatures, an activity that was not properly considered fishing or hunting in the traditional sense of the terms. Geographically stretching all the way from present-day Alaska to southern California, many specialized in netting salmon from the rivers and hunting seals and whales off the coast. Although some might consider these activities closer to fishing or hunting than to gathering, they were so unique that these practices deserve their own treatment. The capture of animals partially or completely camouflaged by their environment required different skills and observation techniques than did the capture of their land cousins. Because fishing gear suffers from the same fragility as other gathering tools, evidence is often difficult to come by when researchers are trying to determine common methods. And when tools are apparently present, it is still difficult to put them into a context and know for sure how and why they were used. This can be done deductively by examining artifact remains in archaeological sites or by inference, based on modern, oral history accounts of fishing techniques. It is even possible for the behavior and habitats of the fish themselves to lend clues to this mystery. Fishhooks, gorges, spears, and netting were the most common tools of the trade. The fishing specialists had to know the environment and behavior of fish well in order to choose the best tools and have a successful catch. Whaling, for example, was just as important to the tribes of northern prehistoric coastal societies as the buffalo hunt was to the Plains Indians. Their social structure revolved around whaling parties and their role in society. The most common method probably involved sailing out in a wide, shallow boat and harpooning the whale with spears tied to ropes and sealskin floats to keep the whale from diving down. Then they could simply follow the whale until it was exhausted. The whale could then be killed with lances and spears and drug to shore for use by the community. The fisherman hunted seal by using ripple indicating devices to signal when a seal might be coming up to breathe. Sometimes they would scratch ice with seal claws to lure the seals up from underneath. Once the animals were within spearing range, the hunter could use a smaller version of the whaling harpoon to spear the seal. They even used

Native Americans of North Carolina using boats, spears, and nets for fishing, by John White, 1885. National Archive Image number 535743.

wound plugs to keep the nutritious blood from draining. Nothing was left to waste in these societies, creating a people and environment that fed off of each other.

One bonus of this lifestyle was that utilizing water animals for food was far more reliable than the hunting and gathering efforts farther inland, so much so that many of these societies established a more permanent residence based on resource availability. Because of the relative consistency of their food supply, aquatic foraging natives had the time to build larger, permanent houses and enjoy leisure activities such as creating complex works of art. Elaborate clothing, masks, and totem poles decorated community life. Their social structure also evolved to a more complex level than did the social structure of their inland cousins, as a result of the stability their environment afforded them. Because of resource consistency, coastal tribes took an entirely different path of social and cultural development, producing one of the most artistic populations in prehistoric North America. Observations and utilization of the local environment and its resources allowed for flexibility and development in many areas of tribal life.

Understanding their environment and the plant and animal species they collected was just as important to foragers as it was to the hunter. Weather patterns, growing seasons, insects, and disease were just a few of the issues important to a successful "harvest." It was important to know which plants and small animals were best to collect, and being choosy about picking could also influence next season's crop or generation. Gatherers had to know which specimens would be the best to harvest, leaving the weaker, less ripened choices to die on the vine. They also had to know *how* to pick their food. Pulling berries too far into the stem or digging root plants incorrectly could damage next year's produce. These bits of knowledge were passed down from generation to generation and were only gained through years of observation and experimentation. It is common knowledge today that some edible-looking plants are poisonous and even deadly, and this information has been known and handed down through the ages in native communities as well. Ultimately, just like hunting specialists in the tribe, highly successful gatherers utilized intelligent analysis of and experimentation with picking techniques, plant growth cycles, and food quality in order to get the most out of their natural habitat.

This brings up a common misperception about the hunting and gathering way of life. For a long time people have assumed that such a total dependence on the natural environment equaled an uncertain existence in a harsh atmosphere—basically, a short, miserable life. This idea is more of an imagined reality than a true description. People that live in the modern world view such a life as drudging, wretched, and completely undesirable. A "civilized" life *must* be the best way to live, and "primitive" culture is something to avoid at all costs, according to this way of thinking. Research and analysis over the last half century has essentially destroyed this false image. Commonly, the food supplies of hunter-gatherer societies were reliable and adequate, and relatively little effort or energy was needed to provide for the basic needs of families and tribes. Nuts, vegetables, fruits, and even protein-rich insects could provide for most nutritional needs and constituted a large majority of the native diet. Even their average life span rivaled that of today's population. Evidence suggests that people often lived well into their 60s, further evidence that "primitive" life agreed with them. Additionally, adults of many tribes dedicated only 15 to 20 hours a week to providing food for the community, and that was their primary role. The rest of their time could be spent pursuing more spiritual or cultural quests. That sounds like a wonderful workweek by today's standards.

WHO IS MORE IMPORTANT? CLASS DIVISIONS WITHIN HUNTING AND GATHERING SOCIETIES

In modern sociological study, "social status" is the honor or prestige of a person's position in their community. Throughout human history, social status has always played a large role in determining how individuals and groups of people within that society interact and function together. Sometimes occupation determined social status and accumulated wealth has often been a common class barometer. In many modern societies, affiliations such as ethnic groups, gender, and religion often play a role as well. A social class then is a group of people who have similar social status and the "class" describes the relationships between groups of people in hierarchical cultures. The next step, social structure, is a functioning, adaptive mechanism that its members use to adjust to their ecological environments. Social class, status, and structure then represent the patterns of community interaction. For prehistoric Native Americans, status and class rarely fell within these modern definitions, although there are some notable exceptions and a few similarities. The majority of native societies used accomplishment and skill as social benchmarks, and fewer saw material wealth as the determinant. Occupation is the area of most similarity between native and modern societies in terms of its relation to status. Out of necessity and common connection, native people who performed similar functions for their tribes made up different classes. Within native social classes, accomplishment and honor further stratified their cultural structure. Artists, hunters, potters, shamans, chiefs, and even water carriers carried their own weight and their own significance based on tribal contribution, creating societies that were interdependent, diverse, and complete.

Individual native groups did not make many conscious choices in creating a particular way of life; what they did, instead, was make unconscious adaptations. Not all societies faced the same environmental challenges and conditions, and the people in those societies did not usually know *why* they adapted the way they did; they simply knew it worked. Because of the dependence on environmental factors, natives in each region of North America evolved socially in different ways. In the northeast and eastern coastal areas, for example, most were hunting, fishing, and gathering societies. In these cultures, skill and contribution played a large role in defining social status. Although every job was important to tribal survival, some jobs played a more central and often more elevated role. At the top of most social pyramids were the chiefs and spiritual leaders. Following them came the warriors, then hunters and fishermen. Next came gatherers and then the laboring members of the tribe. In areas where agriculture took root, farmers would have been ranked at the level between hunters or fishermen and gatherers. Agriculture, in turn, encouraged more complex social development because agricultural society was often more permanent than hunter and gatherer cultures. The Adena culture, an example of a mound-building society, developed as one of the most socially complex, however, the Adena people stand out as an anomaly given that they did not depend on agriculture for subsistence. Everything they did, they developed to perfection, despite the fact that they often had to migrate to sustain themselves, including creating a detailed social structure wherein everyone knew his or her role and place in society.

To get more specific about those roles, the Illinois natives offer a good example for study. How other members of the tribe thought of someone determined that individual's social status. Success as a warrior and a hunter elevated a man's social status because then others saw him as a good provider, both for his family and for his tribe. Illinois tribes celebrated these accomplishments with public feasts and special ceremonies. Women elevated their status level through other methods of providing for the people. Raising healthy, well-behaved children, harvesting plentiful crops, and constructing and maintaining durable, comfortable homes contributed to a woman's social standing. Outstanding leadership ability in women's groups helped as well. When it came to matters of spirituality, however, both men and women often enjoyed equal opportunities for status elevation. Young girls and boys both went on visions quests, where they would travel into the forest and fast for up to a week, hoping to receive a vision from an animal spirit that would then be their spiritual guide. Animal spirits were not bound by gender differences, so it was possible that powerful animal guides would visit both males and females. If it happened to be a spirit with special healing or medicinal knowledge, the man or woman chosen by the spirit could rise in stature to the level of shaman, one of the highest social ranks in Illinois society and most other native cultures. Although status was an indispensable facet of native culture, it differs drastically from today's class definitions.

Social structure, class, and status are difficult to study in Native American society because these ideas did not leave many physical traces. Two of the best ways to study a tribe's social structure are through housing burial remains, however indirect this may be. The way people lived and the way they were buried often tells a great deal about what their peers thought of them. Where they lived in the village demonstrated status also; for example, if a person's home sat in a place of honor or close to valuable resources, scholars to assume that the home's resident was a highly prized member of the community. Respected individuals were often buried in places of honor or great spiritual significance as well. Possessions buried with people also testify to their stature and role. When dealing with artifact challenges, scholars have to carefully study what clues do remain in order to come to the best conclusion possible. Around 3,000 years ago, several cultures across the continent began to practice more elaborate burial rituals, and the differences between practices in the same tribe often suggest higher and lower stations in society. Elaborate art found in wood, stone, and bone also suggests that a huge span of social levels existed within tribes. Archaeological sites such as the one in Scowlitz, British Columbia, imply a detailed social stratification. Complex mound construction and a wealth of contemporary treasures accompanied important community members to their afterlife while leaving behind rare evidence useful in difficult social analysis.

An exception to this pattern of achievement and skill as a determinant of social rank was the Natchez culture of the Northwest. They utilized a distinct hereditary class system. It has sometimes been called a caste system, which suggests a rigid scheme of division in which people could not move between classes. This was not so for the Natchez. At the top was the Great Sun, or the chief of the tribe. They called his mother the White Woman, and in this society, descent was matrilineal, passed down through the mother's side. Her next son would be Little Sun and war chief of the tribe. All of the other brothers were Suns, and then came the Nobles, the Honored People, and finally, the Stinkards. The interesting thing is that all Suns were required to marry Stinkard women, which made their children only Nobles, and each successive male was required to marry a Stinkard woman, constantly lowering the offspring by one class. The daughter of White Woman, on the other hand, became the White Woman upon her mother's death, and as a result, her eldest son would then become the next Great Sun, and so the tradition would continue. As it was with other Northwest tribes, noble classes were set apart by special laws and customs. The location, size, and furnishings of a family tell of these differences. Tattoos and clothing were also used to demonstrate class membership. There were ways for an individual to move up in the class structure, such as distinguishing honorable contribution in warfare. If a Stinkard rose up in the ranks by proving himself a valuable warrior, for example, his wife would move along with him. However, there are some contradictions in this system that scholars have tried to explain. By doing the math, it would seem that very quickly, there would be no Stinkards left. One explanation for this is that through warfare and slave capture, the Stinkard class was constantly replenished. Another is that it seems that the *daughters* of Nobles became Stinkard, rather than honored, and this kept the lowest class populated as well. Unfortunately, there is little oral tradition left on which to base solid assumptions. In the face of French expansion through southern Canada, by 1940 only two elderly people of pure Natchez descent were left. On their death, what was left of their culture and its unusual social complexity died with them.

ART FOR SUBSISTENCE'S SAKE: ART AND ORAL TRADITION OF THE HUNTER-GATHERERS

Although it is generally assumed that sedentary agriculturally based societies encouraged more artistic production than did the cultures of migratory hunter-gatherers, the creative endeavors of mobile societies deserve attention also. Their having, relatively speaking, less free time did not mean they did not *make* the time to express their culture creatively. Visual art, stories, and songs performed many functions for prehistoric native peoples. Art expressed cosmic and spiritual beliefs, social status, family lineage and relationships, history, and societal tradition. Songs and stories taught adults and children alike what was expected of them in society, explained the history and beliefs of their people, and cultivated their understanding of the ways the world worked. Art and oral tradition celebrated the life and environment of native peoples, transforming their stories into vehicles of transmission for future generations. Art was used in rituals and ceremonies ranging from coming-of-age rites to symbolic religious practices. Often when work was less intensive, artisans created amazing examples of native culture. Pictographs or petroglyphs, for example, used mainly by peoples in the Southwest, as well as other areas around the continent, expressed thoughts and experiences regarding people's spiritual realms. Some natives expressed their creativity on a larger scale by constructing aerial image mounds and ground drawings. Ceramics, metalwork, beadwork, quillwork, textiles, leatherwork, sculpture, and painting were all methods of artistic expression and cultural communication. One constant that runs through all Native American art, despite inherent regional and cultural differences, is a deep, fundamental respect and veneration for the natural environment and an elemental bond with the spiritual world, which were inseparably linked in native culture that produced this art.

Basically what this suggests is that art was a part of life, not a separate aesthetic expression. Dancing, the arts, poetry, and song came together as one entity, one all-encompassing expression of life and culture. Art could not be separated from spirituality and healing either. Dance, along with painted drums, shields, and clothing were central to the practice of shamanism, the basic form of most Native American religions. One way scholars know how integrated art was in the indigenous definition of life is that only a few aboriginal languages contained a word or expression that could be translated as the Western idea of art as a separate cultural study. This is largely because symbols were the protectors and reminders of everything around them. They connected the material to the spiritual world. The mandala is a fantastic example of this. It represents the universe in miniature and at the same time also symbolizes the pantheon or entire collections of gods. Stone carvings, pottery, and other art objects have been found across the continent, most with symbolic embellishment.

Available materials, lifestyle, religion, and environment shaped the arts of different peoples to reflect their cultural worlds. Migratory groups, because of their constant mobility, produced lighter, smaller, portable works. Using their natural resources, the Sioux decorated buckskin items and painted buffalo hides. Tribes on the far northern West Coast carved bone and ivory from marine animals and adorned sealskin with paintings and beadwork. The more stationary the people were, the more intricate the art became. The Tlingit produced detailed masks with moveable parts, and the familiar totem emerged from coastal societies as well. The highly decorated kivas of the Southwest testify to the amount of time tribes devoted to artistic spiritual representation. Although they were less settled than their Pueblo cousins, the Navajo created complex sand paintings, beautiful kachina masks and dolls, and silver and turquoise jewelry. It is difficult, however, to discuss visual arts or even oral tradition as a singular and separate entity. Music, dance, drama, poetry, visual arts, religion, culture, and community combined to function as one, and to treat them separately is to lose their meaning and context.

With that in mind, it is clear that oral tradition played a major, integral part in creative life expressions. Songs and stories handed down through generations are the closest the modern world can get to the actual words and thoughts of prehistoric Native Americans themselves. Unfortunately,

Ancient Anasazi pottery for storing and carrying, some with broken handles, photograph circa 1910. Denver Public Library, Western History Collection, Call Number N-247.

oral tradition suffers from the "grapevine" effect. As stories and songs are passed down, they change to meet fluctuating needs and interpretations. But since prehistoric Native Americans rarely "wrote" or illustrated their thoughts, there is little to learn from in this arena. Another problem was early transcription and description; it was often done by European explorers, sometimes with little, if any, input from the natives themselves. Trusting the evidence that has survived, scholars know that ornamentation was the symbolic form of prayer, and words and songs the symbol of spirit. According to many native religions, the creator of all *sang* the world and life into being, so singing was considered a very sacred act with a specific and important purpose. Because modern people revere the *written* word as the primary and often only legitimately reliable method of knowledge and history communication, it is difficult to translate the importance and meaning of American Indian song into western understanding. Different tribes varied in the character of their music, poetry, story, and manner of performance just like they did in every other facet of their lives. There are some general similarities, though. Rhythm, melody, and harmony are the essence of music, but natives also added an element of voice pulsation on sustained notes. Additionally, almost all Native American music is paired with singing. Environment affected not only music composition, but also the details of performance. Natives of the prairies, for example, were constantly exposed to severe weather conditions, which affected the quality of their voices, creating a unique characteristic in their singing. The range of notes and their delivery reflected the sounds of nature they heard every day. Very different sounds emerged from the Pueblos, however. Their rhythms of life and sounds of nature were quite different from those in the prairie lands. Pueblo men sang with a strong, clear voice coming out of full lungs, and women sang with a pure, delicate, subtly suggestive quality in their voices often compared to the austere, pristine desert that gave it birth. Their environment inspired their artistic expressions and shaped their creations as they evolved and expanded to perpetuate the native way of life and teach their children the lore of the land and the ways of the people.

The final area of analysis left in understanding hunter-gatherer societies, often accomplished through art and oral tradition analysis, is the ceremonial and spiritual customs attached to both hunting and gathering. To a certain extent, the hunter was his own shaman. Many saw a close connection between hunting and personal medicine or spiritual power. Hunters needed to be able to contact special spirits, invoke protection and success for the hunt, and interpret dreams regarding hunting. Native Indians considered the prey a sacred spirit that took a sacred material form on earth. Tradition often dictated that tribal members should participate in a dream fast somewhere just outside the village or further away, in surrounding forests or mountains. The first image seen once hunger induced a vision was considered the guardian spirit and could be either animal or element.

Once a hunter identified his guardian, then he could call upon that spirit for help, protection, and guidance. In addition to this personal dependence, there were also public group rituals necessary to the hunting practice. The Delaware, or Lenape, tribe of the East Coast enacted elaborate community rites prior to hunting stag. Members of the community performed recitals and speeches for nine nights. During the daytime there were ritual hunts from the third to the sixth day. These hunts were not for food purposes, but rather to show the spirits of the stag that the people were worthy of their gifts and to offer respect and honor to the spiritual world. After being blessed, the hunting party would travel into the forest and return with their kill. The animals were then ritualistically butchered and offered to the spirit world. Then ceremonies would continue until the 13th night when the women would join in song, completing the almost-two-week festival. The purpose of this intricate process was to show the Great Stag Spirit that the Delaware held the stag in high esteem and would never disrespect or dishonor them. This, they believed, helped ensure successful hunts for the coming season. Native North Americans, the land on which they lived, and their natural environment were tied together by interdependence and respect shown through religious beliefs and practices.

One other nonconsumption purpose of a hunt was the defining of male identity and adulthood. Most hunter-gatherer tribes practiced some sort of coming-of-age ritual that involved the successful hunt of either a boy's spirit guide or another animal considered intensely sacred to the people. A young man's successful hunt demonstrated that he had done everything right; he successfully performed the rituals in the proper way, showed appropriate respect, acquired enough knowledge and skill, and generally conducted himself as a man of the tribe should. If he had not, the animal's spirit would not have let him- or herself be killed. Some tribes used similar ceremonial hunts in preparation for weddings as well. In order to be a proper husband, a man had to provide food for his family. As a ceremonial act of both proving himself as a man and committing to the responsibility of marriage, the husband-to-be would embark on a ritual hunt intended to provide food for the wedding celebration feast. If he was successful in providing enough meat for the entire clan or tribe, then providing for his family would not be a challenge.

Additional rituals accompanied the hunt, no matter what its purpose. By apologizing and offering thanks, natives expressed sorrow for the killing as well as gratitude for the generosity of the prey. Some tribes required the preservation of certain parts of the animal, such as the heart or the brain, in order to sacrifice the organ back to the spirits from which they came. Sometimes killing taboos were extended to cover an entire species during certain seasons, in order to respect the place the animal held as an important part of nature. Even when the prohibition on hunting during certain lunar months was practical, for example, to protect pregnant mothers and their future offspring, the main reason for observing the taboo was not self-interest or for tribal benefit. The intent was to respect and honor both the animal and the Great Spirit of the species. It seems that native hunters rarely, if ever, questioned these restrictions. It was understood that everything ordered by the gods was ordered for a reason, for the health, wealth, or safety of the individual and the tribe. Looking out for the natural environment was absolutely necessary because every tribe was dependant on their environment for survival. To question the natural order would be to put a hunter's family and people at risk, something people are rarely willing to do.

The spiritual tie to foraging and gathering is very straightforward. Animals were not the only beings on the planet with a spirit or essence; plants held the same stature from a spiritual perspective. Every plant species had a representative or "Great" spirit, just like animals. Although plants could not run away when being harvested, showing disrespect could cause the botanical spirit to be slighted. This meant that the plant's Great Spirit could decide not to bless the people with so much bounty, hurting their food supplies and medicinal stock in the future. In this way, special precautions taken when either hunting or gathering showed striking similarities. Other similarities existed in preparation and consumption as well. Even if the plant had been successfully and respectfully harvested, this did not mean that the Great Spirit was not still watching. Careful preparation and cooking was all part of the honor and respect process. In this case, disrespect could not only cause a decrease in availability, but it could also harm the physical health of the individual and the individual's community. Illness and death could be blamed on the spiritual negligence in the improper foods and medicines. The modern world knows this as scientific fact and yet Native Americans intuitively deduced this essential truth. Spiritual rituals may not play such a large role in a majority of food preparation today, but scholars suggest that through trial and error, native societies figured out that consumption of foods and medicines could be dangerous, and so they developed detailed rituals and practices to avoid this. Their explanation for the causes might be different, but the precautions are the same. In order to survive in and utilize their natural environment, American Indians learned from their mistakes and incorporated practices and beliefs to pass that information along.

6

Spiritual Environment: Religious Beliefs and Practices

> You have noticed that everything an Indian does is in a circle, and that is because the Power of the World always works in circles, and everything tries to be round . . . The Sky is round, and I have heard that the earth is round like a ball, and so are all the stars. The wind, in its greatest power, whirls. Birds make their nest in circles, for theirs is the same religion as ours.
>
> *Black Elk, Oglala Sioux*

All people spend their lives making a living and constructing meaning out of it. Prehistoric North Americans carved a life and culture out of their surrounding environment, and when they were not doing that, they were trying to find a meaning for it. This is the birth of native religion. They had to find ways to cure the sick, bring healthy children into the world, and educate the young so that they could become productive members of society. While they were figuring these things out, they also had to devise ways to pass these traditions along and ensure the perpetuation of their people. But "living" is more than just food and survival. The need to give meaning to these struggles is as old as humankind itself. This realm of life is meditative, creative, and artistic. Assumption alone does not work; examination, observation, and faith must be the predominant forces. The *why* of things cannot be ignored; it plays a central role in every society in human history.

Every Native American culture established a religion to answer that question. Many languages did not have a word that translated directly into the Western conception of religion because Native American societies were holistic, making little if any distinction between everyday material life and the spiritual. Religious ideas would not have been thought of as separate or disconnected. Daily activities such as treating sickness, hunting, gathering, celebrating, mourning, educating, and creating art and music—pretty much everything that could be considered culture—came from, was allowed in, or was created in the process of honoring and celebrating the gods or spirits. Individuals were born, lived, and passed on to the next world immersed in their religious convictions. Sacred forces exerted influence over everything, from the success of the hunt to the growing cycles of plants, from conception to death. This does not suggest that all natives accepted their people's beliefs without thought or question. Although there was no culture of skepticism in native beliefs like there is in the modern Western world, some still questioned what they were taught. They could observe human motivation, human desire, and the man-made connections in tradition and understand that sometimes belief and practice were symbolic rather than "real." For example, as soon as Hopi children began to mature, they realized that kachina dancers were not spirits, but people dressed as a representation. The spirits embodied by the kachina came to ceremonies to ensure that the people performed the ceremonies properly as well as to keep outsiders out. As the children grew, they realized that the dancers were real people in mask and costume. They did not, however, question the purpose or meaning of the role or dance. Most Native Americans realized intuitively that the fulfillment of human sacred needs must have a vessel, a vehicle of transmission. They also believed that when dancers put on kachina masks, their conscious state and connection to this plane of existence changed. Symbolically, by putting on the trappings of the spirit world, people moved closer to that space between the two.

In the process, peoples' relationships to the natural world, their sense of tribal identity, their understanding of the individual self, their conception of divine reality and the spiritualities that guided them became blurred. The holistic character of traditional native culture showed itself in the American Indians' relative inability to distinguish between nature and divinity, between the self and the group. There were no rigid lines of distinction between such categories. Rituals and myths dealt with all inclusively. That does not mean that they were simply ants in a colony or the equivalent of worker bees, but it does mean that the Western idea of the individual does not directly translate into native mentality. This is often a major difficulty for the Western mind when it tries to wrap itself around ideas that do not define themselves in Western ways and makes Western understanding of Native American reality difficult. Another issue is that in dealing with early North American culture, especially ethereal, non-material ideas like religion, archaeological evidence is often of little use. The emphasis often has to be on the written record, all of which has been created over the last 400 years. Oral tradition plays a role as well, but is difficult to analyze. With all of this blurring of the lines and the striking lack of evidence, it is also important to remember that in examining such a large continent with so many cultures, generalizations are difficult to make. Some of the most common elements do stand out, and it is useful to look at representative examples, but an exhaustive treatment of all Native American religions would be virtually impossible. Just as natives struggled to find meaning in the world around them, the modern mind must struggle to comprehend cultures very different from its own, and in that way, perhaps the two cultures can meet.

THE EASTERN WOODLANDS: THE FIRST AREA OF EXPLORATION

The Eastern Woodlands people experienced dramatic shifts in their life patterns following the introduction of significant numbers of Europeans during the 1600s. The growth in white population forced many to move from lands they had occupied for generations. Not only did they have to develop new economies and patterns of subsistence, but they also had to adjust to emotional losses brought on by forced migration. The land they lived on and were being forced to leave was not simply an indifferent, inanimate place; it was the living center of their existence. When that center no long existed, their lives changed in many ways. Their homeland was maternal. In their eyes, it gave birth to them, nurtured them, and shaped them as a people. What their adoptive mother would provide, only time would tell. Their traditional habitats had holy sites, places of special beauty and significance to only them. Spiritual forces were strong there. Burial sites kept them close to their ancestors, and the spirit guides of the animals from their native lands were intrinsically part of the people. The changes brought by European contact were permanent and many times devastating. All that remains of what came before are painstaking efforts at re-creating an entire way of life that was quickly and irreparably destroyed.

For most people of the Eastern Woodlands, the point of some of the earliest European contact in North America, the land was a source of power. As the seasons changed, as the sun passed through the sky, or as the earth sprouted new plants and animals, the connections to nature touched the people. This power was a presence of the divine, the sacred, the only true reality and center of reference. The power could not be explained in relation to anything else; it just was. It was every living and natural thing individually and, at the same time, the combination of it all. It was the power to which natives believed humans should submit if they were going to live successful, productive lives and ensure a future for their children. By examining myths of creation, these connections become clear. To the Menominee of Wisconsin, the first human beings came from bears. A male and a female bear rose from the earth at the mouth of the Menominee River and became the first man and woman who then went on to shape and direct the world. The connection was that animal life came from the earth, and the waters were the catalyst for creation, the giving of life. The tie between animal and human life was direct, absolute, and represented by the animal species that humans hunted with the most fear and respect: their ancestor the bear. Another major point of this story is that gender differentiation is basic and aboriginal. From the beginning of time, there were males and females, and this dichotomy ran throughout creation. Because of this, it made sense to organize social and cultural life in terms of gender. Ultimately, all of nature could be understood, according to this story, through the lens of male and female with everything that exists being either one or the other.

In the southeast woodlands, natives viewed the world, its creation, and consistency as having three layers: the sky above, which was an inverted stone bowl; the waters below; and the earth, a circular island, floating in between the two. This was bounded by a superior world and an inferior world. Above the sky resided the sun, moon, and archetypes or Great Spirits of all creatures on earth. Below the waters was a world of both monsters and spirits. Above, order and peace reigned, and below, it was chaos. Both existences were seen as necessary for the world to be as it was. In one creation story, there were at first only the Above and Below. The three layers natives knew as the earth, sky, and waters arose when soft mud from the world below rose up to form an island that depended on ties, almost like physical bonds, to elements of north, south, east, and west. The elements were vulnerable and weaknesses in human behavior could weaken the directions. They believed it was possible that humankind could misbehave so much as to break the cords of the elements holding the earth-island up, and then it would sink back into the netherworld. In this case, native society structured its moral code around an intimate and dependant connection to the earth and its health, tying the two together permanently.

Based on this three-tiered existence pattern and others like it, some interesting and unique taboos emerged in some southeastern tribes. Children, for example, were not allowed to touch moles, because they burrowed into the ground. They saw this as a bizarre trait that was connected to the lower realm, and they believed that physical contact would make the children just as odd as the moles. The basic idea was that touching something would put a person in contact with its spirit and its power, and because of this, no contact could be considered benign. Another widespread custom was to avoid cooking four-legged creatures and birds in the same cooking pot. Southeastern natives considered birds one kind of spirit and ground creatures another. Human beings were a third. Although they shared the same world and could be helpers to each other, it was important to be aware of their basic differences. To mix birds and other animals in this way would be the same as challenging the way that creation had laid out the natural world. Bison could not fly, birds could not breathe water, and fish could not walk on land, hence they should not be cooked together; it was as simple as that. Maintaining harmony and proper balance were of utmost importance to a peaceful, productive existence. It was one of many reminders to Native Americans that being precise, disciplined, and traditional in their thinking and behavior was most appropriate and beneficial for society.

Another important spiritual practice was the separation of males and females on certain occasions. The logic again falls to the importance of difference. Men and women were different kinds of human beings—complementary, but different all the same. They had different powers and played different roles in the natural world. Women carried the power of creation, an awesome ability that inspired tribes to separate men and women during times of menstruation and childbirth, the times when this power would be at its height. Men held the power to kill, and after killing, they separated themselves from the group until the power they had summoned settled back to normal, lest it negatively affect others in the tribe. If the two polar opposite powers had collided, that would have been disastrous in this belief system; the balance of nature would have been destroyed along with the world as they knew it. For eastern tribes, explaining the connections they saw and felt between themselves and the world around them gave them security and structure. With their cultural roots grounded in the earth, everything in life took on rich symbolism. Their religious and spiritual beliefs helped them explain their environment, interact with it, and ultimately succeed in it.

A SEA OF GRASS: PRAIRIE AND PLAINS UNDERSTANDING

When thinking about the general background that geography, diversity, and history provided for Native Americans on the one and a half million square miles of land that is the prairie and part of the plains expanse, what emerges first is the psychological effect of living on an apparently unending expanse with few obstacles to movement of people, animals, or weather. Cold winds from the north or warm winds from the south would arrive and change the weather very quickly. Above was a vast expanse of sky, and below, the endless spread of the prairie. Movement was easy for everything, and the people moved around a lot. Sometimes, as in the case of finding new food resources, movement was a positive thing. In other cases, such as when violent storms blew in, movement was not such a welcome force. The ability to move and the idea of movement colored these peoples' entire religious and social system.

Most plains mythology involving the origins of their resources within this culture of movement was associated with an archetypal female figure. Maize and buffalo are the two predominant nature elements found in their stories. The connection seems to be that these two important resources were so obviously tied to fertility that the female connection was natural. Male symbolism came into play in hunting and horsemanship (after the reintroduction of the horse by Europeans), but buffalo and corn were the gifts of the first woman. Besides the hunt, everything involving the buffalo was the world of the female as well. Buffalo skins provided the material for women to make clothing and construct housing covers. Women prepared the buffalo meat for meals and feasts. Women turned buffalo bones into tools and other implements. Buffalo symbolized the bounty and richness of the prairies and plains, and women embodied the creation and bounty of humanity. This is Mother Nature at her most basic. The sky was usually personified as a grandfather figure, providing sun and rain, the source of nourishment, but the earth was the grandmother, birthing, raising, teaching, and protecting everything on it. The vast openness also bred a special awareness of the different directions of the compass. The weather that came from each direction was different, with a unique purpose and personality. Each direction, as a result, had to be treated differently, with a reverence and respect unique to its character. The prairie peoples were fully aware that they owed much of their fate to the weather, and their rituals to called on each kind of wind to provide good gifts instead of bad. Everything about these societies was a reflection of what they observed around them: power, space, and movement.

The following is taken from the reflections of an elder Omaha Indian in the early 1900s.

When I was a youth, the country was very beautiful. Along the rivers were belts of timberland, where grew cottonwood, maple, elm, ash, and walnut trees ... In both the woodland and the prairies I could see the trails of many kinds of animals and could hear the cheerful songs of many kinds of birds. When I walked abroad I could see many forms of life, beautiful living creatures which *Wakananda* had place here ... but now the face of all the land is changed and sad. The living creatures are gone. I see the land desolate and I suffer an unspeakable sadness. Sometimes I wake in the night and I feel as though I should suffocate from the pressure of this awful feeling of loneliness.[1]

In this man's world, when he was a child, humans did not own or alter the land. They did not transform or dominate nature. They reacted to it but did not try to form it to resemble an idea inside their heads. The loneliness this elder expressed tells much about that connection. He is lonely because he has lost some of his best friends, the animals and plants of his native environment. His love of beauty and enjoyment at being part of the nature around him turned to sadness when that landscape changed. And it is not just beauty and friendship he misses. Within that natural beauty was the divine of his world. Wakananda, the divine creator, fashioned everything on earth with precision and the intention for it to function as a whole. The man was part of that, and with pieces of that whole missing, he no longer felt whole himself. This is not to suggest that all natives revered nature as this man described. He may have even disregarded or disrespected the divine in the past, being only human himself. At the basis of his culture and upbringing, though, was a respect and thankfulness for the gifts of the spirits. Nature was not a separate thing for him to use; it was part of the larger reality that he belonged to, making his self-perception, ideas about the world around him, and nature itself inseparable.

Among all of the plains tribes, the Pawnee gained the reputation of having the most creative sense of the world. In their mythological system, the supreme being, Tirawa, lived in the heavens. Among the lesser beings whom Tirawa used to carry his messages to earth was Teuperika, the Evening Star. She was a young maiden and kept the garden in the West that was the source of all the foods earthly creatures needed. From her marriage to the Morning Star came all human beings, and between her and her husband, the great warrior who cleared the sky, everything came to be. Among the symbols in this brief story is a sense of human orientation and connection to the heavens. Throughout human history, societies have generally seen their gods or spirits above and not below. This would especially make sense for the Pawnee and other plains and prairie tribes, with such an amazing expanse above that provided so much for the earth below. Yet it still seemed so far away that the Pawnee saw the heavens as the realm of "something else," something different, so the spirits residing there did not take on human form. Embedded in this idea was the fundamental belief that nature not only was material, but had vast spirit components as well. Other suggestions running through this story include the earth's connection to its weather, seen in heavenly activity (e.g., Morning Star's warrior status and control of the morning sky, as well as the origin of humans being the joining of Morning and Evening stars). A further examination of this story reveals the details of how these heavenly spirits not only kept the day and nighttime sky calm, but also sometimes influenced the directions to bring winds, rain, and storms. Even today, human's connection to the weather can be seen in the words used to describe moods—for example, "he has a stormy personality" or "her face clouded over." In their search for understanding, the Pawnee incorporated the forces that affected them most: the sky above, the land below, and the meeting, relationship, and interaction of the two.

Not everything is a gift, though, and certainly it would be overstating to say that if it is not good, then it is evil, and this is particularly true for natives of the plains and prairies. Although spirits and the divine played certain definite roles in the native cosmology of belief, there was a vagueness to the boundaries around holiness and divine power. The trickster comes in here as a murky example of the gray area between good and evil. He was a bungler responsible for the limitations inherent in human life and often set a negative example. Children greatly enjoyed tales of the trickster's exploits, but understood that the tales were meant to teach them what *not* to do. Trickster had a great appetite for everything and too much of anything is usually a bad thing. The message was one of moderation and forethought: the children were taught to think before consuming, and that discipline would make for a successful, healthy life. On the other hand, the idea of the trickster tended to encourage a tolerance for and amusement at human folly and foolishness. Having a spirit that regularly messed up suggested that perfection was not achievable, and laughter in the face of mistakes and thoughtlessness was not only healthy, but even necessary. It encouraged mental balance and a tolerance of imperfection that made the prairie and plains tribes amicable and fun-loving. The openness of their environment created an openness of mind and developed a unique personality that included flexibility, creativity, and tolerance.

THE LAND OF THE WEST: COASTAL COSMOLOGY

When studying tribes of the North American West Coast, the first detail that stands out is diversity. The bounty of the sea and forests in this region often made life quite easy on its native tribes. A majority of their meat came from the waters, which were fairly regular in their supply capability. Farming was usually not necessary because they could gather plenty of seeds, berries, and roots to balance their ready diet of fish and meat. The forests also furnished plenty of building materials for houses, canoes, and artwork, such as totem poles. There was so much wood present, especially from large trees, that things like their art expressions and canoes were much larger than those created by tribes in other regions. The typical location of a coastal village was the mouth of a river, giving them easy transportation access. Apparently so much bounty, with ready food sources, building materials, and easy transportation, gave many of these tribes enough time to evolve into more warlike cultures as well. The West Coast also offers one of the exceptions to the rule that most natives did not place great importance on amassing material wealth. For many West Coast tribes, this was of utmost importance. The natural bounty was usually so great that material prosperity rarely suffered, and some suggest that it is that very bounty that created such a focus on wealth accumulation. Readily accessible resources free up a people to seek other pursuits; war and wealth happened to be two of them for this region.

In this unique environment, their rhythms of life were largely focused on seasonal changes. In many areas of the West Coast, seasons were distinctly divided and this influenced the way most tribes lived. During the summer, they spent most of their time outdoors, hunting, fishing, gathering, warring, and preparing for the winter. When the snows came, many tribes redirected their attentions toward taking advantage of the break from providing to rehearse and celebrate creation, their self-understanding, and the mysteries of the natural world. One significant focus of ritual activity was food. Coastal natives thought that the forces driving the world were all competing for a limited supply of food, and this idea leaked over into their belief that they were competing with other communities for a limited amount of souls. As a symbol of their resourcefulness, providing extensive feasts was one method of showing the spirit world that they were good at what they did and thus deserved the souls bestowed upon them.

Their location by the sea also influenced the spiritual imagination of many tribes. The Kwakiutl, for example, depicted spirits moving in their environment as *sisiutl*, or double-headed serpents characterized by wetness and fluid motion. By extension then, they also associated the *sisiutl* with tears and blood in humans and the sea and rain in nature. They characterized their entire worldview through the ideas of the constant motion and fluidity. Human beings could figuratively "stop" the world enough to perceive it as material and deal with it appropriately, but in itself, the world was always moving, always changing. Death, decay, and rebirth were some of the forces of constant change in their cosmic view. Changes in life, losses and gains both mental and physical, and the impermanence of riches were other facets of the cosmic dynamic. One of the ways to see this worldview in action is to examine the religious beliefs and stories of the people.

Take, for example, the story of Bear Mother told by the Haida. Princess Rhpisunt, daughter of the chief of the Wolf Clan, was out one day picking berries. By accident she stepped into bear dung, which upset her greatly. For the rest of the day, she complained about the dirtiness of bears, who had soiled a lady of her high standing with their excrement. At the end of the day, she found herself separated from her companions when she stopped to fix straps on her basket. Before she became upset about being separated, two young men showed up and offered to help. She followed them, not realizing that they were leading her away from the sea where her people lived and into the mountains. After some time, they reached a village with a large house in the center. They led her into it, promising to introduce her to their father. It turned out that he was the chief of the Bear People, whom she had offended by her displeasure at stepping in bear dung. Around the house, she noticed many people who moved as if they were asleep. From a mouse woman, she learned that these were slaves captured because they had offended the bears, either by making fun of them or by mutilating them after a successful hunt. The mouse woman promised to help the princess in exchange for gifts. Her advice was that the princess should always eliminate her waste outside and put a copper bracelet on top of her waste every time. The bears would be spying on her, so when they saw this, the mouse woman said, they would examine her waste and realize she was right to be disgusted at their own, because hers would be shiny and valuable.

The princess followed her advice, was spared enslavement, and married a son of the Great Bear. She learned the customs of the Bear People, including their tradition of wearing bearskins whenever they went outside. The Bear People would move to different caves from time to time, and about the time the princess found herself pregnant and soon to become Bear Mother, they moved closer to her own people's village. Her people had searched and searched for her, killing many bears in the process, so she knew of their sadness in losing her. The princess gave birth to twin cubs, who were lively and beautiful. Her Wolf brothers gradually closed in on the cave where they were living, though, and her husband resigned himself to losing her to her people and dying himself. He told the princess to make sure that her brothers did not mutilate his body, and he promised to use powerful magic to turn their sons into humans that would be great hunters. The princess and her brothers upheld the Bear Prince's wishes, and the coat made from him became a source of great blessings for their father, the head of the Wolf People. The cubs turned into handsome boys, and their new grandfather built them a high pole from which they could see their old home among the Bear People. When the princess grew old and died, the boys put on their bear skins and returned to the Bear People, yet kept in contact with their Wolf relatives. From then on, the Bear and Wolf Peoples considered themselves related, exchanging resources, skills, and knowledge.

This story illustrates the deep connection Native Americans felt with the animal kingdom. In living by hunting, natives of the northwest felt their lives were intertwined with the game on which they depended so greatly.

Kiva of the Pueblo tradition at Yellow Jacket Pueblo, Montezuma County, Colorado. This kiva has two levels and would have been used for religious ceremonies and dances that symbolized American Indian spiritual and cosmological beliefs. Denver Public Library, Western History Collection, Call Number P-627.

How they treated their prey and even how they thought about them made all the difference in their fortune as a people. The fault of the princess was pride: she thought herself separate and superior to the bear that her people hunted. It was this attitude that brought her to potential disaster. The princess had to pay for her arrogance. On the other hand, the story also shows that Native Americans perceived a fluidity and haziness in relationships between species. All species had both strong and weak characteristics. The Bear People, for example showed their pride and confidence by deceiving the princess, but also their gullibility in believing her waste was copper. A mouse-woman was able to spy on them and help trick them, even though she was tiny and insignificant. Also apparent is Haida humor with the focus on human waste or excrement. Natives probably would have found it hilarious that people were so fascinated by this lowest of activities. Also found in the story is the use of and beliefs about totems as seen in the pole built by the grandfather for his grandson to climb and view their distant relatives. The Wolf People and the Bear People both crossed the line between animal and human, which is one of the central themes of totem pole symbolism. Are they wolves and bears or humans in wolf and bear skins? The fact that the story does not make this clear reflects the belief that all animals are "people" in the spiritual sense: intelligent individuals who deserve respect. A final theme is the reconciliation between enemies, important especially given that war was often a central feature of coastal life. By giving and receiving, the two peoples or species in the story come out better in the long run, benefiting from the strengths and skills of the other.

According to the native mind and religious belief, human metaphors and explanation, embodied in song and dance and elaborated through ritual, could never match the complexity or richness of the truth of the universe. Human understanding always had to run to catch up, but would never quite make it. It is an oversimplification to separate the mental world from the physical world of Native American cosmic reality. The two, according to West Coast native thinking, could connect, and although they could never truly be combined, the cosmic world sustained the mental world, providing its energy, sustenance, and meaning. The spirituality of Native Americans of the Northwest sought to honor this interrelation of the physical and spiritual, the connection between human, nonhuman, and more-than-human to describe the totality of their experiences and the meaning of their existence.

RELIGION BORN OF EXTREMES: TRADITIONS OF THE SOUTHWEST

For the North American desert region, the challenge of extremes was the force that shaped native lives. There was very little mobility within these societies, and most built permanent pueblo villages or larger cliff dwellings, utilizing local resources as best they could. Because of the resulting geographical separation, different social structures, economies, languages, and religions evolved across the region. There is a correlation between differences in language and differences in cultural structure, but because of the nature of this region, even within the same language group, cultures could vary dramatically. Rancheria (small, isolated agricultural-ists), permanent villages or pueblo-dwellers, mobile bands or tribes that were sporadically nomadic, and fully nomadic bands all existed within this area, some speaking related languages and some not. The religious lives of southwestern natives, despite this diversity, were divided into two major groups, although there were many exceptions, amalgamations, and offshoots. The agriculturalists usually held communal rituals representa-tive of religious beliefs that revolved around the cycles of nature. Pueblo people developed a hereditary caste of priests to preside over these ceremonies. Many religions of this type focused almost entirely on the community and little on individual concerns. The Hopi, though, varied greatly from this pattern by utilizing individualistic shamans, both male and female, who were more concerned with healing and other personal issues. The second group, which was usually more prevalent in hunt-ing and gathering societies than in those with a more agricultural basis, practiced much more shamanistic-related beliefs and practices. In an indi-vidually focused religion, shamans were more concerned with individual healing than with communal benefit. Healing in the native sense also meant more than just the relief or cure of physical symptoms and often crossed into the spiritual realm as well. And just as the first group found ways to integrate individual concerns into their religious practices, so did nonagriculturalists find ways to include communal practices into theirs. Some peoples explicitly mingled the two forms equally, holding both sha-manistic ceremonies and rituals for natural environmental cycles.

Basically, peoples in the Southwest saw little distinction between the best interests of the people and the best interests of the individual. This might seem contradictory based on the evidence, but the connection that underlies all of the differing beliefs is that health and well-being, whether it is for the one or the many, was as the root of beliefs and practices. The difference in interpretation rests in how they exercised it. Some tribes felt that if the good of the community was taken care of, then individu-als would have nothing to worry about. Others flipped that around and believed that healthy individuals created a healthy tribe. Still others addressed both concerns equally in ritual and ceremony. Many pueblos developed a complex view of the world and a parallel sophistication about ritual. Although their worldview was often reserved in its interpretation while being creative in its ritual expression, everyone demonstrated sen-sitivity to and understanding of the cycles of nature and the impact and role of spiritual beings. Harmony between humans and the powers of the natural world insured prosperity on earth.

The Papago of southern Arizona illustrate the intimacy that traditional peoples felt for their little part of the planet. The crops they depended on became fully living, personified beings in their religious beliefs. In many planting and harvesting rituals, for example, first the singer sang of the crops *to* the crops as part of the audience. Then the singer identified and connected with the crops, by singing of laughing and dancing with the corn and other produce. In the next part of the song, the crops sang back, and then finally, when the harvest lay in the arms of the people, plant and human would sing together with contentment, completing the duet. Although all of the "real" singers were human, the connection between humans and the nature around them was embodied in song and ritual. The wind blowing through the crops made them sing, and the human imagination gave them voice. This sense of identification meant that people could not treat their brothers in nature with indifference. Because of their kindred spirits, animals and plants had rights in the world, including the right to respect and appreciation. Destinies were tied together. The happiness expressed in the embrace at the end of the harvest suggests that it was the crop's destiny to nourish humans, so through planting and harvesting, humans helped the crops fulfill their providence. When people expressed thankfulness for this relationship, showing the proper respects through religious discipline, the songs were transformed into blessings. The world then moved as it should, with all of nature's children offering each other mutual respect and service.

In another example, the Navajo hogan or house song demonstrates one native attitude about nature and environment in the southwest:

Far in the east far below there a house was made; delightful house.
God of Dawn there his house was made; delightful house.
The Dawn there his house was made; delightful house.
White corn there its house was made; delightful house.
Soft possessions for them a house was made; delightful house.
Water in plenty surrounding for it a house was made; delightful house.
Corn pollen for it a house was made; delightful house.
The ancients make their presence delightful; delightful house.
Before me may it be delightful; behind me may it be delightful; around me may it be delightful; below me may it be delightful; above me may it be delightful; all (universally) may it be delightful.[2]

Similar songs, using themes of the west, complemented this song of the east, along with songs of the north and south as well.[3] The world "delightful" should be interpreted as "beautiful" or "holy." The point was to create human dwellings in concert with the surrounding environment and the homes of other creatures who shared the earth with people. The beliefs expressed in this song suggest that, left to itself, uninjured by disrespectful assaults of human beings, nature and its directions, dawn and dusk, corn and water, were simply beautiful, peaceful, delightful. In times of religious insight or connection, the Navajo felt and understood the beauty and presence in this song. Ultimately, nature was perfectly ordered, not having to think about planning, building, planting, hunting, and everything else necessary to human survival. In honoring and connecting to this perfection, the Navajo hoped to enjoy some of these blessings.

The Hopi, another representative southwestern society, traditionally celebrated a cycle of festivals designed to help crops along the way to maturity. Through an examination of how the Hopi regularly reasserted their ties to the land, their myths of origin, and their relationships to the spirit world, the ritualistic self-definition process of many southwestern natives becomes clear. The Hopi were rather typical of southwestern natives in that they organized their culture around religious societies. The typical society had both priests and lay people. Men's societies received more attention, but women's societies may have been equally important, especially given that many ceremonies centered on fertility, which in a ritual sense as well as a physical sense required the participation of both males and females. There were three levels of religious societies among the Hopi. The lowest were the Kachina and Powamuy. These were open to children age six through ten, both girls and boys. The kachinas were spirits whom masked dancers represented in rituals and celebrations, and the Powamuy society focused on the success and health of bean planting and harvesting. These societies represented the introduction of religious education and participation at a young age, breeding respect in the young for the natural world and its power. The second-ranking groups included four societies for men: the Blue Flute, Gray Flute, Antelope, and Snake. At this level, there were also two societies for women: the Maraw and Owaqol. These were open to community members between the ages of 11 and 16. At 16, they were eligible to enter adult groups at the third and highest level of social ranking. As one of the most elite, only males initiated into other societies could participate in the very important Soyalangw society, which carried out the holiest of ceremonies, but had no special initiation of its own.

It is clear that through these societies, the Hopi filled most of the calendar year with rituals and dances. Their religious activities were not a part-time aspect of their cultural life. What they did to maintain their homes and fields, care for their children, hunt, and cure was permanently intertwined with their dealings with the spiritual world. This was a dramatic way for training society members to think of their real identities, communal and individual, as intimately tied to the unseen forces of nature. One of the results is that in Hopi psychology, the self often became almost godlike. Kachina, for example, were dancers with masks that in the Western mind represented guardian or protective spirits, but the Hopis would not have described themselves as masked humans. When donning the costumes of the spirits and performing the correct rituals, the human *became* the spirit. The self moved so deeply into the mysteries of the supernatural that a person could not tell the difference between the

Arapaho Ghost Dance, circa 1900. National Archives Image number 530915.

two. This implied that Hopi social and cultural life was filled with the sacred, and so, daily life was inseparably tied to the spiritual. A human spirit that did not wonder about the rocks and clouds and nature around them was smaller, more restricted than it should be. With that shrinking came loss of dignity. The Hopi would suggest that present-day alienation from nature, the self, and a higher power comes from our doubts that modern humans play a significant, necessary role in the cosmos. The remedy? Take time to wonder, the Hopi would say.

INSEPARABLE ELEMENTS: RELIGION AND MEDICINE IN PREHISTORIC NORTH AMERICA

This is another area in which it is difficult for scholars to make definite assumptions about prehistoric Native American practices. Of all areas of study, herbal remedies and medical practices left little if any evidence for scientists to study, so what the modern world knows has been passed down through generations of tradition and practice. Native American medicine in general combined spirituality, herbalism, and magic to treat a wide range of mental, emotional, and physical ailments. Like other ancient healing systems, Native American medicine was a holistic approach that emphasized the treatment of body, mind, and spirit as a whole regardless of the physical origin of the ailment. Because they believed that humans were inextricably linked to the people, objects, and environment surrounding that person, their healing practices focused on harmony in the community, nature, and the spiritual world. Although across the continent there were many variations, there were four basic common practices. These practices, according to tradition, are at least 10,000 years old and include the involvement of "professional" healers or medicine men and women, the use of herbal remedies, ritual purification or purging, and the observance of symbolic rituals and ceremonies. There was no way, according to native belief, to take only pieces of the practice and use them effectively. Most would say that in order for the treatment to be affective, the entire process must be enacted. At the least, partial treatment would not work, but at its worst, it might harm. Everything was linked according to native belief, and a whole without all of its parts was dangerously incomplete.

Not only was everything in nature connected, but each human spirit and object on the planet also had a corresponding presence in the spirit world, the primary origin of good health and illness. Because of their direct responsibility, spiritual rejuvenation and achievement of physical, emotional, and communal harmony were at the heart of medical practice. Typically a healer was used as an intermediary or go-between with the spiritual world. Sometimes a healer or a trained herbalist would also prescribe herbal remedies for symptom relief. Purification rituals cleansed the body, and other ceremonies promoted spiritual healing, personal contemplation, and internal growth. Treatment also relied on the community coming together to support the sick individual, so tribes conducted many ceremonies as groups, with the entire community physically surrounding and supporting the patient. What the Western mind thinks of as medical practice, with one-on-one doctor–patient interaction, would not have been recognizable to Native North Americans.

Specific healing practices utilized in Native American societies differed from tribe to tribe and depended on the patient and nature of the illness. Causes of disease always played a role, be that past deeds, state of mind and emotions, or level of harmony with the spirit world. Healers could be trained and initiated, could have powers transmitted from another healer, or could inherit their powers from an ancestor. They performed complete examinations that were more in-depth than those of today's practitioners. A "check-up" included an assessment of not only physical symptoms, but also mental and emotional issues, nonverbal cues, and spiritual connections. Then the healer might use prayer, meditation, symbolic rituals, and counseling to treat their patient. These practices would rid the ailing person of impurities, appease spirits, and restore harmony. In some cases, the healer might have gone into a trance state to petition for help from the spirit world in retrieving part of the patient's soul that might have been commandeered by someone else. Possession was a possibility, and healers used trance states to treat these issues as well. Herbal connections to health and wellness were also handed down through generations, and stories of the origins of the herbs functioned as ways of preserving the benefit of the plant to society. When given herbal remedies, the ill might ingest them directly, drink them as tea, or mix them with another drink or food, depending on the knowledge of the healer and guidance of the spirits. Burning herbs such as sage, sweet grass, or cedar during a ceremony could also play a role in treating and purifying the patient. When performed in a sweat lodge, which often symbolized the womb and rebirth, the combination of the steam and herbal smoke would purify both body and spirit. Final elements might include medicine wheels, the sacred hoop, and communal "sings" along with dancing, painting, chanting, and drumming. The combination, whatever its final elements were, treated the whole person—body, mind, and soul—using humans' connections to nature and the environment to heal and maintain individual health.

Through the use of both spiritual and material tools, native medicine men and women treated many ailments and illness with great success. The root of the wild yam was a very effective painkiller used in childbirth and menstrual cycles as well as a balancer for hormones. The Cherokee used passionflower as a poultice or medicinal pack for injuries and bruises and for relaxing the muscles and easing tension. The root of this plant also helped earaches and boils. Sage treated colds, bruises, and upset stomach and could also work as a deodorant and insect repellant. Natives used purple coneflower for simple things such as sore throats, toothache, swollen glands, and headaches, but science now knows that it functions well as an antibiotic and antiviral treatment also. Healers employed juniper for arthritis, coughs, and diarrhea. Willow has been used for centuries to relieve pain and dandelion for improving circulation and blood cleansing. Although many centuries ago they may have been guessing, very quickly natives amassed an immense amount of knowledge concerning what herbs could help people. Many are still in use today or are used as the foundation for modern medications to serve the same functions. Trial, error, and observation can be the best teachers of all.

EMPIRICAL OR ETHEREAL: ASTRONOMY AS RELIGION

As a generalization, it is fair to say that less is known about the early inhabitants of the Great Plains than about any of their contemporaries on the continent. The American Indians of the plains left no written language or well-developed preservable art. Unlike their Anasazi neighbors to the south, the Plains Indians did not build much. And unlike the woodland tribes to the east, intensive observation of the Plains tribes by Westerners did not really begin until around 200 years after they had started adjusting to white presence. Observing and recording the culture of equestrian natives tells us little about their prehistoric pedestrian ancestors because they quickly adapted to change and abandoned earlier traditions. In fact, it is difficult to know much for sure about these societies, considering how few of them there were spread out over such a large expanse. Some of these nomadic people did leave behind relics and constructions that suggest they followed an interesting belief system and placed religious significance on astronomical events. They left behind many stone circles, ranging from 6 to 18 feet in diameter, which are now called tepee rings. They are simple circles, made of football-sized rocks and spread out over the plains from Texas to northern Canada. There were so many of these rock circles, some guess six million in the North American Great Plains, that they must have performed an ordinary function, most likely holding down the edges of tents (hence the name). What sometimes accompanies these millions of circles is what drew astronomical interest. Plains inhabitants also constructed large effigy figures drawn with stones on the ground's surface and a number of enigmatic large wheel patterns on the ground now called medicine wheels. These medicine wheels consisted of a central circle or rock pile from which lines radiated out like spokes. Often there were other piles of rock or cairns and one or more concentric circles. Medicine wheels were larger than tepee rings, ranging up to 300 feet in diameter. The word "medicine" implies magic or supernatural and was probably used for lack of a better translatable word. They are somewhat of a mystery and are generally so old that their purpose and creator identity have been lost to history. They could be 1,000, 5,000, or 10,000 years old, but based on artifact study, oral history, and scientific analysis, it seems many were used as calendars. Marking the solstices was definitely part of their purpose considering that most cairns and spokes line up with major astronomical features. The purpose of this type of calendar would be to schedule and perform rituals that had to do with astronomical events and changes in the seasons. Most of this evidence is based on observation and experimentation because by the 1700s, much of the native lore concerning the behavior of the skies was gone. Traits are too easily lost in society when there is no written record for preservation in the face of the challenge of European contact.

The Pawnee, as a southern plains example, based much of their religion and ritual on star knowledge. The principal deities were identified as Morning Star and Evening Star, which were male and female. Next in rank were the gods of the four world quarters, standing in the semi-cardinal positions and supporting the heavens.[4] The gods of the four cardinal directions were created first, with Evening Star in the west and Moon as her helper and with Morning Star in the east with Sun as his helper. Then there was North Star, "it which doesn't move," and South Star or "Canopus." Several constellations were recognized and named by the Pawnee, who were apparently aware of the variations in their rising and setting. There is even a Pawnee sky map at the Field Museum of Natural History in Chicago that some suggest is evidence of a detailed knowledge of the sky before the coming of the white man. How a map would have survived that kind of transfer and handling for over 300 years is questioned, but its existence alone suggests advanced astronomical knowledge. They held rituals around their star gods and even planned and constructed their earth lodges based on constellational observation. Everything from animals to man-made objects had a direction association to go along with its purpose on the planet, showing how ingrained astronomical understanding was to the Pawnee.

Of all North American native peoples, the Anasazi showed the greatest incorporation and understanding of astronomical phenomena. Solar observation for the purpose of establishing a yearly calendar or marking religious ceremonies was a strong part of historic Pueblo Indian practice. Discoveries in Chaco Canyon support the idea that the ancestors of historic Pueblo Indians utilized sun-watching practices and perhaps even carried it further than their descendants. There are several buildings or sites aligned to significant solar directions. Not all of them could be used to observe the sun, but they all performed some astronomical role for the people of the area. These observatories fell into one of four basic categories. The first was a site used solely for gaining information, being used as or with a measuring instrument. The purpose would have been either to expand their understanding of the sky through observation or to develop a calendar. The second type of site was built directly from observations

Sun Temple Shrine, Native American Anasazi ruins, Mesa Verde National Park, Montezuma County, Colorado. Denver Public Library, Western History Collection, Call Number P-639.

made at the first kind of site. Rather than being used to observe, these marked or demonstrated the knowledge gained and were built close to the observatories themselves. The third type was also built on the basis of sun observation, but the phenomena in this type were *not* directly observable. Using cardinal or semicardinal directions to position buildings close to the observation point is a good example here. The final type is the same as the third, except the buildings were built at some nonvisible distant location. The only way the people could have been accurate with this would have been to use some type of measuring instrument, aligning one parallel line with the sun and then determining all other positions geometrically from that point. Although definite conclusions are difficult, it is apparent that the Anasazi and their ancestors used their observatories to determine solstices for ceremonial purposes, to establish calendars, and to incorporate the sun into their dwellings, ceremonial structures, and settlement blueprints. Despite these understandings of the Anasazi and other North American tribes, there remains much to be done in order to fully comprehend the place and role of astronomical practice in native life on this continent.

THE YEARLY CYCLE OF INDIGENOUS LIFE: NATIVE EXPLANATION OF THE SEASONS' UNAVOIDABLE CHANGES

Take a moment and consider everything that is known today about the changing of the seasons. Then stand in the shoes of Native Americans and imagine what kinds of explanations there could have been for seasonal change 1,000 years ago. Rotation of the earth and distance from the sun are factors Native Americans would not have had the science or technology to understand. One misconception to avoid in this study, however, is the idea that seasonal changes looked then like they do today. During ice ages, most areas of the western hemisphere would have had only two seasons—summer and winter—but they would have been colder than today's seasons. There were climatic periods in which four seasons were the norm, but the summer would have been hotter and the winter colder than what modern people are used to. Even at the greatest extent of the glaciers, it was not all bad, all cold, all the time everywhere on earth. During the last period of minimal glaciation, hippos were calling the Sahara their home. Ice Age Florida, although not as warm then as it is now, would have been a perfect wintering spot. With all the differences, prehistoric humans lived through the cyclical change of seasons and searched for meaning in what they saw.

In one Native American legend, spirit hunters in the sky slew the Great Bear (a constellation) during the fall. The bear's blood dripped onto the forests, changing some of the leaves to red. Some turned to yellow because bear fat splattered out of the kettle hunters used to cook the bear meat.

Color changes are caused by chemical changes in the leaves instigated by dropping temperatures, but for Native Americans to understand and appreciate their environment, they often turned to natural connections and relationships as an explanation.

Long ago, the trees were told they must stay awake seven days and seven nights, but only the cedar, the pine and the spruce on that seventh night. The reward they were given while all the other trees slept was that the sleeping trees must shed their leaves to nourish them. So, each autumn, the leaves of the sleeping trees fall. They cover the floor of our woodlands with colors as bright as the flowers that come with the spring. The leaves return the strength of one more year's growth to the earth. This journey the leaves take is part of that great circle which holds us all close to the earth.[5]

It is that connection holding native peoples close to the earth that drives stories like the one just presented. Most cultures across the continent have different versions of the same themes. Very often the participants in stories came from an unnamed tribe or a society of ancients, making them easily communicable across traditions. Because of these ambiguities, the culture of origin often gets lost in the telling, retelling, and translation. The connections that all native religions seemed to share concerning the ties between everything in life means that these stories best represent what native cultures have in common. Take a look at this closely related example.

Many moons ago when the world was still young, plant and animal life was enjoying the beautiful summer weather. But as the days went by, autumn set in and the weather became colder and colder. The grass and flower folk were in a sad condition, for they had no protection from the cold. Just when it seemed there was no hope, He who looks after the things of His creation came to their aid. He said that the leaves of the trees should fall to the ground, spreading a soft, warm blanket over the tender roots of the grass and flowers. To repay the trees for the loss of their leaves, he allowed them one last bright array of beauty every year before they fell.[6]

By looking at stories that ignore cultural boundaries, it is easier to see the normally subtle similarities between tribal worldviews and religious beliefs.

The story of Glooskap and his search for Summer was told through the lore of many tribes as well. This is how the story goes. Long ago, a mighty tribe lived near the sunrise. They called themselves Wawaniki, or the Children of Light. Glooskap was their leader, and he was kind and giving. Once during Glooskap's reign it grew extremely cold. Snow and ice covered everything, and his people suffered and died from cold and famine. Glooskap set out for the north and, in a wigwam, found the giant Winter, whose icy breath had frozen the land. Glooskap entered the wigwam and they smoked together, talking of past times when Winter had ruled the

earth. Glooskap fell under Winter's charm for six months and slept until
he was too strong for the charm. The Loon then brought him news of land
to the south where it was always warm because of the all-powerful giant
Summer, who could easily overcome Winter, so off went Glooskap to find
Summer and save his people. Whale, a friend of Glooskap's, gave him a
ride to southern waters, and once he was on land again, Glooskap traveled into the forest. There he found a beautiful woman with long brown
hair, crowned with flowers, and arms filled with blossoms. He captured
Summer, and together they traveled back to Winter's lodge. Winter
invited him in, hoping to freeze him to sleep again, but Glooskap did
the talking and melted Winter's home. With Winter no longer protected,
Summer worked her magic, and everything in nature awoke while Winter
wept. Then Summer said, "Now that I have proven I am more powerful,
I give you all the country to the far north for your own, and there I shall
never disturb you. Six months of every year you may return to Glooskap's
country and reign as before, but you are to be less severe with your power.
During the other six months, I will come back from the South and rule
the land." With nothing left to do but accept this, Winter agreed, and seasons have been set ever since.[7] By giving the seasons godlike powers and
humanlike impulses, natives demonstrated their observation of the sway
nature held over their lives while simultaneously expressing the understanding and connection they felt to these beings in their world.

    In the Southwest, Pueblo natives told the story a little differently. Blue
Corn Maiden of the Pueblo people was responsible for the growth of the
blue corn that they depended on for nourishment. One day she went out
to gather wood, which she normally did not do and encountered Winter
Katsina. He instantly fell in love with her and invited her to his home,
an invitation that she could not refuse. Once they were there, Winter
Katsina iced the windows and blocked the door with snow so that she
could not leave. Although he loved her dearly and was very kind to her,
she was sad not to be with her people, helping to make the blue corn
grow. One day while Winter Katsina was out doing his work, spreading
winter around the world, Blue Corn Maiden went outside to dig in the
snow for some of the plants of summer she loved so much. From the few
she found, she built a fire, which she was not allowed to do when Winter
Katsina was home, and it melted all the snow and ice in the house. When
the door opened fully, Summer Katsina came into the house. When
Winter Katsina arrived, it seemed that they would fight, but Winter's ice
and snow was no match for Summer's fire. As a truce, they decided that
for six months, Blue Corn Maiden could return with Summer Katsina
to her people. This pleased everyone but Winter Katsina, who would
have preferred to have Blue Corn Maiden all year long. When it snowed
or cold wind blew in the spring, this was Winter showing his discon-
tent as Blue Corn Maiden left for her six months with Summer and her
people. Through these stories, natives explained the good and the bad

as necessary to the proper functioning of the earth and its cycles. As an old Seneca tale proclaims, "the kinsmen of Pine hold forth the promise of Spring's return, and their green robes are the despair of Winter and all his furious hosts."[8]

In the prairies, one of the most magical, beautiful times of the year is spring. The colors of prairie flowers carpet the grasslands. In an effort to explain the beauty, many plains and prairie tribes adopted different version of the same story, which told the story of the sacrifice of a young girl for the good of her tribe. As the story goes, drought and famine killed many members of the Nawyaka band of nomadic Plains Indians. In order to sooth her loneliness and hunger pains, She Who Is Alone, an orphan, spent all of her time with her only possession and friend: a warrior doll left to her by her parents before they died. Because her people had experienced years of famine, the Shaman of the tribe went to the holy hill to ask the Great Spirit why there had been no rain. The response was "you mistreated the earth, killed bison, and moved on without replenishing the land. You must sacrifice your most precious possession." When the Shaman told of the Great Spirit's charge, She Who Is Alone decided that the most precious possession of the tribe was her warrior doll. Deep in the night she left her tent, made a fire on the holy hill, and sacrificed her doll. When dawn broke, the rains came, causing bluebonnet flowers to open all over the hills. The tribe understood that the sacrifice of She Who Is Alone was responsible, and they then welcomed her with open arms as her new family. The native culture was trying to explain the appearance of the rains and blossoming of spring, but the parallel moral of the story is that all must sacrifice for the health of society, even if society has caused its own ills. And ultimately, no matter whom the story belonged to or how it was told, respect and proper use of the land was what ensured continued good fortune.

SCIENCE BEFORE THERE WERE SCIENTISTS: NATIVE NATURAL LAWS OF INTERDEPENDENCE

The result of all of this was the definition of place and person, a sense of space and individual identity. The key questions ask how individuals and the community ecologically respected the place they lived and how a conversation between the individual, the community, and the environment could be established and maintained. Wherever there were Native Americans, they developed ways to answers these questions of survival and sustainability in profoundly insightful, creative, flexible ways. The Lakota belief in *mitakuye oyasin*, or "we are all related," was shared by all Native Americans, just expressed differently depending on their natural environment and cultural perspective. Guided by this metaphysical principle, people understood that all entities of nature were interrelated and that this relationship must be honored. The language of that relationship was what made up the intricacies and details of Native American religion. It was through these interactions, which natives examined and developed over hundreds and hundreds of years, that they accumulated ecological knowledge.

In contrast to the modern view of nature and reality, Native Americans perceived multiple realities, and the one they lived in was one of many possibilities. With so many dimensional realities, knowledge was received from both human and nonhuman beings. Animals and plants interacted with each other in many ways, and according to native beliefs, each had a sense of purpose and meaning as part of the world around them. Over the last 500 years, profound changes have altered the land and environment in North America. When Europeans arrived, they saw a wilderness that needed to be tamed, a land of unlimited resources for their use and gain. Unfortunately for the native population, native peoples were viewed as a resource to be dealt with and used, just like the rest of the landscape. Before Europeans arrived, the balance between nature and people was harmonious and sustainable. The changes the people and land experienced disrupted that balance irreparably.

At the center of the native aspiration for balanced existence was the idea and concept of place. To know a landscape, to really know it, the place had to be experienced firsthand, and the observer had to be a part of it. The idea of place was directly connected to the worldview of both individuals and their communities. The complex, dynamic nature of Native Americans' cosmic view resulted in a multifaceted, dynamic definition of place. Place, then, was a living presence in the context of both physical and spiritual meaning. An example of the Navajo perception and description of their "place" is the way they tied their idea of homeland to sacred mountains.

The Navajo view their Fifth World as a pattern of physical landmarks that are imbued with mind and vital force. The basic model consists of four outer sacred mountains. These are called: *Sisnaa jini* (Blanca Peak), *Tsoo dzil* (Mount Taylor), *Dook o oosliid* (San Francisco Peaks), and *Dibenitsaa* (Hesperus Peak). They are positioned cardinally around a Navajo world axis whose earthly form is considered to be Huerfano Mesa in northern New Mexico. Its Navajo name, *Dzilna' oodilii,* meaning Mountain Around Which Moving Was Done (Encircled Mountain), refers to the early movement of the clans during the settlement of the Fifth World.[9]

The sacred mountains were the boundary to what the Navajo considered their place. The stories, experiences, and rituals associated with the mountains were the context for Navajo participation and interaction with plants, animals, earth, and sky. The land nurtured them, and they returned the favor. The separation of culture and nature would have been unnatural, even impossible, just as it would have been unnatural to separate humans from their places. All natives used landscape in ways that benefited them and ensured their survival. The main difference between their methods and modern Western uses was the idea of reciprocity, a relationship of give and take, guided by cultural values, ethical beliefs, and spiritual practices.

Language was one element that was inseparable from native landscape. Native cultures talked, prayed, and chanted the landscape into their reality. The animating power of language connected the breath of each person to the breath of the world. Words held great power in Native American culture. They "talked the land" by naming its places, singing its virtues, and telling its stories. Native languages paid special attention to describing natural places as alive and in constant motion. The verb-based nature of these languages was connected to the native cosmological assumption that everyone lived in an interrelated world that acted as a living being made up of many parts. The human body was often used in native lore and belief as a metaphor for the world as a living being. Native religion often portrayed the sky and earth as two separate bodies that came together to create life; the body of the earth united with the body of the sky to create existence as they saw it in nature. Native perceptions of life and origin, unlike more Western cultures, focused on the earth and its feminine qualities of creation. Most other creation ideas suggest that a masculine sky is the ultimate realm of godhood and conception. Everything that exists on the planet had its roots in the creative Mother Earth, whose collection of living organisms was viewed as one human body analogy in its role and character. Ultimately, in the traditional native perspective, place was an integral part of the larger order. Native stories, languages, and rituals gave meaning to people's participation in their landscape. It was sacred, creative, nurturing, and in motion; the totality of this was the "place" of Native North America.

NOTES

1. Joseph Epes Brown, *The Spiritual Legacy of the American Indian* (New York: The Crossroad Publishing Company, Inc., 1984), 12.

2. George Wharton James, *Indian Blankets and Their Makers* (Chicago: A. C. McClure and Co., 1920), 5.

3. This does not suggest that geographically the peoples who created songs came from the north, south, east, and west, but that the songs represent powers and forces *of* the north, south, east, and west.

4. Semicardinal suggests northeast, northwest, southeast, and southwest, whereas the cardinal directions are north, south, east, and west.

5. Neil Philip, ed., *In a Sacred Manner I Live* (New York: Clarion Books, 1997), 20.

6. Ibid., 28.

7. The story of Glooskap and his finding summer for the native peoples can be found in print in many versions. This summary represents a compilation of read-

ing both online and in-print versions and presenting the most common elements of all of the stories.

8. Just as in the story of Glooskap and Summer, this story of Blue Corn Maiden was written from readings of different version in different sources.

9. Sam Gill, *Native American Religions: An Introduction* (New York: Wadsworth Publishing, 2004), 79.

7

MOVEMENT IN THE ENVIRONMENT: MIGRATION AND TRANSPORTATION

Never criticize a man until you've walked two moons in his moccasins.

Native American Proverb

From the very beginning of their arrival in the "New World," European explorers wondered about the origins of the Native Americans. Where did they come from? Had they always been here? If not, when did they arrive? Because of the natives' exotic customs and their unusual clothing, or lack thereof, some explorers conjectured that the American Indians might not even be human. Pope Julius II declared in the early 1500s that Indians were descended from Adam and Eve, making them human in the church's eyes, but that did not stop speculation on how they reached the New World. One popular idea was that the Indians were the children of Babel condemned to a primitive existence in a harsh land because of their past sins. The belief that the natives descended from Israelites experienced a brief moment in the spotlight, but that proposal died quickly. The revered Cotton Mather of the Puritan faith suggested that the devil led the Native Americans to the New World to prevent them from finding salvation. Everyone from Egyptians, Trojans, and Greeks to the Chinese, Huns, and ancient Irish were suggested as possible ancestors on the North American Indian family tree. It was not other-worldly intervention or wayward sailing ventures, however; it was a journey of hardship, challenge, and discovery that brought the earliest known humans to North America.

A process of massive migration, which apparently took place sporadically over tens of thousands of years, brought the first humans to this continent. The first major human movement to consider then would be the proposed trek into North America from Asia. Movement from place to place has been an integral part of humanity's interaction with the environment for thousands of years. For most tribes, until they adopted agriculture as their main form of subsistence, migration was a common and frequent occurrence. The search for more and better resources, the advent of war, and issues of mutual toleration often forced peoples from one land to the next. Migration was the main force behind social, cultural, and technological change, with every move bringing out the need for flexibility and adaptation to new environments. Studying this major catalyst of change would not be the job of a historian, especially when examining the earliest periods of human movement. A combination of archaeology, anthropology, physiology, genetics, and linguistics offers the best glimpse into prehistoric daily life, culture, biology, and social structure, with each specialty doing what it does best to help recreate a picture of ancient life. Unfortunately it is difficult for specialists in different fields to come to definite agreements, even when analyzing the same site or collection of information. Careful synthesis of analysis and interpretations is necessary to come to any strongly supportable conclusions. Modern technological methods and tools also affect conclusions made about prehistoric North Americans. Scientific dating is the largest of these challenges. Although multiple datings using different methods is the most reliable way of determining age of a prehistoric site, it is often not possible, because of lack of evidence and artifacts for testing and analysis. This means even the basic "facts" such as times, chronology, and dates are not certain, making the job even harder.

As a result of these difficulties and uncertainties, theories abound as to how and when these first residents arrived. Everyone pretty much agrees that they have been here for at least 15,000 years, but some suggest humans arrived as long as 50,000 years ago. "Doubling time" estimates, or assumptions made about the time it takes for a population to double itself in numbers, influence these dates. Other issues are life span assumptions and rate of expansion across the continent of the migrant population. If the doubling time was long, around 70 years, the life span short, about 20 years, and the population dispersal slow, then 50,000 years would make sense. If these assumptions are exactly reversed, then the later estimates must be right. Using these determining factors alone makes it difficult to utilize demographic analysis to come to clear-cut conclusions. Two other methods that could determine these dates are based on archaeological artifact dating and linguistic, physiological, and genetic differentiation between populations in northern Asia and North America. One popular model based on this evidence is the "three wave model," which suggests that three different "waves" of migrants populated the continent. The three linguistic groups in the Americas provide the strongest support for this theory. DNA evidence, though, suggests one genetic connection with language differentiation evolving after their arrival and a very early arrival date range of 41,000 to 28,000 B.C.E. Whom to believe and what evidence to accept ends up being the final, most important question.

As far as the evaluation of physical evidence goes, it depends on what evidence is accepted as signs of human occupation. Charcoal and stone chips suggest possible human habitation, but could also be the remnants of a forest fire or some other accidental work of nature. It is because of evidential uncertainty that it has been difficult to conclusively prove the existence of humans in North America more than 40,000 years ago. Sites with simple hammers, choppers, and hearths have been dated back as far as 50,000 years ago, but questions over the accuracy of dating procedures brings question in there as well. Additionally, there are only three separate times the Beringia Bridge would have been exposed: between 40,000 and 50,000 years ago, between 32,000 and 36,000 years ago, and between 13,000 and 28,000 years ago. When the land bridge was submerged, the sediment and water would have erased or buried most evidence, and since the bridge remains relatively inaccessible anyway; hard material evidence may never be available. As for skeletal remains of the people themselves, that is even harder to come by in an archaeological site. Some of the oldest known human remains in North America are those of the Kennewick man, found in Washington State and dated at approximately 9,600 years old. There is a woman's skull and leg bone, though, that jump further back in time, with her remains dating at approximately 70,000 years old. Subsequent testing and the development of new techniques put this date into serious question, but with such a widespread scale of evidence and time frames, factoring in the reliability issues in dating procedures, concrete, unquestionable analysis becomes nearly impossible.

Debate also surrounds assumptions about *how* they got here. The most common and well-known theory is that a low sea level caused by extensive glaciation exposed at certain times in history the Beringia Bridge that spans from Siberia to Alaska. Ice sheets locked up large amounts of the world's sea and ocean water, lowering the sea level 150 to 300 feet. This exposed a land mass that was anywhere from 600 to 1,000 miles wide. It is suggested that when exposed, it blocked off cold Arctic waters, creating a warmer climate on the bridge than might be expected and encouraged the presence of lakes and plentiful vegetation. This would have been necessary for animals and humans to survive the long trek across. Pollen analysis, though, suggests several different interpretations of climatic conditions, only some of which would have been agreeable to human migration. In response to this, some scientists theorize that migrants reached the Americas at least in part by boat. Many anthropologists believe that the traditional seagoing cultures of the Arctic and West Coast did not develop independently, but rather through the influence of their earliest North American ancestors. Some scholars embrace a combination of both theories despite the lack of evidence for early coastal societies.

Most of the lands containing evidence potential have been submerged by rising sea levels over the centuries, thus adding one more obstacle to definitive analysis of early migrants. Then in a leap away from this family of suppositions, some think ancient migrants found South America first by leaving south and east Asia in boats. This is probably the most controversial theory, given that these ancient people would have needed advanced deep-sea sailing technology to successfully travel such a long distance. Although many have tried to prove that primitive vessels could have reached the continent, there is very little evidence to support this line of assumption. Even what caused these early people to migrate remains unknown. They could have been big-game hunters, and in following their resources, as in the land bridge theory, they would have reached North America when their prey crossed the bridge. Population pressures could have played a role as well because hunting and gathering societies could only support one person per six square miles and perhaps migrant societies needed more environmental and food resources to sustain their numbers. Warfare and conflict cannot be ruled out either. It is possible that curiosity about the unknown, a natural human urge for knowledge and exploration, drove them also. What better reason to climb a mountain than simply because it is there?

Once they arrived on the continent by crossing the land bridge, humans made their way south either down the coast or by passing through ice-free corridors, which opened intermittently between 23,000 and 13,000 B.C.E. Either route would have been dangerous and intimidating. The coastal route would have forced the boats to navigate through ice-free pockets and the land route involved traveling down a harsh, barren valley between two massive glaciers. There is no hard archaeological evidence to support either theory and both theories contain their own strengths and weaknesses. Linguistic evidence weighs in on the side of the coastal route, suggesting much longer periods of habitation there rather than inland because of their diversity in language development. Most scholars support the coastal path because it offered fewer physical challenges to the migrants, and what evidence does exist from later peoples suggests a sophisticated understanding of water travel and navigation. As migration continued, by about 12,000 years ago, the Americas were populated from the Arctic to the tip of South America. And then history, evidence, and historical study cannot help but throw a wrench (or several wrenches) into the theories. Oddly enough, most of the sites with the oldest dates are located in the lower United States and down into Mexico with no northern sites in Canada or Alaska being able to compete in age. Clovis Culture, named because it was found near Clovis, New Mexico, demonstrates some of the earliest widespread common traits in Paleo-Indian society; however, no one has been able to locate the place where this technology was invented. It seems to have appeared all across the continent all at once. Furthermore, Clovis has never been found anywhere else in the world except in North America. If Clovis traits did not evolve within North America, where did they come from? Although spontaneous emergence of a culture seems unlikely, how else could it have emerged in North America? Until more conclusive hard proof emerges, that question is difficult, if not impossible, to answer.

WHAT THE BONES TELL US: MOTIVATIONS FOR MIGRATION

Once people arrived and spread out across North and South America, resource availability, geography, and climatic changes influenced the patterns of movement within the continents. Climatic conditions affected how and where people moved; for example, as the glaciers retreated at the end of the last ice age, humans followed them returning north. The funnel shape of southern Mexico, on the other hand, forced people into close proximity and encouraged the development of more complex societies. Although prehistoric migrants came to North and South America as rather amalgamated, primitive cultures, very quickly the character of their new environment shaped people into unique, diversified societies that stayed on the move, constantly looking for greener pastures. This largely resulted from their methods of providing food for their tribes. From the time that humans arrived in North America until the melting of the last ice age approximately 7,000 years ago, two basic forms of subsistence prevailed: big-game hunting and the foraging of small plants and animals. The gathering method would have provided more consistent food supplies than the large-game hunts would have, but both played an instrumental role in the survival of native peoples. Although more evidence is available for the analysis of the hunters in a society, that does not mean they played a more predominant role. The tools used by gatherers would have been made of wood and fiber, so they would not have stood the tests of time and decay like a hunter's projectile point could. Another misconception is that all native societies focused on conservation and appropriate use of their resources. Some of these hunter-gatherer societies left behind evidence suggesting not all natives were concerned with only killing the animals they needed to survive. Many migratory societies used the cliff-drive method of hunting, driving herds of large animals such as the bison off of cliffs to their deaths. There is no realistic way this could have been efficient. An entire herd of any animal would have been too much for even several societies to use, so waste was more common in Native American societies than is often believed. Migration resulted from many different ways of living, from the most stingy to the gratuitously excessive. No matter what they were looking for, there was rarely enough in one place to sustain a community for long.

Take the Mississippian culture of eastern North America, for example. Much of Mississippian culture resulted from an outward diffusion of

Mexican native migration. Trouble in Mexico meant that societies migrated in the effort to escape physical and political conflict. The Natchez tradition resulted from migration out of a troubled Mexico, Mississippian platform mounds began to appear during a turbulent Mexican period, and Mexican maize played an instrumental role in Mississippian development. Ultimately, Mississippian society was a result of the combination of these Mexican influences, and local innovation and regional interaction modified and individualized the culture. "It was not until after many generations that the Great Suns came and joined us in this country, where . . . we had multiplied like the leaves of the trees," as native tradition says, with time and multiplication here meaning division and dispersal.[1] The farther migrant Mexicans got from home, the less their descendants felt and behaved like their ancestors. And a strong pattern of cultural differentiation suggests that a condensed core of middle Mississippian cultures spread out aggressively in spokes to become their own entities. Later, the culture disappeared in the Wisconsin area around 1300 C.E., and it most likely was increased aridity that encouraged a stronger dependence on hunting and fishing rather than planting and gathering. In the Southeast, however, the Mississippian culture flourished through the 1500s until Hernando de Soto arrived. Climate did not force the change for them; outside intervention did. Although the catalyst of change was different, the result was the same: migration and subsistence shifted as a result of natural and unnatural environmental factors.

Another tribal group affected by Mexican contact and influence was the many Algonquian-speaking peoples of eastern North America. They followed a different pattern of migration traveling initially eastward from Alaska instead of south to begin their residence on the East Coast. The Ojibwa tell that their ancestors traveled all the way to the coast and then reversed their path to eventually settle at the shores of the Great Lakes. Northern Algonquian speakers, who lived where planting was impossible, continued a highly mobile hunting-and-gathering way of life, whereas others to the south found themselves more settled. The tales that have survived suggest that interaction among different people influenced these movements the most. According to Algonquian Delaware tradition, they made it all the way to the Atlantic, and the story told to Moravian missionary John Heckewelder recounted a tale of different directions of influence. Speakers of the Algonquian and Iroquoian languages came to the Northeast from apparently different directions: the Delawares came from the West and the Iroquois joined them. At some point (native histories rarely speak of time in an understandably Western way), the two peoples joined together and made war against the Allegewi people east of the Mississippi, apparently a Mississippian tribe. When defeated, the Allegewi fled the area, moving south along the Mississippi, never to be seen by the Delawares again. The Allegewi would have brought Mexican influence with them as a Mississippian people, but war and defeat forced a permanent southern migration that left the eastern lands to the Delaware and Iroquois. War is a man-made element, certainly, but still part of native environment and also potentially a force of change. Migration happened for many reasons, all culminating in the native effort for survival and prosperity.

In studies of how this happened, the forces behind migration must be considered. The Nez Perce of the Pacific Northwest claimed a migration territory that covered parts of Washington, Oregon, and Idaho close to the Snake and Clearwater Rivers. As a traditional migratory society, they traveled with the seasons, following appropriate food sources for the time of year. Movement followed a predictable pattern, which included leaving permanent winter villages every year as spring returned to travel through several temporary summer camps, usually utilizing the same locations year after year. They went as far east as the Great Plains, hunting bison and fishing for salmon, following resource availability. Patterns such as these especially apply to Plains Indians like the Lakota Sioux, for when a people depends entirely on, for example, the buffalo for all survival needs, the people move when the animals move. Dr. Pius Moss, an

A winter village in the Dakota lands. National Archives Image number 530977.

elder of the Arapaho tribe, another Plains society, describes the story of his people's movement:

Indians depended on the buffalo, which roamed the vast North American plains area. That was his way of life . . . the buffalo. Complete dependency on this animal. Wherever the animal was, that's where the Arapaho was. If the animal moved, he moved. He didn't wait to send scouts out to see where the animals were. At a moment's notice, when he was notified that the animals were moving, he moved and that is the reason why the structure that we call a tipi was adopted by the Plains Indians. It was easily taken down and easily put up in no time at all. Because of the buffalo's migration, the Arapaho had to be nomadic, in quest of the buffalo from time to time. Now the Arapahos moved all over the plains area, eastern slope of the Rockies, into Canada . . . east to the Mississippi River and south to the Mexican border . . . and at times, skirmishes would happen between tribes . . . and later, the Sand Creek Massacre . . . [made] the Arapahos leave the area. Their belief and custom is that wherever death occurs, they do not go back . . . because of that happening, the Arapahos did leave and never return . . . but that was their home country.[2]

Although the idea and definition of "home country" differed for every nomadic native band, each held their understanding of territory close to heart in their roaming searching for survival.

Because of the temporary and mobile nature of these people's daily lives, many cultures left behind sparse evidence for analysis and understanding. The Apache tribes of the southwestern desert region are some of the most elusive cultures, remaining among the more obscure civilizations in pre-contact Native American history. Their territory included Texas, New Mexico, Arizona, and parts of northern Mexico. Living in a harsh, arid environment forced them to rely on scarce resources of the desert. The nature of their surroundings affected every aspect of their society. Having to be constantly on the move and invested in providing basic resources, they had little time to spend on less necessary elements such as art or religion. The belief system of the Apache was less intricately developed than other, more settled tribes. Their beliefs focused less on gods and goddesses and more on supernatural spirits or figures that were less detailed and less involved than other culture's higher beings. These spirits interfered little in the daily lives of the Apache unless they were called upon to help. Time was a critical factor for native communities, and certain things had to be sacrificed for survival: for the Apache, the sacrifice was elaborate religious beliefs and ritual practice. Because they employed no agriculture, they had little reason to celebrate the seasons or hold periodic gatherings based on seasonal changes. They spent all of their time and energy on survival. An example of this is that the Apache lacked formal ceremonies for marriage and death, two events on which many societies placed a great ritual importance. Morris Edward Opler, an expert on Navajo and Apache culture, suggests that marriage among the Apache was "less the founding of a new social unit than it was the absorption of the couple into an on-going extended family."[3] Death was the "ultimate foe and its triumph was not to be celebrated." Sickness and death were problems that needed constant effort at overcoming; the Apache did not even have an organized detailed belief in an afterlife. This meant that most Apache ceremonies that did exist centered on healing or continued good health, the most important element in the rugged struggle for survival in the southwest. All attention focused on success in this world, and people very rarely looked on to the next. Individual relationships with the supernatural was the foundation of Apache religion, and therefore, the Apache were encouraged to establish their own connections with spiritual forces. Life for the Apache, then, was a struggle for survival as a community, interspersed with individual interactions with supernatural forces.

THE MECHANICS OF MASS MOVEMENT: THE CHALLENGES OF MASS MIGRATION

Throughout their history, Paleo-Indians moved as nomadic bands across the landscape in response to the rhythm of the seasons and availability of resources. This means that from 20,000 to around 8,000 B.C.E., they traveled on foot in extended families of perhaps two dozen or so individuals, carrying their belongings on their backs. On the American continent, large creatures suitable for use as draft animals had become extinct by the close of the last ice age. Not only did people not have domestic animals to haul things, but furthermore, the wheel had not made its way into society because there was nothing to pull it. Over time, this pedestrian wandering scattered the people across the American continent. They took shelter where they could find it or slept out in the open. They constructed clothing out of animal skins and plant fibers, using and discarding natural resources as they outlived their usefulness. In the process, they developed other forms of transport and transportation systems to facilitate their passage across the continent.

Prehistoric nature trails and roads grew to lace the North and South American continents in a well-developed system of transportation paths. One trail ran along the eastern edge of the Rocky Mountains from present-day Alberta all the way to Mexico, spanning over 3,000 miles. The road system built by the Anasazi people in and around the Chaco Canyon complex covered an area almost as large as Ireland. To top it all off, there were smoke-signaling and reflected-light–signaling stations that natives used to communicate across miles of the travel network in mere seconds. The Oregon Trail, the Central and Southern Overland Trails, the Cumberland Gap-Wilderness Road, the Natchez Trace, and the Santa Fe Trail all saw centuries of human use before European feet ever tread their lengths. Working in concert with their environment, natives carved into the land paths of easy access, connection, communication, and defense, one footstep at a time.

As one example of an extensive road system, Chaco Canyon seems like an unlikely place for a native culture to take root and call home. In desert country, with long winters, short growing seasons, and little rainfall, survival often depended on hard, consistent effort by everyone in a community. But that's exactly what the Anasazi did; they built large towns connected to each other through an intricate road system and farmed in the lowlands, which helped the towns benefit from each other. Architecture, complexity of community life, and social organization of the Anasazi all reached a level of sophistication rarely matched in native history. The growth of their culture began in the early 900s C.E. As they started building on a large scale, using the same materials and techniques but going much larger and much higher than just a generation earlier, a pattern emerged of building a large pueblo with oversized rooms surrounded by more conventional villages, and the pattern caught on and spread. Eventually there were almost 80 of these towns, most of them connected to the Chaco center by the extensive Anasazi road network.

Within 100 years, Chaco Canyon stood as the political and economic center of the Chaco Plateau. There were anywhere from 2,000 to 5,000 people living in the approximately 400 settlements that made up the complex. With Chaco functioning as a hub of political and economic activity, the road system reflected its growing complexity and importance. One theory of development is that Chaco Canyon became an important societal center in response to environmental fluctuations that made farming unreliable. In this theory, Chaco would have controlled the agricultural life of the region by storing and redistributing food as needed to compensate for draughts and low harvest yield. Then the smaller towns would have played the same distribution role, except in their more limited locality. Ultimately nature caught up with them, and an extended drought between 1130 and 1180 C.E. finished off Chaco Canyon. Even the ingenious irrigation methods could not compensate for the profound lack of rainfall. Under these pressures, people drifted away in bands to find areas with better natural-resource reserves. Although the society experienced not even 200 years of prosperity, the evidence they left behind gives archaeologists a detailed snapshot of Anasazi life.

The extent of the ancient Chacoan road system impressed scientists. What they saw when they got into the air was a vast network of over 400 miles of roads connecting Chaco and its more than 75 satellite communities. The longest of the roads runs 42 miles, and most of the settlements sit at one-day travel intervals. They are not roads simply worn in by foot travel either. They were the products of energy, engineering, and thought, all necessary for the planning, construction, and maintenance of their unique system. The Anasazi laid out the roads in long, straight lines about 30 feet wide with little concern for terrain. They date from the 11th and 12th centuries, which was a period of population expansion for the southwest. Easy travel within the Chacoan world was definitely the main goal, but that means that many things traveled these roads, not just people. Communication, goods, and material exchange all benefited immensely from the road network, helping create one large society of Chacoan culture.

Traveling offered particular obstacles and difficulties, and in response, many cultures created innovative footwear and travel aids to deal with natural and climatic elements. In the northern parts of the continent, where climatic conditions kept snow on the trails for long periods of time, Native Americans invented unique contraptions to make travel easier. Snowshoes are well-known native inventions, but toboggans, sleds, and travois join them in the collection of native innovations. Two other contributions to land transportation should be mentioned here also. The moccasin used by Native Americans provided a pattern for comfortable, lightweight, breathable, flexible footwear. Made out of tanned hides, these all-purpose, all-weather shoes served natives well across the continent, no matter where they lived. When combined with the South America rubber-soled shoe, the product became the most widely recognizable and

Travois, one of which is shown here being pulled behind a horse, were a traditional method of village relocation for centuries before the horse arrived, being pulled by domesticated dogs or people instead. National Archives Image number 523855.

most-used kind of shoes in the modern world: the sneaker or tennis shoe. In making the best of their natural environment, natives developed technologies that not only influenced, but sometimes even directed modern society to the most efficient, adaptable solutions.

Other inventions and adaptations in native transportation that have stood the test of time include watercraft and travel techniques. Ocean-faring vessels were usually large dugout canoes, but plank-hulled boats and skin-covered kayaks were also utilized, especially on the West Coast and farther north into Canada. Inland waters encouraged the development of lighter, shallower dugouts and other kinds of small watercraft. Bark-covered canoes worked well for the waterways of the Northeast because they were easily carried between the many lakes and rivers. Hide-covered, round-bottomed "bull boats" were favored on the Missouri River. In many lakes and marshes, natives used canoe-shaped craft made of dried reeds lashed together. The northeastern woodland's birch canoe and the Inuit kayak survive today as the most popular of native boat inventions, both for their hardy structure and for their flexible use both as sport and functional transportation. Although there were common traits across the continent, each cultural creation was different, conforming to the resources and needs of individual environments. On the southern California coast, the Chumash built a type of boat that was distinctive. Formed of planks lashed by sinew or plant fibers, the Chumash waterproofed the boat by coating it with naturally occurring asphalt. These boats would carry the Chumash over 25 miles to the islands lying off the coast of California. Further north, several styles of canoes developed, many very large. These came from cultures on the coasts of northern California, Oregon, Washington, British Columbia, and all the way up into Alaska. Generally of exceptional craftsmanship, some of these boats reached 60 feet in length. What made each area's canoes distinctive was often style: some were shovel-nosed river canoes, some were large whaling vessels, and others with a substantial frame structure were freighters that had a carry capacity of up to five tons. Environment determined function, though, so in other areas, like the northeastern woodlands, lightweight canoes made of birch bark were the rule. Thin, water-resistant bark was peeled off of birch trees in strips. Then when the canoe was sealed with glue made of tree resin, the result was a hardy, watertight craft that was portable and durable.

Although somewhat in danger of puncture damage, smaller craft worked well on the river waterways of North America. Damage was a concern, but the availability of construction materials made maintenance and repair easy. The trade networks and routes were later of great use to Europeans because of their accessibility and efficiency. American Indians developed, explored, and perfected these routes over centuries of native travel, and as a result, there were no better experts than the natives themselves. One well-studied example is southern New England. It is crisscrossed with ancient pathways blazed by the Algonquin tribes who lived there before Europeans arrived. Maine also contains many native paths and canoe routes. In a larger context, the eastern United States was one large canoe route composed of the Connecticut River, the Hudson River, and the Susquehanna River, which connected Chesapeake Bay with the Great Lakes. The role of the canoe in New England life was so important that language developed around it. *Wangan* is an old Indian word that means any and all cargo and other encumbering issues associated with canoe travel. Typical cargo would have been hides, meat, equipment, trade items, and personal supplies, as well as the people themselves. Whenever travelers needed to change rivers or pathways, they had to unload the canoe and carry the craft and its contents. This process was so integral and important that it received its own word: *ahwangan.* This was used to signify the laborious process of traveling from one river or watershed to the next. Natives also used these two words to symbolize many things in their lives that resembled heavy loads and hard transfers. It would be like today's equivalent of saying "he has a cross to bear" or "she has a lot of personal baggage." Humans create metaphors in order to communicate ideas that they want everyone to understand, using images that everyone in a society would recognize. Natives took these words that had a large cultural significance and turned them into metaphors that everyone understood because of their important environmental role.

One of the mysteries of prehistoric culture, especially during the earlier Archaic period on the East Coast, is the use of large, ocean-capable vessels, especially when considered along with the people's utilization of deep-sea food sources, such as swordfish, whales, and other creatures. Toward the end of the Archaic period, East Coast tribes began reducing their dependence on ocean animals and increasing their use and utilization of more inland resources. At this point, it seems, tribes began expanding their inland waterway network, while simultaneously developing more complex trading relationships with neighbors. Another area of transportation that is often difficult to study is the extent and use of foot trails. Looking at tribes that resided more inland, although their primary mode of travel would still have been the canoe, foot trekking must have played a major role as well. In the winter, when foot travel would have been more difficult, inventions like the sled, toboggan, and snowshoe came into play. For example, because beaver were usually trapped during the winter, cold weather transport would have been used to move the trapped animals and resultant trade goods. The option to stay put was not simply impractical; it was often impossible. Survival depended on trapping and trading, especially during the winter when natural resources were in short supply. The trails and canoe routes used to obtain and transport necessary resources were employed for centuries.

Footpaths and waterways, then, were obviously extremely useful for facilitating the movement of goods and people across native territories.

"Relics of an Ancient Race," circa 1880. The irony here is that natives did not utilize the wheel for transportation until after the arrival of Europeans, making this not-so-ancient of an idea. The photo was taken at San Juan Pueblo, New Mexico. Denver Public Library, Western History Collection, Call Number CHS.J1361.

They served a dual purpose in providing goods exchange, as well. As natives traveled, they could forage in the swamps, bogs, riverbanks, and forests for food. In Maine, for example, 35,000 miles of rivers and streams alone provided a great deal to the tribes that called the area home. Native transportation devices were an elegant solution to some of the Native American's greatest needs: transportation and survival. Long-distance travel became possible because of these innovations in technology. Waterways and footpaths connected ancient North American people in ways modern scholars are just beginning to understand.

NOTES

1. M. Le Page Du Pratz, *The History of Louisiana; or of the Western Parts of Virginia and Carolina, Containing a Description of the Countries that Lie on Both Sides of the River Mississippi: With an Account of the Settlements, Inhabitants, Soil, Climate, and Products* (London, 1774), 293.

2. Dr. Pius Moss, "The Story of the Origin of the Arapaho People," *The Wyoming Companion* (Laramie: High Country Communications), available online at http://www.wyomingcompanion.com/wcwrr.html. *The Wyoming Companion*, to the best of their ability, transcribed the stories of Dr. Pius Moss, preserving both his word usage and terminology. As a direct descendant of Chief Black Coal of the Wyoming Arapaho (the major leader of the Wyoming Arapaho in the late 1800s),

Dr. Moss draws the stories of his people from oral tradition passed down through his family.

3. Morris Edward Opler, *Myths and Tales of the Chiricahua Apache Indians (Sources of American Indian Oral Literature)* (Lincoln: University of Nebraska Press, 1994), 72.

8

THE ART OF FUN AND GAMES:
NATIVE AMERICAN LEISURE AND
THE ENVIRONMENT

To celebrate each noted event, a feast and dance would be given . . .
When the feasting and dancing were over, we would have horse
races, foot races, wrestling, jumping, and all sorts of games . . . I was
always glad when the dances and feasts were announced. So were all
the other young people.

When I was eight or ten years old, I began to follow the chase
(hunt), to me this was never work.

Geronimo, Chiricahua Apache

Leisure, according to Webster's dictionary, is the "freedom provided by
the cessation of activities; *especially* time free from work or duties." In
order for leisure to be "leisure" by this definition, the following conditions must be met: the activity must be chosen freely, must be considered
enjoyable by the one participating, and must not be viewed as a regular,
necessary action. Mentally and psychologically, leisure is closely related
to play; leisure activities involve either individual or group imagination
exercises and could be considered almost the exact opposite of work. Leisure activities do not *have* to be "play" activities, which are intentionally
imaginative, but play is often important to adult leisure pursuits. Leisure
time also can involve the absence of mental effort. There are some similarities and some differences between the Native American expression
of leisure activities and the Western idea of nonwork pastimes. Native
communities had extensive, healthy, and complex leisure traditions rift
with entertaining yet socially instructive activities that were vital components of native experience: games, dance, sports, ceremony, humor,
art, theater, and more. For American Indian societies, leisure functions

included expressions of social meaning and definition, symbols of the cultural norms and values, and vehicles of social process and adaptation. Ultimately, however, it was much more difficult to distinguish between work and play, between necessity and leisure, in Native American culture because these societies saw everything as one big interconnected circle of cause and effect, making the native definition of leisure much more complicated.

Prehistoric leisure had many functions, making it different from today's equivalent activities. Physical games, sports, and competitions helped participants develop skills that contributed to tribal welfare, such as hunting and defense abilities. Team sports and ceremonies helped reinforce relationships and interpersonal networks within the community and between neighbors. Festivals and dances served as mingling places where singles could meet and get to know each other in the early courting phases. From a more specific cultural perspective, there were many other uses as well. For example, a study among the Cree identified three central themes in their definition of leisure: the pursuit of personal freedom or solitude, extrinsic or nonessential motivation, the sense of being close to nature, the inner drive to be outdoors, and the potential for interaction. Natives in Canada believed leisure to be important for relaxation, stress reduction, health, social development, and cultural expression. Early archaeological records suggest a rich leisure practice across native North America. Although science can draw only limited conclusions about the details of leisure activities, many tools used in these activities survived the test of time. Also, oral history and cultural tradition preserved these practices and handed them down through the generations, although many changed as they were passed along. Additionally, it is important to remember that it was much more difficult to separate leisure time and activities into categories disconnected from more necessary daily routines. Everything was intrinsically connected to everything else, not separate and distinct like today's view of societal elements. To separate activities and their significance from one another was to destroy their place in daily life and society. Once again, combining disciplines such as history, ethnography, anthropology, and archaeology offers the most complete picture of American Indian leisure life and the best possibility of understanding both leisure itself and its societal significance in Native American culture.

The detailed information that remains concerning Native American leisure largely exists in records of European contact experiences. By starting there, it is possible to move backward in time, retracing the details of native culture to create a more complete precontact picture. By the 19th century, for example, white observers were writing quite a bit about the presence of gambling in Native American leisure life. Gambling took on a different form and significance, though, than it does in today's modern world and had been a part of native culture for much longer than suspected. People placed wagers on the outcomes of games, but there were no odds, betters only bet on their own team, and the winner took everything. Betting almost seemed more of an obligation than a moneymaking venture. It showed faith in the better's team, as well as a willingness to risk major loss based on that faith. In some ways, this could be viewed as a contribution to the game process. Some donated physical energy and activity by playing the game, and others gave spiritual support and material goods through betting, all in the hopes of producing a successful outcome. When communities came together to play competitive games, everyone would bring piles of supplies and personal goods to bet. It seems that in addition to providing added sport for the game, this also helped ensure a rather fair distribution of surplus goods across regions. This was probably not a conscious goal, but rather than engaging in conflict over issues of economic equality, riches were more evenly and less violently distributed by gambling. Religion played a role in competition and gambling as well, contrary to modern religious roles. It was normal practice in most cultures to solicit the help of shamans, medicine people, and other religious figures to affect the game's outcome. At least that is how it appeared on the surface. In reality, rather than influencing who won, the rituals served to make a statement about the inevitability of fate. This represents one small piece of the larger Native American worldview that people must work in harmony with their environment, not try to control it. They were basically petitioning the spirits to have thing work out as they should, whether that was in their favor or not. According to native belief, rituals played a role in making things work out as they were supposed to, which led to the belief that games of chance directly demonstrated who the fates favored, while games of skill did not. This is why games of chance enjoyed more general popularity; fate favored the lucky, and the lucky were favored by the community.

Among the activities difficult to distinguish as solely for leisure purposes are ceremony and dance. Although these activities were designed for specific religious functions, it is clear that both participants and observers viewed them as leisure also. For example, the dances of Native American tribal groups were often associated with elements of nature, and natives viewed them as appeals to those corresponding spirits, but they also used the events as social gathering opportunities. As communal entertainment *and* a plea for nature's favor, dances served as effective dual-purpose activities. Dances varied in seriousness and intensity from the most solemn, as in cases of body mutilation and pain, to the more lighthearted expressions of comedy, color, and costume. Even the most serious of dances, the Sioux "Ghost Dance" (included here despite the fact that it was a postcontact invention), had obvious leisure connections. The dance itself was designed to drive the white man away and return the natives' lands and resources to them, restoring the old ways. Along with the Ghost Dance, there was a game that participants played called the "Pawnee Ghost Dance Hand Game." In an effort to guess which hand held one, two, or no bones, players placed bets, and ritualized gaming practices accompanied the game, although the game played no direct role in the ritual. After a while, it became difficult to separate the game and the dance, with the two almost always being enacted together. This insepara- bleness represented much of the natives' ideas about the universe; every- thing was a part of a larger whole, and separation of those things was not the natural order. Fate and religious appeal went hand in hand.

Arts and crafts were also components of Native American leisure. In many ways, it is difficult to draw a clear line between "arts" and "crafts." Basket designs, pottery paintings, and wall art all testify to the rich artistic culture of native life, but was it for fun or considered necessary? With the introduction of Western contact and context for comparison, the nature of native arts and their place in society became clearer. Using rug weaving in Navajo tradition as an example, it is easy to see that the arts were often labor by choice and for pleasure. In the 1950s, women spent many hours preparing the wool, spinning thread, coloring it, and then weaving the rug, only to sell the rug for very little money, for the equivalent of about five cents per hour. The women pointed out, though, that weaving was not work; it was pleasure, an end goal all unto itself. Eventually, after con- tact with Europeans, many traditions died out, changed, or were outright outlawed, robbing native communities of unadulterated leisure time. During the latter half of the 20th century, many cultures began to revive lost leisure practices, fostering a sense of identity and belonging. Despite all of the changes, both natural and forced, the foundation of these things suggests that natives often created art simply for art's sake while combin- ing that art with the creation of necessary items. Native American leisure practices reflected the fundamental values of native culture, its methods of environmental adaptation, and the nature of native social life. Studying those leisure practices then provides an excellent window into under- standing American Indian history and culture on a larger scale. Leisure activities served a variety of functions that enriched and strengthened community life, retaining even through hardship and challenge their distinctive characteristics, cultural significance, and fundamental role in native society.

ARTISTIC EXPRESSIONS: FINDING INSPIRATION IN THE ENVIRONMENT

Prehistoric art does not translate easily into present-day categories or definitions of artistic effort. Modern people often speak of prehistoric art with a certain equality suggested, but this is misleading. Today, art is a specific field of culture with boundaries and specialization understood by both creators and viewers of art, but in the past, those ideas were much less defined. Art, just like everything else in the prehistoric person's envi- ronment, could not be separated from life and nature around it. Art was part of the never-ending circle of native existence. In one similarity to today, it seems only a few people possessed the ability or the right to create artistic illustrations. Tribes recognized artistic talent as a gift from the spirits. It is possible that there were artists and viewers separate from each other, but it is also possible that people participated on both sides of the brush. The major determining factor here was cultural. Since ancient leisure time bore little resemblance to today's reality, it is difficult to define early aesthetic creation in modern terms. There was no period of time left in ancient daily life unfilled by some sort of activity viewed as beneficial to the individual or the community. Idleness was not a possibility; if not engaged in providing material goods for the community, then members worked toward prosperity in spirit and health. Art was, in many ways, an expression of this drive for survival.

Animal skin depicting the combat history of Shoshoni chief Wahakie. National Archives Image number 530876.

As a result, most American Indian art was functional and often adorned basic useful objects, such as pots, tools, weapons, or costumes. Often, when the object held ritual or religious significance, the designs on them were thought to produce or enhance the magic that made the object sacred. A few areas of the continent employed full-time artists, specifically in the Northwest and Southeast, who produced works of art for wealthy patrons, priests, and rulers. The pieces were respected for their technique, form, and color, but still performed more functional roles in society. Once Europeans began introducing their idea of culture, many native artists began to produce work with no practical function at all, changing the definition of native arts. Several dozen art styles existed in prehistoric native North America, but many shared cultural connections and significant similarities, especially styles common to geographically close neighbors. Most of the time, the major artists in tribes were men and this was a trait common to many cultures. Women produced mostly folk art, whereas men created larger, more elaborate carvings and paintings. Some suggest this is indicative of men's and women's roles in their society. Folk or domestic art reflected the domestic world of women, while men's contributions were on a "grander" scale. That does not mean that their significance was greater, but instead demonstrates the different circles of influence men and women occupied. Between the two genders, everything in native life that deserved the honor and respect of artistic adornment received it, and as a result, art effectively fulfilled its role in society.

Beginning with the Northwest, one major art style dominated this regional culture. Coastal natives carved or painted figures of animals, mythical monsters, and human beings onto totem poles, house fronts, boxes, canoes, and other daily objects. Red and black paint provided color and relief to both carvings and smooth surfaces. The animal, monster, or human depicted represented supernatural beings who had revealed themselves to the ancestors of the person who owned the objects. All art symbolized religious and social organization, and ownership, display, and production of the art proved noble descent and rapport with the supernatural. All artists of this type were men, although not all men were artists. Women did weave designs into baskets, blankets, and costumes, but the male designed the pattern that she followed. Boldness, individualism, and vigor characterized northwest regional art, as did size and complexity. The dramatic intricacy of their designs stood unmatched by any other society north of Mexico.

Another area that produced decorative or applied art was the plains. Plains Indians did not create art to display, but rather to adorn useful, functional items. Almost all plains artwork appeared on animal hide, the most commonly available material. Artists used two techniques, painting and porcupine quill embroidery, but painting was more common. Anything made of animal hide—from shirts, robes, and shoes to tepees, drums, and shields—was fair game for artistic creation. Colors made of clay and charcoal, such as brown, red, yellow, black, blue, and green, brightened the detail in the designs. Generally there were two styles of painting, and they corresponded to the two sexes. Men usually painted more natural figures of horses, humans, buffalo, and other animals. Women painted geometric figures and designs. In keeping with the idea that men and women occupied different spheres in society, the two types of art were rarely seen together on the same object. The objects themselves were rather flat and two-dimensional, and often the scenes lacked perspective or relative size depiction. There were no highlights or shadows, and rather than making a distant figure smaller, artists simply placed the more distant figure above or below the closer figure with no difference in size. Artists also decorated ceremonial objects with paintings, feathers, quills, and beads, emphasizing their significance. This type of art was often the woman's realm, as might be expected given the domestic nature of the decorated items. Porcupine quill embroidery was the only known embroidery form until the introduction of beads by Europeans. The art involved softening and dying selected, stiff porcupine quills and weaving or sewing them onto leather. Plains Indian war shirts offer the most spectacular examples of embroidered beauty. Each shirt would take a weaver at least one year to complete. Beads were much easier to use, so natives quickly replaced quills when they were introduced. Although many legends tell of the porcupine's misfortune (and sometimes punishment) in being given ugly quills instead of beautiful fur, natives found that the quills were beautiful and glossy when carefully selected, softened, dyed, and applied. Some of their most sacred images and objects were created using this unlikely, yet readily available, natural resource.

Another area with a particularly unique artistic style was the Southwest. Pottery, baskets, cloth, jewelry, walls, and many other objects sported the desert-dwelling people's artistic efforts. No one material dominated their art in the way that wood did in the Northwest or animal hide on the Plains. Scholars have a relatively comprehensive archaeological record to study as well. The dry climate encouraged artifact preservation, leaving behind many clues for analysis. Decoration could be applied by weaving in colored materials or by painting images onto objects. Visual symmetry, color contrast, and pattern repetition characterized early design elements and quickly became standard in desert and Pueblo native art. Some unique expressions include kiva wall painting for religious and ritual purposes and elaborate colorful ritual costume. The most distinctive form of Pueblo art, though, was sand painting, which were created on the floors of *kivas* in front of alters. Dry materials such as sand, ocher, dried plants, petals, leaves, and corn pollen offered artists many colors from which to choose. The creators carefully sprinkled handfuls of the materials from between their thumb and forefinger. Every element of their religious art, such as kiva floor sand paintings, was symbolic and thought to be beneficial to the society that properly produced and displayed the art, according to the directions of the spirits. The purpose was to influence the weather, personal health, or good luck, but despite these very utilitarian functions, the practice survived as a unique expression of Pueblo creation and perception.

The art of the Southeast was probably as rich and varied as that of the Southwest, but European contact disturbed the East Coast much more than other areas of the continent, and as a result, their cultures suffered more aggressive European cultural influence than did other regions. Most of their art simply disappeared before later European observers had an opportunity to examine or analyze it. One form of expression that survived, however, was personal adornment. Objects made of wood, bone, stone, shells, and copper decorated East Coast native bodies. Paint was also applied to the skin for game, hunt, and ritual purposes, functioning to call the spirit of the image to the wearer's aid. Another material art form that survived despite European intervention was basket decorating. This was most elaborate around the lower Mississippi River region. Artisans decorated baskets by plaiting and weaving in previously colored materials, often made red, yellow, or black by vegetable dyes. Pottery, however, did not draw nearly as much artistic expression. The designs were more simplistic and often had a geometric focus. Clay was readily available, but less utilized in the production of artistic and sacred objects. Shells, stone, and metal were used more extensively. Southeastern natives carved stone into sculpture, engraved shells with elaborate designs, and cold-hammered copper into body ornaments, ultimately producing some of the most elegant imprinted art north of Mexico. As tribes across the North American continent experimented with and perfected their artistic techniques, their connections to the environment that inspired them strengthened and grew more complex.

A DIFFERENT FORM OF CONFLICT: GAMES OF SKILL AND COMPETITION

"The games of the American Indians may be divided into two general classes: games of chance and games of dexterity," suggests Stewart Culin, a foremost authority on the tradition of native games and their significance in society. Games that focused solely on skill and strategy seem to be entirely absent from native culture. All tribes across the continent played games very similar to each other, suggesting similar roles in society. Young men and women also played different games than did children because they needed to learn different things for their roles in their tribes. Religious stories or myths of different native belief systems all include games. The very idea of competition, either with others or with the self, holds a special place in North American native culture. Competition teaches many things including religious morals, physical honing, and social skills. A sharp wit, analytical thinking, and the ability to fool an opponent were all prized abilities that could be taught and perfected through games. Understanding of the workings of the earth, cycles of weather, rhythms of nature, and the importance of teamwork are just some of many '"side effects" of native game-playing. Tribal environment determined the nature of the games, and the cultures adapted those games to necessity and available resources, interpreting, understanding, and interacting with their natural environment through the educational lens of play.

Many games played by Native Americans focused on the development of the skills necessary to be a successful hunter and warrior. Boys had to be well-trained while they were young in order to assure the proper development of those skills. Quick eyes and ears were the foundation for interpretation of the environment and immediate conditions. A keen sense of smell helped the warrior-hunter in his evaluation. Steady, silent feet in the forest and on the warpath were required for success. Perfect coordination of mind and muscle, thought, and movement produced the perfect hunter, the perfect warrior, and that perfection was not possible unless training and practice started early. Stamina and strength were also important, but these qualities were easily produced and improved upon in comparison with the technical skills. The training had to be rigid and strict because less-than-perfect abilities could mean a tribe would go hungry or a warrior would lose his life. Interpretation and understanding were necessary as well: simply hearing a sound in the forest was not enough; both hunter and warrior needed to know what that sound meant in order to react appropriately. A small splash in a nearby lake could mean that a bird was disturbed by a predator's approach. It could also mean that another animal startled the bird. Worse yet, it could mean that another human in the area was the cause of the flight. Understanding or misreading the cause of a sound could very well mean the difference between life and death. Because real life training often posed great danger, a considerable part of the earliest training of warriors and hunters was through the use of games.

Competitive races, such as the ones Geronimo mentioned following feasts and dances, appeared in native culture from the Arctic all the way down to Meso-America and was one of the most popular game types on the continent. The formats varied widely, but the expression was the same. The Crow of Montana used a 300-yard track, whereas in the Dakotas, racers cleared a three-mile track shaped like a horseshoe that put the start and finish lines only 100 yards apart. Observers crowded into the "U" of the track to watch the three heats necessary for the winner to be crowned with a red-painted feather, which gave the winner the rights to significant betting spoils. The Osage used a two-and-a-half-mile track where runners from other tribes could challenge Osage members, helping keep them in peak performance condition. Along the Colorado River, young boys and girls were encouraged to run from a young age. They enjoyed kickball and relay racing as both fun pastimes and preparation for the future. As they grew, for example, boys eventually became able to run deer down on foot in the hunt. Running also prepared young men to be the "Legs" of their tribal leaders. A "Leg" would sit behind his assigned leader, ready to carry messages such as game announcements, tribal news, and even messages of war to distant neighbors. The integration of leisure and friendly competition with preparation for survival and success was a necessary part of North American native life.

In New Mexico, Taos Indian runners participated in relay races as part of annual feast days. There is little explanation for the native interpretation of the races, but the best analysis suggests a dual purpose. As with most tribes, running and training for such events helped keep warriors and hunters in peak condition to contribute to the health and welfare of the tribe. It also seems that racing was associated with the sun, and the runners, through their efforts at running the length of the track, strengthened the sun's trek across the sky. Southwest Indians called the racetracks "sun roads," and the roads followed, from east to west, the path of the sun. The competitions also traditionally occurred at the changing of seasons, so the races could have encouraged strength for the participants in enduring through the coming season. The competitiveness helped reinforce bonds between villages as all participants came together for larger, cosmic goals such as the ones mentioned. Because each runner represented the health and welfare of the entire tribe, before the race, medicine men would exorcise the track from any sorcery cast by the opposing side or other natural, but evil influences. They used eagle feathers and eagle down to bless and adorn the bodies of the competitors to make them light and swift on their feet. With the entire community and supernatural world watching and with the success of the tribe, both physical and spiritual, dependant on good, strong runners, anything that might help ensure victory played a role in these important seasonal games.

The "Running Wheel" is another game with many manifestations across North American cultures. The spiritual significance of the game was the focus on the force of human control and place in the circle of life, and that the circle is inseparably tied to the earth itself In a common variation, a racer rolled or pushed a hoop made out of flexible wood, using a stick as his or her pushing tool, never being allowed to touch the hoop with their hands. Strength, coordination, and endurance were the focus of this game. Another form had the hoop hanging, and the competitor would about-face and walk away a certain number of paces. On the count, the participant would turn and "blindly" throw his or her stick in an effort to get it through the hoop. Hunting and defense skills were the focus here. In yet another form of the game, small animal shapes were cut out of hide and hung inside the hoops. Then the hoops were sent rolling across a field or down a hill. The players would then try to shoot the animals as moving targets, offering great practice for the challenges of hunting small game. With practice, those that played these games became familiar with the earth and the obstacles presented, while honing and perfecting their skills as food providers.

In an even more complex game of training and skill, "chunkey" proved to be a difficult game to master. The game was usually played by two men and featured a notched pole (one for each man) and a polished, wheel-like stone, the "chunkey" stone. One player would set the stone to rolling, and just as it was about to stop, both players would throw their poles much like they would a spear. The person hitting the ground closest to the stone (which would have stopped by now) received a designated amount of points based on the pole's distance from the resting stone. Usually American Indians played the game on a smooth court or chunkey yard that was sometimes covered with packed sand. The stones were carefully crafted and polished, with one or both sides concave. They were owned by either the village or a clan of the community. Because they were fashioned out of hard quartz, a very difficult material to work with, the stones were valuable to those who owned them. This was very much a spectator sport with large crowds gathering to cheer the players on and significant betting occurring when two communities came together for a match. Most chunkey artifacts have been found in Mississippian digs, as far south as Arkansas and Tennessee and as far north as northern Illinois, suggesting widespread popularity.

Another game that saw great fame across the eastern portion of the continent was stickball. At the time of European contact, its popularity was high. Attempts to reconstruct the history of the sport, though, hold little promise of detailed accuracy. It seems to have been played throughout the eastern half of North America, mostly by tribes in the Southeast, around the western Great Lakes, and in the St. Lawrence Valley area. Today it is played further west, but this distribution is solely because of European-instigated relocation of Native Americans. This "little brother of war" held a significant place in eastern native culture. Apart from its recreational value, stickball played a more serious role as well. Its origins were rooted in legend; the game was played for therapeutic purposes and was immersed in ceremony. Both game equipment and players were prepared for play by medicine men, and participating tribes believed team selection and victory to be supernaturally controlled. The game was used socially to vent aggression, and sometimes even territorial issues were solved through tournament match rather than conflict. The biggest connection showed in the fact that the ceremonies of preparation for the game and the rituals performed by the players were often identical to the rituals practiced before leaving on the warpath. Once properly primed, opposing teams used handcrafted sticks with small nets, or *kabocca*, and a woven leather ball, or *towa*. Each team tried to get the ball down the field to the other side's goalpost using only the *kabocca*, never touching or throwing the ball with their hands. When the goalpost was hit, the team scored a point. Games could involve as few as 20 or as many as 300 players. The health value of exercise along with the communal value of nonviolent methods of dispute resolution made stickball and games like it, including shinny or field hockey, centerpieces of native culture. Today this game would be best recognized as a close cousin to lacrosse. Both societal and environmental connotations combined in the one leisure practice of stickball to affect and direct the course of community health, relations, situation, and success.

A LONG HISTORICAL CONNECTION: GAMES OF CHANCE IN NATIVE SOCIETY

Just like games of skill, games of chance appeared in all North American native cultures, yet took many different forms. They generally fell into two categories: (1) games in which dice-like pieces were thrown to determine numbers for keeping score and (2) games that had the players guessed where an object was hidden under two or more covers, and correct and incorrect guesses created a tally. References to these types of games are found in many native myths. They usually consist of several contests in which the hero overcomes an opponent through skill, cunning, or magic. Fate and chance appear in all of these myths, as well as figuring heavily into native leisure gaming practice and belief. The ultimate goal of these games of chance was to accumulate the highest score based on chance and fate combined. There are four basic forms of guessing games. In the first, bundles of sticks with one oddly marked stick were separated into two hands, and the purpose was to guess which hand held the marked stick; these were commonly referred to as stick games. In the next, two or four sticks were used, with all but one marked. The sticks were held in the hands that covered where they were marked, and the object, then, was to guess which hand held the unmarked stick. These were called hand games. Then there were games in which two pairs of marked sticks were mixed and covered, and then it was the player's job to guess in what pattern the sticks lay. Finally, one small object was hidden in a tube, in a moccasin, or under a mound of earth with other empty containers around it. The player guessed where the object lay, much like the hidden ball and cup game of today. "Dice" games, on the other hand, involved implements marked with different values and some type of counting apparatus. The dice were thrown and scores were counted in many ways, but the end goal was to either get the highest score or reach the target score first. Relying on chance and fate, players often bet goods and supplies in order to show their faith in the surrounding supernatural forces that affected every aspects of their lives from the most serious conflicts to the most leisurely of games.

In one expression of Hand Game, the Paiute and Shoshone tribes of the Great Basin used the game to determine land-use rights and female companionship. The game was played with one white and one black or striped stick or bone and ten "point" or counter sticks. Two teams sat opposite each other with the first team hiding the bones under their hands while singing and drumming to distract the guessing team. The leader of the guessing team then guessed which member or members of the hiding team were actually hiding the bones. Each time there was a wrong guess, the guessing team had to hand over one counting stick. If the team found both sticks, then the roles reversed until all point sticks were held by one team. In tribes that relied heavily on hunting, the Hand Game was a part of rivalry between warrior cultures. Each society tried to outdo the other, not only to gain prestige, but also to gain riches bet on the game. Originally, only males could participate in the games, although females could often help with the singing, but in some nations, females held their own matches. Never in the games, however, did opposite sexes participate together; that would have been against the natural order. Today there are professional Hand Game teams in many native communities. In centuries past, the game would have been played for many days, day and night, essentially nonstop, until one side ran out of betting goods. Today, tournaments are often held at tribal celebrations or powwows. According to the best scholarly analysis, the Hand Game has been part of most native cultures for centuries, and although the stakes and meaning may have changed, the game's position in cultural identity remains relatively the same.

Music was a major component of the Hand Game. Drumming and chanting were used to distract guessers and boost a team's chance of winning. One musical technique used was to coordinate the drumming "against" the human heartbeat rhythm. The counter-beat created a psychological distraction, hopefully confusing the guesser and raising tension in the game. Many songs survived the tests of time and European contact. The following is an account handed down through Cheyenne tradition and recounted by Mu-u-sinim No-otz.

In the winter the Cheyennes often meet in little companies to play the hand-game . . . The company sits on the ground, with four of five leaders of the singing grouped around a drum and the rest line about the circular wall [of the tepee]. The game opens with a prayer, delivered by the one who may be, for the night, the leader in the game . . . This leader has usually beheld in a dream the arrangement of the game . . . or he has been taught by some spirit how the game is to be played of the night of his leadership . . . [As the game is played,] with the winning of the counters from one side to the other, there comes a cry of triumph from the men, a trilling halloo of victory from the women, and laughter from all. The drum-beat changes, a dance-song is struck up, and then the tipi is filled with the rhythm of dancing feet and jangling ornaments. During the whole game the hand-game songs are sung . . . [and] at the close of the game there is a dance, and then the feast is brought in by the women . . . When the feasting is over, the guests quietly disperse without formality . . . In a few short moments the gay hand-game company has melted away in the darkness.[1]

The following Hand Game song refers to the search for sticks hidden in the hands of players, using symbols of everyday life familiar to all. When combined with off-rhythms and motions of the singers, sometimes the distraction served its purpose, and the defending team successfully confused the guessing challengers.

Now I go to seek my horses!
So here I stand and look about me!
So here I stand and look about me!
Now I go to seek my horses![2]

The interpretation of this song suggests that the singer is making fun of himself because only a truly careless person would lose track of something as important and as noticeable as his horses. Although the games and betting played a serious role in society, this account and song show the importance of the games as leisure activities as well.

In dice or bones games of chance, players truly put their fate in the hands of supernatural forces. Unlike in Stick and Hand Games, fate was the true determinant of the victor. Played with dice-like pieces of polished wood or bone, carved with dots or chevrons as value symbols, and counting sticks for score keeping, betting played just as large or larger role in these true games of chance as it did in the Hand Games just discussed. Obviously skill and strategy were involved in Hand Games, and when people were betting on those, faith in both spiritual favor and human ability were important. In dice games, it was the luck of the draw or roll. As a general rule, dice games were played in silence, whereas singing and drumming often accompanied guessing games. The wide distribution of both stick and dice games across the continent suggests they are old, and this conclusion is supported by artifacts found at various dig sites. They played a large role in both daily and ritual life, but their presence in native culture also shows through the cultures' myths and legends. The following Seneca legend provides an example:

A poor old woman lived in the woods. She was only skin and bones and cried all the time. Her blanket was so old and dirty that nobody could have told what kind of skin it was made of. She had seven daughters, but six had been carried off and one died. One night, though, she found a naked baby boy crying on her seventh daughter's grave and she took him in. He grew very fast and one day, she came home and he was not there. That night there was a storm with thunder and lightening and the next morning the boy was home.

"I have been with my father; we have been here all night. Hino (the storm) is my father and your daughter was my mother."

The woman believed her grandson. As he grew, he often made the noise of thunder and spent time with his father. After a time, the boy asked where his six aunts were and the grandmother told him of a mother and son who lived by playing dice. Her daughters went there with some others, played, lost, and then lost their heads. Many had suffered the same fate. The boy set off to the woman and her son's house and beat the woman at her own game of dice. In order to keep her head, she asked for a ball game contest with her son. Unfortunately, he lost as well and the woman and her son were killed. The boy and his grandmother then made the dead players' longhouse their new home and they were welcomed by the tribe in recognition of the boy's skill, favor, and power.[3]

Although the cultural role and significance of the dice game is difficult to tease out, some general assumptions and interpretations can be made. What stands out the most is that apparently playing betting games could be used for both good and bad purposes. The old woman and her son who made their living by throwing dice killed the people that lost. Eventually, though, the young boy came and challenged them, and because of his power, he was able to win the games and adopt the people as his own. As an integral part of cultural life, the games functioned as a method of determining social standing, as well as a meter of supernatural favor, a perfect system of lifelong conditioning and training.

PLAYTIME AS A TOOL: TEACHING THE YOUNG ABOUT THEIR ENVIRONMENT

Today it is common knowledge that some of the most effective ways to teach a child involve embedding educational methods and information into play activities. The way a child learns is vastly different than the way an adult learns, and the methods used to teach must reflect that difference in order to be successful. Spiritual beliefs, physical prowess, and mental discipline were all necessary in prehistoric native life and children needed to start learning these things at an early age. Many of the games prehistoric children played resemble activities that children create on their own today. Some of these childhood amusements have been handed down or have survived cultural changes so that they may still be studied. Almost every lesson involved children learning about their connections to their environment. If they were not learning new knowledge or skills, they were practicing and refining information they had gleaned before. Just as adult games and leisure activities fell into certain categories, so did children's play. Some were a copy or reflection of adult behaviors, such as war, hunting, religious, and domestic activities. A contemporary example would be "playing house" or pretending to be soldiers going off to battle. Others were competitions, and some were simply personal amusements. Many games had special times of the year in which they were played, and boys and girls rarely, if ever, played together. Sleds were very popular across the continent and were common to most native cultures. Another common item or set of items was playthings or toys made out of wood or clay. It seems native children enjoyed making things out of materials in their environment, but even this helped prepare them for their future as adults by letting them experiment with available resources and their possible uses.

Even seemingly pointless activities of childhood translated into knowledge and skill for future use.

Training for young boys to become warriors and hunters involved not only physical skill and stamina, but also keen observation abilities. In order to evaluate what could happen in a hunt or battle situation, a warrior or hunter had to be aware of and understand everything that went on around him. The rolling-wheel games mentioned earlier played a large role in teaching children some of these skills. Another category of play, however, contributed as well. Guessing games were popular in many cultures, and both children and adults participated. One game involved children sitting in a circle with two different-colored balls of clay or two differently shaped or colored stones. The first person held one in each hand and passed one to the player on his or her right. That player then guessed which ball or stone had been passed to him or her. If the child guessed correctly, then the balls or stones went to that child, and it was the next one's turn. If the player guessed incorrectly, then he or she stepped out of the circle. Although this game may seem like a pure game of chance, children could increase their chance of success by observing the characteristics of the objects and the behavior of the player holding the objects. If they paid close enough attention to detail, certain clues could ensure that they won the game. A game that helped children learn about their culture and religion involved dreams and interpretation. The Iroquois, among many others, placed great importance on dreams. Children were encouraged to make up puzzles or riddles about dreams they had had so that others could try and guess what the dream was about. They also drew symbols that represented things in their dreams and had others guess the story line from the drawings. In the process, they learned the meaning and significance of dream elements, which often revolved around their environment and their place in it. They even played a form of charades to communicate dream elements for others to guess and put together. Once the other children teased the dream out of the child who received it, they tried to interpret it, often with contributions from community adults. The story behind another game called "Rub the Clouds Away" helped demonstrate humans' relationships with nature. The child would choose a cloud and focus on it. Then the child licked his or her fingers and rubbed them on the top of the other hand. While doing this, the child tried to communicate with the cloud, encouraging it to disappear. The child was supposed to continue this until the cloud actually moved or disappeared or until the child gave up. The underlying lesson is that although humans can affect nature, they do not and cannot always control it. Sometimes natural forces just had to be accepted, a lesson easier learned when little was at stake.

Another game that appeared in all Native American societies, as well as most indigenous cultures around the planet, was the making of string figures or "Cat's Cradle." It was played using one loop of string woven by the hands and fingers into certain patterns using specific finger movements. The result was an intricate pattern that represented or resembled familiar objects. The games appealed to the young and old and were especially useful to those restricted from more physical activities as a result of age, physical condition, or weather. During the late 1800s and early 1900s, Alfred Haddon conducted an exhaustive, comparative study of Cat's Cradle traditions around the world. Inspired by the "elaborate string figures of savage peoples that put our humble efforts to shame," he set out to collect as many examples as possible.[4] The necessity emerged for a language system that would allow people to easily relate the process of making the figures to other people. Caroline Jayne stepped in and wrote a volume consisting of over 100 string figures with images and instructions. Based on observations, interpretations, and translations, comparative study of native culture around the world became possible through a child's activity.

This activity, though, was not only contrived to pass the time. In western Canada, traditional legend suggests that people played string games at the coming of winter because "while the sun was going south in the fall, the game of cat's-cradle [was] played to catch the sun in the meshes of the string, and to prevent his [complete] disappearance."[5] Other beliefs surrounded this game, such as the idea that boys should not play the game because later in life, their fingers might get tangled in their fishing nets. Some hunters who lost their fingers as a result of net or bow accidents believed it was because they had played Cat's Cradle as a child, so basically this was always a young girl's game. The large number of figures that could be made from one loop of string is surprising, as is why it was played. Words and chanting often accompanied the string figure game, and all cultures included figures that were religious or mythological in nature in their image repertoire. It could have been merely a pastime, a reflection of beliefs and stories of a community, but as demonstrated in the quotation about the sun's disappearance, it may have held magical significance as well. Strings, cords, knots, and circles played a role in many systems of religious belief, as did representations of natural figures. Everything humans do has significance to them, and to understand the ways they think and act, it is sometimes necessary to examine seemingly casual, trivial activities.

NATIVE AMERICAN DANCE AS A REFLECTION OF ENVIRONMENT

"Dance (dan(t)s) v., to move or seem to move up and down or about in a quick and lively manner," as defined by Webster's Dictionary. Dancing seems almost instinctual to humanity and is found in the animal world as well as the human. For Native Americans, the idea and definition of dance moved far beyond movement into an art form. Nearly all natives in North America danced at many points during their lifetimes. Before children could crawl, they were immersed in the movements and rhythms of dance. Dances imitated animals, plants, and natural forces in their environments and told the stories of society. Native American dance included physical exercise, dramatic and imaginative interpretation, rhythm, symbolism, history, and beauty in one activity. The occasions calling for dance varied greatly, from family events and religious ceremonies to hunting celebrations and preparations for war. Almost every native dance recognized or included some element of the culture's environment. Even dances of war and victory celebration thanked the spirits of the land and sky that played roles in their success. No matter what the purpose of the dance or the props and music used, two things remain constant in all cultures: dramatic action and rhythmic precision. "The White man dances with his legs; the Indian with his individual muscles," an anonymous Native American once said.[6] According to *Dance Rituals of the Pueblo Indians*, "the spirit of these dances is so pure, so genuine; they spring so inevitably from a primal source, that a comparison with our more artificial art is almost impossible."

In looking at the dance connection to natural environment, it is often not necessary to go beyond the names of the dances—Mountain Chant, Dog Dance, Deer Dance, Eagle Dance, Coyote Dance, Harvest Dance, Rain Dance, Corn Grinding Dance, Snake Dance, Dance of the Moons, Sun Dance, The Desert Wind; the list could go on. But even dances such as the Hoop Dance of Taos and the Basket Dance of the Cochiti, which have names that do not seem so related to the environment, actually are. In the case of the Basket Dance, first, the dancers performed in traditional Corn Dance costumes, symbolizing the husks often used for basket weaving. But the basket weaving itself was another symbol as well. The dance was performed as a fertility rite. Plants often represented birth and rebirth, and combining that imagery with basket weaving suggested the interlocking of past, present, and future generations to ensure a successful and continuing society. The Hoop Dance focused on the shape of the hoop: a perfect circle. In every native cosmology, the circle played an integral role, from symbolizing the cycle of birth, death, and rebirth to the idea that a circle represents all of nature, with each element depending on and being depended upon by every other element. All of these dances employed the imagination and the physique, while endeavoring to support and educate the community on its place in the natural world. The dances were but a part of a harmonious, interconnected world. Without them, Native American environments would have been sorely incomplete.

Each region developed its own unique dance expressions even as the dances performed similar functions across cultural lines. Subarctic communities in Canada, for example, relied heavily on drum dancing in

Papago basket maker at work in Arizona, circa 1916, following the traditional methods and patterns of her ancestors. National Archives Image number 532042.

half circles, using their arms and upper bodies to convey emotion and meaning. In Washington and British Columbia, the potlatch offered the opportunity to host or celebrate family events, and dancing was always present. In Spirit Dancing at potlatches, for example, young men and women would "catch" a guardian spirit through the dance, creating unique songs and movements to represent their spirits. In the Great Basin, natives danced the Bear Dance for food and the Sun Dance for the favor and protection of the sun. Pueblo dwellers danced in prayer for their most precious resource: water. In the Plains, different tribes came together for powwow dances, a series of dances performed in a certain order that often included dance competitions designed to show whom the spirits favored for the coming year. Up and down the East Coast, social dances were popular, in which many people from different tribes would get involved. Sometimes these dances forged ties between communities, sometimes between individuals as a sort of meeting and courtship ritual. The health and wealth of both communities and individuals relied on the meaning and function of dances, and without them, the never-ending circle of cause and effect in native life would be broken.

ACTING OUT IN THE ENVIRONMENT: THE PLACE OF NATIVE AMERICAN PERFORMANCE

In the centuries prior to European contact, hundreds of Native American tribes enjoyed many performance activities, few of which, unfortunately, have survived in pure form. It is difficult to separate dance performance from ritual dramas or prayer dramas and in fact, the two are often the same. It is important, though, to also look at the entertainment value of the "show" as well as its religious significance, or its role in native culture would not be complete. The entertainment value of costumes, masks, and clowning often drew not only everyone in the hosting village, but outside observers as well. The best method of comparison is to look at secret rites and rituals in contrast to the theater-like performances for public viewing. Using Pueblo culture as an example, although preparation began in private in the village kiva, often consuming days inside the structure for purification and adornment, once the public scenes began, the *kachinas* were provided a foil to their solemn role in the performance antics of clowns. Pueblo cultures tended to value secrecy, privacy, and demure, proper behavior very highly, but in the case of public dancing, the entertainment took over providing distraction for the crowd, yet also ensuring their patience and participation as observers while the *kachinas* rested.

In other areas, public performances fulfilled similar purposes. Among the characteristics and social structures shared by numerous tribes of the Plains were warrior societies or "fraternities." All of their performances reinforced their relationship with the unseen spirits and forces of nature. They did not, however, only perform the dances for their own personal benefit. Their dedication to the performance ensured that the entire tribe would enjoy good relations with the surrounding natural forces. For the Lakota, the Sun Dance epitomized this role in society. Performed in early summer, the yearly Sun Dance brought together the many tribes that had scattered during the winter. Some participants danced, while other prepared themselves for a painful rite that was seen as a sacrifice to the sun. During the preparation, the dancers and "actors" performed rites and reenactments of recent events, both for the purpose of appeasing natural spirits and to demonstrate to the gathered communities important battles and other activities of the previous year. At the end of eight days, the Sun Dancers would be bound together by leather straps threaded through their skin, and then they would try to break free from each other. If they were unable to do so, they would be cut free on the next morning. The Plains tribes expected that the suffering of the Sun Dance warriors would bring blessings to the entire band and induce trances in the dancers that would bring them closer to the spiritual world to receive messages and visions. Although this is an extreme example, dancing and its performance clearly filled religious, social, and historical (or communication) roles in tribal life.

Many cultures across the continent also engaged in different pantomimic or imitating performances. The most complex were those of the coastal Northwest. Because those peoples could obtain ample food reserves in short periods of time, they had plenty of opportunity to create intricate works of art, performance included. Their acting told elaborate stories of individuals, clans, and tribes. A particular clan's ancestor legends, songs, dances, names, and masks were thought of as spiritual gifts from guardian beings, and these were passed down through the generations. An entire tribe's culture was contained in its dances, and every physical piece, every song, every movement helped to preserve it. One unique theatrical expression of this region defined the roles of men and women in society. The conditions, time, and details of the performance were kept secret under the threat of death among the men who performed. At a time when some of the village's men were off "hunting," the men at home would pretend to be nervous. When some of the party returned at night, terrible noises would be heard throughout the village. Investigation would show a devil in their midst, which the men would drive out. After the scuffle, one man would be missing, and a woman of the tribe would be carried out as a sacrifice to the devil for the return of the man. The man's "corpse" would be brought back along with the "sacrifice," and the man would then be "beaten" back to life with inflated animal bladders (symbolizing the organ's life-sustaining importance in society). A few days later, the rest of the hunters would return and listen in pretend amazement to the events that transpired in their absence. Although very useful to the Northwest natives that employed this practice, there is also an important use to more recent generations and today's scholars. Rituals and performances such as the one just described not only tell the modern world of a history gone by, but also embody the definition and meaning of the culture from which they were born. Without these artistic expressions, little evidence would survive today to give Native North Americans a sense of their historic identity and origins.

NOTES

1. Stewart Culin, *Games of North American Indians: Volume 2—Games of Chance* (Lincoln: University of Nebraska Press, 1992), 275.

2. Ibid., 286.

3. Natalie Curtis, ed., *The Indians' Book: Songs and Legends of the American Indians* (New York: Dover Publications, 1968), 416.

4. Caroline Furness Jayne, *String Figures and How to Make Them: A Study of Cat's Cradle in Many Lands* (New York: Dover Publications, 1962), vii.

5. Ibid., 122.

6. Alice Corbin Henderson, "The Dance Rituals of the Pueblo Indians," *Theatre Arts Magazine*, 7 (June 1923).

9

Two Halves of the Same Environment: Gender Roles in Native American Society

[Woman] has been given by natural laws the ability to reproduce life, the most sacred of all things in life . . . the woman is the foundation of the family [so] we treat our women with respect and understanding . . . as if they were [our] own female relatives. This, I vow.

White Bison, Inc.[1]

I have seen that in any great undertaking it is not enough for a man to depend simply upon himself.

Lone Man (Isna-la-wica), Teton Sioux

Of all of the topics in Native American prehistory, gender is one of the most debatable and one of the most significant as well. Archaeological analysis consistently removed gender from the equation during the 1970s and 80s. The belief was that if the gender relationship to an artifact could not be known or tested, then it was not important. Three assumptions encouraged this ignoring of gender issues and identity: gender was unimportant to the study, gender assumptions seemed improvable, or the investigator assumed that all (there were not always just two genders) genders participated equally. Ultimately, how visible gender was in archaeological study came to be an important concern as scientists came to realize they had been overlooking and misreading signs of gender differentiation. The analysis of the role gender played in native society followed closely behind a new focus on evidence interpretation. Some ways to look at this include the consideration of resource access. It is possible to make detailed assumptions about men's and women's roles according to the access they had to important life-sustaining or rare resources because society valued people who had more access to certain materials than others. Autonomy or personal power is another consideration, but that is even harder to analyze because of the lack of physical evidence. Even the assumption that prehistoric natives defined gender in the same ways as modern society holds many problems. In some societies it seems that although they had two physical sexes of people, in social function, there was only one gender. In others, gender definition included male, female, and what today would be considered a transgendered identity, the self-definition of someone who feels and identifies with a gender that does not match the individual's physical sex or who has a sense of containing *both* genders within the body. It all depended on the roles of gender in individual societies. Once again, environment played a large part in determining an important area of native culture and daily life.

But why bother with gender definitions in the first place? A common assertion is that native communities, in fact most human societies, delegate work duties according to gender. This, however, could stratify social structure to infinity, with each job having its own set of gender characteristics, creating a rigid system of social functioning. Is gender defined by sexual partnerships or something as simple as the shape of a person's body? In most of human history, it is a combination of these two things. To determine the role that gender played in prehistoric society, archaeologists must understand the definition of "gender" itself as well as determine exactly who fit into those categories *relative to the society being studied.* Once again, all scholars have to rely on are the physical remains of the past. And even then, what they are studying is collective, not individual behavior, and gender is not always a collective matter. Some general patterns stand out, though, especially in hunter-gatherer societies. It is no surprise, for example, that in these societies males generally made war, hunted, and conducted intertribal business, while women focused on gathering, home-tending, and child rearing. There are many ways to study the role of gender in prehistoric native societies, including through the study of art, mythology, burial practices and remains, and physiological evidence, and all of these things are important to gender understanding. Because of the level of interpretation necessary in these methods, incorrect conclusions are a real possibility. For example, even if a society followed a belief system that put a female deity at the top, this did not mean that women were elevated to a higher status in that culture. In Medieval Europe, the Virgin Mary was one of the most holy, most sacred images for the Roman Catholic Church, but despite this, society in general did not treat women with the greatest respect. Just as in other areas of historical study, analysis is a fragile thing, full of the danger of misinterpretation and misunderstanding. What analysts know is sketchy at best, but this still helps to create a more complete picture of prehistoric North American daily life.

THE ENVIRONMENT OF FAMILIES: DEFINING FAMILY RELATIONSHIPS IN PREHISTORIC TERMS

Two of the most obvious and natural roles of women in any society are childbirth and mothering, and they are both biological and social. Each tribe had its own ideas about the role of "mother," about what they were expected to do and contribute outside that role, and about how important motherhood was in the community. In today's culture, biological mothering and social mothering are often one and the same. It is usually considered rude to tell a mother how to take care of her children and even worse to step in and intervene, even if the interloper is a family member. Interactions in prehistoric societies were not so cut and dry. First, it is important to keep in mind the fact that most North American tribes relied heavily on the extended family structure as the basis of their social organization. The relationships between family members were not as strictly defined. Terms such as "mother," "grandmother," "aunt," and "daughter" were much more permeable and did not always refer to someone connected by "blood." The question concerning value of the role rarely concerned native societies; families and tribes needed to procreate and increase their numbers. Childbearing was not easy or safe, and cultures valued a woman's willingness and ability to risk their health and even their lives for the benefit of society. And it is not true that native tradition always strictly delegated women and men to their respective, expected societal places. In examining the stereotypical jobs of "mother" and "father," it is also important to note that neither of these roles demanded a fulltime commitment. Ultimately, the goal was to perpetuate society, and everyone in the community had a hand in ensuring societal growth, creating one large extended family at the tribal level. Each role was important—indispensable, really—and all of those roles intertwined to create a successful society.

For Native American cultures, the extended family was by far the most commonly found social structure. This means that two or more "nuclear" families (meaning a father, mother, and children) lived together or very close to each other; they were of different generations or different immediate families but were still extensions of the same genetic line. Aunts, uncles, grandparents, and cousins depended on each other both for survival of the family unit and for collective contribution to the larger tribe. The extended family unit also suggests a certain hierarchy within the family based on experience and generation. Different patterns of family connection determined who lived together, depending on the larger social structure and tradition of the tribe. In patriarchal societies, sons lived with their fathers, bringing their wives and children along with them. In a matriarchal community, it was the husbands and children who followed the wife/mother to *her* mother's residence. In some societies, there was a mixture of the two traditions, depending on family needs and wishes, although this mixed form was not nearly as common. If a society did not function with extended families, then the more familiar "nuclear" family was the rule, although the connections between nuclear families and generations were closer than by today's standards. Traveling across prehistoric North America, natives utilized many different styles of family organization for their benefit, and those choices reflected the environments in which they lived.

On the Northwest Coast, tribes functioned within a rather strict pattern of extended family residence. Across the region, arrangements varied between matriarchal and patriarchal structures, but regardless of which form the organization took, natives respected their traditions as strict guidelines for social structure. Farther down along the coast, the guidelines became less rigid, although extended families were still the rule. Sometimes the families lived in single structures, but more often they lived in several smaller structures positioned close together. The differences between more northern and more southern tribes resulted partially from the fact that the environmental resource supplies in the north, specifically food and wood, were more stable and plentiful than they were further south. Without the worries of varying resource availability, cultures had time to develop more strict, less interdependent ways of living and interacting. This meant that northern natives easily functioned with less flexibility in their social structure than did their southern cousins. The extended family as an organizational umbrella, however, was constant in West Coast societies and served their environmental conditions well. Especially in areas where building more permanent villages was reasonable, even preferable, the extended family structure answered the different interdependent needs of more sedentary societies. Luckily for nomadic peoples, versions of this same extended family structure offered enough flexibility to encourage success for them as well.

In the Great Basin, for example, the independent nuclear family was much more common. Although sometimes these individual families grouped themselves into something that resembled an extended network, those groups were so flexible and impermanent that the extended label really did not apply. The mobile nature of their existence required family groups to work together, but successful survival often proved easier with a smaller number of people to support. The plains and plateau areas are difficult to classify as a whole, however, given that their regional environment varied so much that it produced very different forms of family structure. In some areas, loose, extended families served as the rule, whereas in other regions, independent, polygynous (having multiple wives) families made more sense. The prairie region exhibited more consistent extended family structure, though, based on regional environmental consistency. The most common form followed the patrilineal pattern, with the men in the family cooperating in hunting efforts and sharing the spoils. During farming seasons, a matrilocal (meaning temporarily matrilineal) structure took precedence, which complicated the picture. The result was tribes that used both farming and hunting switched their living styles at least once or twice a year. In farming, women did most of the work, so those family connections became more important during those seasons. This certainly created complicated arrangements, but also made the appropriate human resources available at different times of the year. Basically, whoever did the work for most of the food provision ended up being the organizing factor in the social structure of the Prairie Indians, and because that changed regularly, so did family organization. The Woodlands natives utilized much of the same basic extended family structure, but their region did not experience the drastic seasonal changes of the prairies, and so the longhouse functioned as the main form of familial residence. In the Southeast, for example, the matrilinear extended family prevailed, but by the time European observers began consistently recording southeastern native culture, it was on its way out because of the influence and pressures of European contact. As native cultures evolved, many of these familial structures changed out of necessity in response to their changing environments.

Another stationary North American culture was the Pueblo tradition. The core of the family line was the maternal connection, and as a result, the female side of the family owned farmland and houses, passing them down through their daughters. In their large, apartment-like complexes, extended families lived together (meaning many extended families lived within one structure), but individual nuclear families lived separately in their own rooms. The rooms of nuclear families connected by marriage or blood connected to each other, physically creating a nucleus for each extended family. Each extended group handled its own economic activities, ritual practice, and sustenance provision, but often shared with other family units or the larger pueblo population. This social structure relieved the burden on nuclear families to provide for themselves, helping ensure the success of all within the community. In areas where hogans were utilized, such as by the Navajo peoples, although the hogan structure grew larger over the centuries, hogans continued to house individual families and group together in extended family clusters. The function of these groups was mainly economic without a ritual component like that of the Pueblos' grouping, with the men contributing to hunting and the women working the farms. Basically all cultures used the extended family form to some degree, but the strictness of inheritance rules and cohabiting practices defined the character of each individual social culture. In order to understand family interactions and cultural history, it is important to define in detail "family" in order to illuminate native history as well as interaction with the environment.

ONE HALF OF A FAMILY CIRCLE: NATIVE AMERICAN WOMEN'S IDENTITY AND ROLE IN THEIR ENVIRONMENT

When defining gender roles in Native American society, the easiest and most obvious factor in creating those definitions was labor division. In smaller, nonfarming societies such as the Clovis cultures, subsistence activities were allocated by age and gender. Based largely on biological characteristics, adult women took responsibility for nourishing and educating the children of the tribe. Because of this primary role, women in hunting and gathering societies assumed only other roles that did not conflict with this primary duty, mainly doing things that kept them close to home and that did not interfere with their responsibility for the children. Cooking, preparing hunted animals for food and supplies, and the creation of goods and materials for village use all fit the bill. In many areas, a woman's role as a forager and gatherer made her indispensable as a primary provider while keeping her close to home. This elevated her status, and as a result, her social power increased. In desert tribes where foraging and gathering were extremely important for survival, tribes greatly respected and admired their women for their contributions. Sometimes these cultures gave their women the opportunity to serve as tribal

Apache Bride in traditional dress. National Archives Image number 530903.

shamans and allowed particularly prosperous women to take several husbands. Both of these privileges were rare for women and suggested a high level of respect. When women were scarce, they were so important to the social structure that men would often share a wife rather than go without or let others in the tribe suffer. In the desert, men moved into the women's homes, given that women were more familiar with local environmental resources. Because of their central role as food suppliers for the family and tribe in foraging societies, women often enjoyed status benefits of heightened honor and respect.

One interesting role that women played in North American history was as the continent's first farmers. Plants grow best in disturbed soil, and the soil around native encampments provided a good environment for growth. It seems that when women brought home plants from their gathering efforts, they accidentally scattered the seeds in their handling of the plants. Once the women realized that the plants they had gathered were growing in their front yard, so to speak, they started an elementary experimentation process that led them to an understanding that seeds from old plants grew new plants of the same type. This, to scholars, is the most plausible explanation for early gardening and farming efforts. Throughout the continent and its various cultures, women retained, preserved, and utilized local botanical knowledge as part of their social contributions to and duties in society. The women knew which plants were best for food and which created the best for clothing and dyes, as well as the best time to harvest for all of these uses. Women knew which plants and their individual parts cured diseases, eased pain, and kept people healthy. Because women had such power and understanding of the means to support and feed a people, it is no wonder that many cultures determined kin relationships and family lines of inheritance through the female side of the family. Ultimately this foundation proved very practical, especially for tribes that sent hunting parties far away from home or that were warlike. With large groups of men gone for extended periods of time, women needed the knowledge, social power, and respect to lead village life during the men's absence. Rather than reverting full power to the men upon their return, it made more sense to have women in permanent positions of respect and authority, so as to perpetuate continuity and success within the tribe.

From a larger societal perspective, women were the central organizing force in matrilineal cultures. Generations of mothers and daughters formed matrilineal social units all across the North American continent. Mothers and their children, both male and female, composed the matrilineal structure, with male positions of power and authority passing from brothers of women to the senior matron or mother's son, basically from maternal uncles to nephews. These lineages formed the basis for tribal politics and leadership. A male member of the matrilineally connected elite led the community and functioned as a tribal pivot point for economic and religious relationships and networks. Biologically speaking, this structure was the only one that could not be questioned; no one could doubt whose son someone was when the parentage in question was matrilineal. Tribes that functioned this way always knew that their leaders were biologically rightfully part of the leading clan. Motherhood simply could not be faked. Even in societies that put the power in the hands of patrilineal decent, women were still valued for their contributions in foraging and gathering as well as for their role as child-bearer and raiser. Without women, native societies would not have seen their way through the seasons, much less been able to perpetuate their people and culture through the generations.

THE OTHER HALF OF A FAMILY CIRCLE: NATIVE AMERICAN MEN AND THEIR ROLE IN THEIR ENVIRONMENT

The easiest assumption to make would be that the men in native societies did what the women did not, but that would be too easy. As mentioned, physiology determined some divisions of labor. While women stayed home in hunter-gatherer societies, men traveled off on the hunt and to wage war. These skills designated the man as the protectors of the

A Sauk native man and a Fox native man, each with traditional war paint. National Archives Image number 530973.

home and village. Together men and women created a perfect partnership for family and tribal success. Not all men and women "pulled their own weight" in a community for a variety of reasons, though, so what happened to them? One of the basic secrets of survival on the tribal level was the idea of reciprocity, or "share and share alike." Regardless of who killed an animal, foraged a basketful of food, or harvested a plant, everyone in the community enjoyed a fair share of the product. Even the most skillful hunters and adept farmers failed sometimes, and often the failure occurred through no fault of their own. Sharing among community members protected everyone from short-term and individual setbacks. Tribes gave great honors to those who could provide well, but also to those who willingly and unselfishly shared their bounty. They considered the hoarding of resources a serious social transgression and sometimes even a criminal offense. Because of the necessity of working with and within their given environment, native cultures developed social structures of responsibility that ensured the survival of all within their community.

For men, biology dictated other responsibilities. Hunting ranked at the top of their priority list, and the large majority of hunting responsibility fell on the shoulders of the men. As discussed, gathering women trapped small animals as a food and as material resources, but the methods and tools placed this activity within the sphere of gathering or foraging. The other major biologically appropriate duty was war. Warfare, just like every other aspect of native life, possessed a strong, obvious environmental connection with society and a way Native Americans viewed and interacted with their natural surroundings. Bravery and honor were important to the identity and social status of Native American men. One surefire way to prove bravery was through warfare. Some cultures were more warlike than others, and many reasons for conflicts between tribes might seem trivial to modern society. Very often, conflict was not even political, something difficult to understand or relate to today. In general, conflict began over goods, resources, revenge, or general aggression. Each society had different reasons for going to war, as varied as the environments in which they lived. Territorial boundaries arose often, a common issue for cultures that engaged in farming, hunting, and foraging, but generally only in areas where larger populations lived. Raiding, on the other hand, appeared in both high- and low-population–density areas because societies both large and small needed to replenish both captives and supplies. No matter what the reason, warfare in native society was rarely simple, and patterns changed depending on environment and location.

With land as the most common factor to all tribes, the ideas of possession and use must be considered because they differ greatly from Western norms. Tribes had specific, traditional, sacred territories that defined who they were, and the spirits that resided in their areas functioned as an integral part of that self-definition. These lands usually did not sit right next to another tribe's traditional territory, instead areas that could be considered "no man's lands" sat in between. This meant that those lands were open to several bands or tribes for hunting, fishing, or gathering purposes, owned by no one but accessible to all. Although conflict might have taken place on these lands, it was never considered for settlement or "ownership" purposes as Westerners would think of it. Lands passed down through traditionally defined communities, and until the arrival of Europeans and the forced removal and relocation of Native American populations, those definitions never changed. Instead of fighting over ownership, which really did not exist in native mentality, the most common form of conflict was raiding activity. Raiding helped accumulate wealth, material resources, and goods for a tribe. Raiding helped provide new tribal members as well; when people were captured in a raid, they were often adopted into the tribe. There was also a more subtle function. By obtaining goods from other tribes, those who participated could share those rewards with others who were less fortunate in their own tribe. That helped raise the standing of the less fortunate and often made it possible for them to continue to spread the wealth by having enough resources to participate in future raids. Without disrupting tribes' traditional places on the land, warfare helped ensure tribal success, gave men in the community chances to prove their bravery, raised their status, and contributed to tribal health and wealth, while simultaneously preserving a balance between local native powers.

Native American warfare also served to honor kinship losses and nurture spirituality. Many tribes participated in "mourning" warfare. If a relative died as a result of conflict between tribes, kinsmen often went on the warpath to obtain revenge and restore the spiritual balance disrupted by the relative's death. The goal was to exact the same amount of loss from the enemy tribe, thus ensuring a return of spiritual balance. A member of the enemy was either killed or kidnapped and adopted into the tribe as a replacement. Some widows literally wiped their tears away with the scalps of the enemy. Ultimately, this type of warfare served its purpose both for the avenging tribe and for the larger native environment by balancing tribal membership, varying the genetics of each tribe, and providing an outlet for vengeance. Additionally, spirituality also played a role in native warfare. There were rigid lines of definition drawn between wartime and peacetime activities, and they involved the nature of the spiritual forces at work in both categories. In order for societies to successfully make the physical and mental transition from peace into war and back to peace again, Native Americans practiced religious ceremonies each step of the way. They considered individual and community spiritual preparation extremely necessary in order to provide the best chance at success. Upon a war party's return, tribes felt it important to cleanse the warrior and the society as a whole of aggressive wartime energy and return the warrior and the people to a state of peaceful being. Prehistoric natives believed that unless the war party could be cleansed of battle trauma, it was possible that warlike patterns of behavior would infiltrate the community, bringing about negative consequences. Basically, it was best if the men not bring work home with them; it could create an unpleasant family and community environment.

Just as there were strict lines drawn between war and peace, strict lines also defined "male" and "female." Native Americans saw warfare as a purely male-oriented pursuit and an outlet for male youthful aggression. In some ways it could be considered an elaborate game through which young men worked off their natural tendencies while at the same time perfected skills necessary for tribal benefit and to assure their own place in that society. The tradition of "counting coup" in the cultures of the Great Plains is a perfect example. Coup was a specific war honor that emphasized stealth, skill, cunning, and bravery rather than the actual killing of an enemy. The process of "counting coup" involved a warrior being able to get close enough to his enemy to touch him with either his hand or a "coup stick." Touching an enemy in the heat of battle left the enemy alive, but aware of the fact that he had been bested and thus humiliated. Another way for warriors to gain respect and status was to participate in the ceremonial rituals of war. In many ways, war defined and embodied the more aggressive native societies. Although one tribe might hate their enemy with great passion, that enemy was worthy of the conflict and was needed to help define basic tribal identity. There were other reasons, though, for having traditional enemies. Despite the bloody nature of conflict and the inevitable deaths that occurred, annihilation of the enemy was rarely, if ever, the goal. Destroying the enemy completely could effectively devastate both tribes as balance of people, supplies, goods, and resources often depended on war itself. If one of those tribes disappeared, their resource supplies also disappeared leaving the future needs of the surviving tribe unfulfilled. Even the native words that different tribes used to mean "warrior" translated into ideas that contained a specific male component. Some societies had female warriors as well, but this was definitely an exception, not the rule (remember, in the rigid lines drawn between the sexes, most societies considered war tendencies the complete opposite of female nature). For most native cultures, "warrior" and "male" were practically synonymous, each identity helping to define the other in society.

ONE PERSON OF TWO SPIRITS: MORE GENDER CLASSIFICATION IN NATIVE SOCIETY

> The men are strongly inclined to sodomy; but the boys that abandon themselves thus are excluded from the society of men and sent out to that of women as being effeminates. They are confused with

the hermaphrodites, which they say are found in quantity in the country of the Floridians. I believe that these hermaphrodites are none other than the effeminate boys that in a sense truly are her-maphrodites. Be that as it may, they employ them in all the diverse handiworks of women, in servile functions, and to carry the muni-tions and provisions of war. They are also distinguished from the men and the women by the color of the feathers that they put on their heads and for the scorn that they bring onto themselves.

Francisco Coreal

This was how a Spanish traveler who visited Florida in 1669 described the people in native society known as Two-Spirit people or *berdaches* (a term used by anthropologists, but considered offensive by most Native Americans today). Observers have documented in almost 200 native tribes men who assumed women's roles, and nearly half of those tribes also had women who assumed men's roles as well. In the tribes where only men filled this role, the *berdache* functioned as a third gender identity, and in those tribes with women who fell into this category, then there was a fourth identity definition. It is danger-ous to rely too heavily on European descriptions such as this, however,

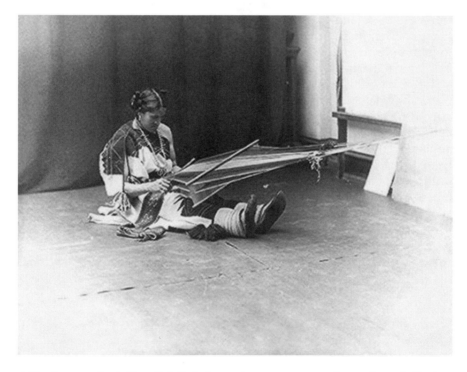

A Zuni man who is Two-Spirited, dressed as a woman and weaving a belt, circa 1879. National Archives Image number 523796.

because Western beliefs and interpretation presented a picture of rejection and disdain of these people by their own tribes that often did not exist. Many studies indicate that native culture actually held both male and female Two-Spirits in high regard and believed them to have exceptional talent, productivity, and originality. Despite differences in detail, Two-Spirits across the continent shared some similarities in traits and roles. Everyone in a native community described and identified male and female Two-Spirit people as the opposite-sex role in which they lived their lives, *not* as what biology dictated. It was not just work that defined them either; in every physical, social, and religious sphere, they functioned as the gender of their identification. Two-Spirit identity originated, natives believed, as a spiritual intervention and blessing. It often made itself known through visions or dreams, and native mythology and beliefs supported the existence of these additional gender identities. Two-Spirits most commonly formed sexual and emotional relationships with members of their own biological sex, but the community did not consider their partners Two-Spirited or even "homosexual" in the Western sense of the idea. Because they accepted the gender of behavior as the gender of identity, if a man married a Two-Spirit man, both he and his tribe considered him to have married a woman because that is the role the spirit world gave him. As celebrated members of the tribe, Two-Spirits were the embodiment of both Mother Earth and Father Sky, a male and female heart or spirit within one body, therefore twice as powerful. Of all the things early European explorers encountered that they interpreted badly, this element stands out as one of the most contentious.

The problems with Western understanding of this very non-Western tradition are many. Simply viewing Two-Spirited people as homosexual does not even approach what Two-Spirits represented in their communities. They were not transsexuals either; the Western connotation of this word suggests that they were a spirit born in an inappropriate body, and that does not apply to native reality. They also were not cross-dressers or transvestites. They were not simply donning the trappings of another gender; tribes considered Two-Spirited people a natural occurrence, and no explanation for aberration was needed because Two-Spirits were not considered anomalies in most native societies. "Transgendered" is the only Western term that comes close to describing the occurrence of Two-Spirited people in native societies except that "transgendered" suggests to many a gender dualism or trade when in native reality, Two-Spirits were simply male or female regardless of biology as identified in their vision or dream. It certainly does not suggest the sacred role of *berdaches* (both male and female in one person) and so still falls short of a true modern analogy.

As evidence of their accepted role in society, there are many historical descriptions of Two-Spirit people as having strong mystical powers.

In one example, raiding warriors of a Plains tribe attacked a group of working women, but when they identified one woman who did not run away as a Two-Spirit, the warriors immediately ceased their attack out of fear of powerful retribution many cultures not only accepted these additional genders as normal, however rare, manifestations, but often welcomed and revered them. This does not hold true for all Native American tribes across the continent; the Iroquois and some other warlike communities seemed to have little tolerance for Two-Spirited identity, but all that is known of this comes from the observations of Europeans. One theory suggests that the Iroquois perhaps once held the Two-Spirit tradition as sacred, but through introduction of Western ideas, came to see alternate gendered people negatively. This is only one theory, though, and it is possible that some tribes were traditionally anti-*berdache*. For many more tribes there is no record to the positive *or* the negative, so the truth about the frequency and extent of Two-Spirit occurrence and acceptance will probably never be known.

The first recognition of a person as Two-Spirited could have come as early as childhood. If parents noticed that children did not take interest in things considered traditional to their physical gender, they performed a ceremony to determine how to raise the children. If the ceremony named the child a Two-Spirit, from then on, the parents raised the child to learn the work and traditions for both genders. The child often spent time with healers as well, not in an effort to be "healed," but to be taught the special ways of the child's unique gender. Above all, it seems the children generally enjoyed acceptance and understanding, and although kids might tease, Native American society taught that the Two-Spirit was a natural and valued part of the community. As Two-Spirits matured, although they predominately dressed and acted as the "other" gender would, natives often still considered Two-Spirits to have both identities residing within one body. In Native American religion and belief, nature did not make mistakes. Things were the way they were because of nature's larger design, of which an individual could only know a small part. If nature created something a certain way, then that was the way it must be. Besides their spiritual importance, their capacity for work, at least in the case of physically male Two-Spirit people, was often greater than the average one-spirit person, adding to their societal value and prestige. Because of this, men prized Two-Spirit women as wives for the work they could contribute to the family. Legend also tells that Two-Spirits seemed gifted in relating to children, possessed a generous nature, and exhibited exceptional intellectual and artistic skills. Rather than characterize something nature produced as odd, evil, or a mistake, many native cultures worked this part of their environment into their larger circle of understanding, just as they did every other naturally occurring element. Modern society must study, evaluate, and understand the pre-contact native worldview differently than expected in order to better understand the culture for what it truly was, an interconnected a communal life surrounded by and immersed in the environment that has long defied western empathy & under standing.

NOTE

1. This quote was collaboratively written at a gathering of more than 2,000 Native Americans representing more than 100 tribes. Taken from "Seven Philosophies of the Native American Man."

EPILOGUE

ENTER THE EUROPEAN: WHAT CAME NEXT FOR NATIVE NORTH AMERICA

> I am a red man. If the Great Spirit had desired me to be a white man he would have made me so in the first place. He put in your heart certain wishes and plans, in my heart he put other and different desires. Each man is good in his sight. It is not necessary for Eagles to be Crows. We are poor . . . but we are free. No white man controls our footsteps. If we must die . . . we die defending our rights.
>
> *Sitting Bull, Hunkpapa Sioux*

As stated by William Bradford back in 1620, the "vast & unpeopled countries of America . . . being devoid of all civill inhabitants, [populated by] only savage & brutish men" were fruitful and fit for habitation by Europeans.[1] The time span of this book covers upwards of 50,000 years or more, and yet it is only one part of the story of native North America prior to European contact. What came next was a long period of change and adjustment punctuated by violence and bloodshed. Sometimes, initially, the aggressors were Native American. As Europeans spread across the continent, gained a solid foothold in the land, and ultimately created their own country, however, they became the aggressors and eventually successfully took control of the entire continent. It is only fair to say that some Native American cultures were aggressively violent from the beginning when confronted with European colonists, but many more were not. Native North Americans expected beliefs and behaviors somewhat similar to their own from the newcomers, but were caught off guard by the reality of contact. In every definition and context, the presence

V.

FRANCISCVS DRACO CVM
IN LOCVM QVENDAM VENIS-
set, à Rege istius regionis conuenitur.

Drawing and reflections of Theodor de Bry. He was
the first to create detailed copper plate engravings
with great accuracy of detail and scope of travels
through the Americas. These images are the first
ones that much of European would have seen of
Native Americans. *Source:* Collection peregrinatio-
num in indiam orientael et indiam occidentalem,
XXV partibus, comprehensae a theodore, joan.
Thodoro de bry, et a matheo merian publicatae. Ser
1. Historia americae sive nove orbis. Continens in
XIII distinctis partibus . . . Francofurti ad Moenum:
M. Merian, 1590. Courtesy of The Bankcroft Library, University of California, Berkeley.

of Europeans created a so-called New World for the Native American.
Some therefore hid themselves away as far as they could and avoided as
much contact as possible with the white man. Of all cultures, the Inuit of
Northern Canada were the most successful at this. When John Frobisher

came to the continent in the 1570s, natives met his ships in canoes, offering friendship and trading. He sent men to speak with them, but ordered them to remain within sight. For some reason, they disobeyed this order, and Frobisher panicked when they failed to return. Before he set sail for home, he lured natives to the boat again and captured a man, woman, and young child to take home as evidence from his visit. When Frobisher returned over a year later, he and his crew saw Inuit men, women, and children on the shore, but not surprisingly, this time the natives tried to avoid contact. Instead a firefight broke out between Frobisher's men and the Inuit people with most of the Inuit group being driven to jump to their deaths from the seaside cliffs.

Interestingly, Inuit legend tells a story that could be about the men Frobisher first left behind. The tale says that white men did live among the Inuit for several years in peace, but eventually they built a craft and sailed away, never to be seen again. When Frobisher returned, he and his men found clothing that only could have been European, but no sign of his men. Frobisher's assumed the worst and reacted to the Inuit based on that negative conclusion. The Inuit people hid themselves away from Europeans as best as they could, and today's scholars suggest that because of this, Inuit tradition and culture is the closest thing to what native culture might have looked like with little European intervention. Ultimately, over 99 percent of North American natives came into regular contact with Westerners, and this changed their culture and lifestyle forever. Until that meeting, however, the circle of existence that was the native environment nurtured, educated, sustained, and defined Native American identity. Their own "New World" that included Europeans changed that environment irrevocably and forever.

NOTE

1. William Davis, ed., *Bradford's History of Plymouth Plantation, 1606–1646* (New York: Charles Scribner's Sons, 1908), 14.

Annotated Bibliography

Abarr, James. "A Look Back." *Albuquerque Journal*. http://www.abqjournal.com/venue/travel/tourism/heritage_walnut.htm.
> This article explores the discovery of and analysis of Sinagua sites dated to the 12th century C.E. James Abarr looks at the history of treasure-seekers in the late 1800s and their contributions to both artifact preservation and evidence destruction. Abarr's article summarizes that process of analysis and evaluation as well as the resulting story of the Sinagua of Walnut Canyon.

Adovasio, J.M., with Jake Page. *The First Americans: In Pursuit of Archaeology's Greatest Mystery.* New York: Random House, 2002.
> This book focuses entirely on discussing who the first natives in America were and how and when they arrived. Within this exploration, the author includes a history of the study of this question and a history of archaeology itself. Not only does the book give the reader a more detailed understanding of the ancient history of the first Americans, but it also provides an exploration of the difficulties, obstacles, and rewards inherent in archaeological study.

Altschul, Jeffrey H., and Donn R. Grenda, eds. *Prehistoric Context of the Southern California Coast and Channel Islands.* Tucson: University of Arizona Press, 2000.
> Using comparative studies of island and coastal cultures from the Pacific, the authors show how the study of southern California's past can expand knowledge about coastal adaptations worldwide. Drawing on sources from anthropology, ethnohistory, geoscience,

and archaeology, the authors present their detailed findings in a readable fashion for both scholars and a general public audience.

America's Stone Age Explorers. London: BBC Horizon. Television Program. Original broadcast November 9, 2004.

This made-for-television program focuses on in-depth exploration of the discovery, analysis, and origin of the Clovis point and Clovis culture. The most recent discoveries and studies are used to come to the most detailed and up-to-date conclusions possible. The accompanying NOVA Web site (www.pbs.org/wgbh/nova/ stoneage/about.htm) offers extra activities and information beyond the program's coverage.

Aveni, Anthony F., ed. *Native American Astronomy.* Austin: University of Texas Press, 1977.

This book, written on a subject about which very little is known, is a collection of essays aimed at explaining what is known about prehistoric astronomical beliefs and knowledge, most of it coming out of Meso-America, the source of much of the surviving evidence. Although it has been critically and somewhat negatively reviewed, the work does provide the reader with an overview of knowledge and understanding on this subject as well as can be expected perhaps. The book also makes it clear that there are many holes in this knowledge (and few have been filled since the book's publication), and what is "known" is often an educated guess. Overall, this book provides a good collection of the modern understanding of pre-Columbian astronomy, geographically focused largely on Meso-America.

Barton, Miles, Ian Gray, Adam White, Nigel Bean, and Stephen Dunleavy. *Prehistoric America: A Journey through the Ice Age and Beyond.* New Haven, CT: Yale University Press, 2003.

This book travels across the continent region by region, introducing the prehistoric animal life and environment of each area. Using extensive fossil evidence as its base, the book is illustrated by computer-generated panoramas of what the landscape of prehistoric North America would have looked like.

Brown, Jospeh Epes. *The Spiritual Legacy of the American Indian.* New York: The Crossroad Publishing Company, Inc., 1984.

The book reads like a handbook to generalizations that can be made about Native American religion across the continent. Based on many primary sources including interviews and oral tradition, there is a passion in the writing that can lead a reader to feel more like they are being preached to, but if read carefully, this could be seen as a reflection of the emotion contained within the sources Brown uses for analysis.

Cajete, Gregory. *Native Science: Natural Laws of Interdependence.* Santa Fe, NM: Clear Light Publishers, 2000.

For the author, the phrase "native science" serves as a metaphor for what happens when humans experience and participate with and within the natural world. What the book hopes to explain is the "collective heritage of human experience with the natural world," taken from the experiences of thousands of generations. Although this is not a comprehensive treatment of native science knowledge and practices, it offers useful examples of the interaction with and understanding of environment in traditional Native American belief by examining some of the most common and recurring examples.

Carmody, Denise Lardner, and John Tully Carmody. *Native American Religions: An Introduction.* Mahwah, NJ: Paulist Press, 1993.

This look at Native American religion organizes its treatment geographically and looks at North American, as well as South and Central American, traditions. Its format is geared toward the student; accompanying each chapter are study questions, notes, and a glossary. It is written as a surface treatment that looks at tradition in general, both prehistoric and historic, but gives enough detail and information to get the reader started at looking deeper into the history of Native American religions.

Clark, Jeffery J. *Tracking Prehistoric Migrations: Pueblo Settlers among the Tonto Basin Hohokam.* Tucson: University of Arizona Press, 2001.

This book takes a look at migration using various ethnoarchaeological and ethnohistoric case studies. The book looks specifically at migration of the Pueblo people into the Tonto Basin of east-central Arizona during the early Classic period—the 13th century C.E. This community had been developing with substantial Hohokam influence until this interval. Clark identifies Pueblo enclaves in the indigenous settlements based on culturally specific differences in the organization of domestic spaces and technological styles reflected in wall construction and utilitarian ceramic manufacture. Limited Pueblo migration resulted in the coresidence of migrants and local groups within a single community. Short-term and long-term impacts of migration are studied through this interaction.

Colinvaux, Paul. *Ecology.* San Francisco: John Wiley and Sons, 1993.

Colinvaux explores life on earth from a paleoecological perspective by examining ecosystem processes, species strategies, social systems, community building, ecosystem stability, population ecology, individual adaptation, and species diversity. Written for higher level popular consumption, this book translates often complex ecological theories and assumptions into understandable language.

Collins, John J. *Native American Religions: A Geographical Survey*. Lewiston, NY: E. Mellen Press, 1991.

John Collins organizes his study of Native American religions around regional divisions, rather than around topic or categorical designations. One of the strengths of this type of approach is a clearer perspective on how environment and region influence the development of change in culture and society. Although the author does not always directly focus on this connection, there are several areas in the book where the connection is made clear.

Crawford, Michael H. *The Origins of Native Americans: Evidence from Anthropological Genetics*. Cambridge, England: Cambridge University Press, 2001.

This book is a synthesis of the genetic, archaeological, and demographic evidence concerning the native peoples of the Americas, using case studies from contemporary American Indian and Siberian indigenous groups. It largely focuses, though, on examining the collision between European and Native American cultures following contact and exploring the legacy of increased incidence of chronic diseases that still accompanies the acculturation of Native American peoples today.

Culin, Stewart. Introduction by Dennis Tedlock. *Games of the North American Indians: Volume I—Games of Chance*. Lincoln: University of Nebraska Press, 1992.

This publishing is a reprint of an original 1907 edition first published as the *Twenty-fourth Annual Report of the Bureau of American Ethnology, 1902–1903, Smithsonian Institution*. Stewart Culin and Hamilton Cushing began a joint project in 1891 to describe and document Native American games across the continent. Cushing died shortly after they began, and Culin continued on alone until the work was finished in 1907. It remains the only comprehensive documentation of Native American games. Originally, it was one volume, but in the 1992 publishing, it was divided into two volumes: one for games of chance and one for games of skill.

———. *Games of North American Indians: Volume 2—Games of Skill*. Lincoln: University of Nebraska Press, 1992.

Games figured prominently in the myths of North American Indian tribes, as well as in their religious ceremonies. Many games in very different areas of the continent evolved in much the same way, with similar rules and structure. Volumes 1 and 2 of this collection reflect Culin's categorization divisions, as well as his perspective on where these games fit into Native American culture and life.

Curtis, Natalie, ed. *The Indians' Book: Songs and Legends of the American Indians.* New York: Dover Publications, 1968.

    This edition in an unaltered, unabridged republication of a second edition published in 1923. Natalie Curtis spent years studying the songs and stories of Native Americans in North America and published her first collection in 1907. She then continued her studies, but died suddenly before she was able to incorporate her newly acquired information. Each section includes culture discussion, and many of the individual stories and songs have explanations regarding where Curtis heard them; the text also explores the stories' meaning and connections to life as explained to the author by the Native Americans themselves.

Davis, William T., ed. *Bradford's History of Plymouth Plantation, 1606–1646.* New York: Charles Scribner's Sons, 1908. Electronic edition available from http://narcissus.umd.edu:8080/eada/html/display.jsp?docs=bradford_history.xml&action=show.

    This is a full electronic text of a 1908 publication of the "History of Plymouth Plantation," written by William Bradford, governor of Plymouth Colony.

Delcourt, Paul A., and Hazel Delcourt. *Prehistoric Native Americans and Ecological Change: Human Ecosystems in Eastern North America since the Pleistocene.* London: Cambridge University Press, 2004.

    In making an effort to address the long-running controversy between ecologists and archaeologists concerning the role of Native Americans in prehistoric ecological and environmental change, the book uses data from both fields to examine the woodlands of eastern North America. The authors come to the conclusion that human interaction affected different areas and environments on different scales and suggest that looking at those changes over time will help present-day scientists understand what natural environments should and would look and behave like without human intervention in order to further understanding of natural restoration and preservation of ancient natural environs.

Dewar, Elaine. *Bones: Discovering the First Americans.* New York: Carroll and Graf Publishers, 2001.

    This book focuses almost entirely on different theories of migration of ancient Americans: how they came, where they went, and when they got here. The book relies heavily on examining physical remains, specifically skeletal remains, to present its case. A large part of the analysis, though, details the problems and holes that exist in prehistoric North American studies. Rather than treating prehistory chronologically, the book looks at all of the major theories to answer the questions just listed and tries to educate its readers on the most possible, while still explaining how not everything can be known.

Driver, Harold Edson. *The Americas on the Eve of Discovery.* Englewood Cliffs, NJ: Prentice-Hall, 1964.

> This is another dated study, but still is considered an important work concerning the state of Native Americans and their culture just before the arrival of Europeans. Written during a time when the history of Native America was still a young field, this is one of the earliest efforts at being objective and honest in the treatment of Native American history. The work suffers partially because of imbedded prejudices of the time, but does its best (for 1964) to overcome some of those. It also suffers because it has very few works to follow as precedents, but the author is aware of that limitation, and the work does a good job of circumventing those problems when possible. Gives a great picture of the state of knowledge during the 1960s.

———. *Indians of North America.* Chicago, IL: The University of Chicago Press, 1969.

> The strength of this book is its extensive maps and easily understood geographical divisions. As one of the most comprehensives works in existence on Native American culture and society, every subject is touched on for every region on the continent. This edition is a revision of the first and provides more detail, research, maps, and analysis than the first work. Rather than using a chronological treatment form, *Indians of North America* describes each tribe and culture at its height, thus providing the most extensive, prosperous examination of each American Indian culture.

Du Pratz, M. Le Page. *The History of Louisiana; or of the Western Parts of Virginia and Carolina, Containing a Description of the Countries that Lie on Both Sides of the River Mississippi: With an Account of the Settlements, Inhabitants, Soil, Climate, and Products.* London, 1774.

> This is a detailed account of first-hand observation of Native American culture through what is today the southern United States. Natchez observation and analysis was of particular use in this study, and although much of the analysis is heavily biased from a Western observer perspective, the primary source preservation of this publication is a valuable contribution to evidence preservation from the point of European contact.

Emerson, Thomas E. *Cahokia and the Archaeology of Power.* Tuscaloosa: University of Alabama Press, 1997.

> Emerson evaluates the span, reach, and extent of chiefly power using Cahokia as a central point, but focusing on Cahokia's surrounding rural communities. It looks at ritual and ceremony as the

cornerstones of power. One of the book's strengths is its approach to settlement analysis and economic structure, coming to some interesting and rather unique conclusions about how the region functioned and how economy and power structure affected the society.

Fallon, Sally, and Mary G. Enig. "Guts and Grease: The Diet of Native Americans." *The Weston A. Price Foundation.* January 1, 2000. http:// www.westonaprice.org/traditional_diets/native_americans.html.
    The authors suggest that native diets high in fat, other animal byproducts, plants, and fermented foods lead native communities to enjoy an extremely high level of societal health with fewer instances obesity, heart conditions, diabetes, hypertension, and even cavities. They use evidence from written sources and biological remains to come to the conclusion that today's food and health guidelines are not only inferior, but perhaps damaging to human health.

Farb, Peter. *Man's Rise to Civilization: The Cultural Ascent of the Indians of North America.* New York: E. P. Dutton, 1978.
    This work begins by explaining culture and how it changes, and then the book combines that discussion with an examination of the first Americans as examples of culture and change. From there, the author uses regions throughout North America to explore different styles of living and processes of adaptation and change. Although the details of history play a large role in the analysis, the focus of the work is to explain historically how human society has developed as civilizations and in its patterns of living.

Frison, George C. *Prehistoric Hunters of the High Plains.* St. Louis, MO: Academic Press, 1991.
    This book takes a detailed look at many of the tribes that inhabited the High Plains and their subsistence patterns, which were largely based on hunting. It begins chronologically with Clovis hunters and ends at the peak of Plains buffalo hunting, giving detailed overviews of different tribes across the Plains, how they hunted the buffalo, and some insight into how they used the animal. Particular attention is paid to the symbolism and ceremony embedded in hunting.

————. *Survival by Hunting: Prehistoric Human Predators and Animal Prey.* Berkeley: University of California Press, 2004.
    Using artifacts and other clues from the Great Plains and the Rocky Mountain region, the author—an archaeologist, hunter, rancher, and guide—illuminates ancient hunting practices in new ways. By incorporating into the study his understanding of animal habits and behavior and his familiarity with hunting strategies and techniques, the author comes to conclusions that suggest that the inclusion of personal knowledge and experience is necessary to understanding prehistoric hunting.

Gill, Sam. *Native American Religions: An Introduction.* New York: Wadsworth Publishing, 2004.

This is a very brief overview of general and shared characteristics of Native American tribes from an anthropologist's perspective. Most of the conclusions and detail come from oral history and tradition, and as a result, this book offers a more recent perspective on historical Native American religion and practice, making little distinction between what might be prehistoric and postcontact manifestations. The author not only details the inherent diversity of Native American religions, but also makes a case for Native American religious studies as a subfield of religious studies in general. It also looks at different aspects of European and American perspectives in order to understand and correct traditional misunderstandings about Native American religions.

Glenbow Museum. "Tepee Design." *Niitoy-yiss: The Blackfoot Tipi.* Available from http://www.glenbow.org/exhibitions/online/blackfoot/main_eng.htm.

Based on an archival collection of Native American culture, the Glenbow Museum created a Web site to share both the archival materials and their analysis. Of particular use in this book was the many images, descriptions, and analyses of Blackfoot decorated or painted tepees.

Gould, Stephen Jay. *Ever Since Darwin: Reflections on Natural History.* New York: W. W. Norton and Company, 1991.

This book uses a variety of popular references and metaphors to help illuminate his rather unorthodox views concerning evolution and biology. In many of his works, he addresses environment and its affect on the creatures within the environment, providing a valuable supplement to archaeological analysis.

Guthrie, Dale. *Frozen Fauna of the Mammoth Steppe: The Story of Blue Babe.* Chicago: University of Chicago Press, 1989.

A find in 1979 of a frozen, extinct steppe bison allowed Dale Guthrie to perform the first excavation of an Ice Age mummy. Guthrie uses evidence from living animals, other Pleistocene mummies, Paleolithic art, and geological data to come to conclusions about steppe environment and the mummies life experiences. Important to this study are the assumptions he makes about the nature of interaction between humans and bison during the last Ice Age.

Haines, Francis. *The Buffalo: The Story of American Bison and Their Hunters from Prehistoric Times to the Present.* Norman: University of Oklahoma Press, 1995.

This book gives a history of the rise, fall, and reemergence of the buffalo on the North American continent. The book's strength is its accurate, detailed accounts of native hunting techniques and uses for the buffalo by prehistoric Native American tribes.

Henderson, Alice Corbin. "The Dance Rituals of the Pueblo Indians." *Theatre Arts Magazine* 7 (1923).

This article explores the dance rituals of the Pueblo Indians through observation and cultural analysis of the symbolism and role of dance in native Pueblo society. Of particular use to this study is the analysis of the role and meaning of dancing itself, not just individual dances.

Hutchinson, Dale L., Ann Kakaliouras, Lynette Norr, and Mark Teaford. *Foraging, Farming, and Coastal Biocultural Adaptation in Late Prehistoric North Carolina.* Miami: University of Florida Press, 2002.

This work looks mostly at the adaptations prehistoric Native Americans in North Carolina underwent to continue successfully existing in their environment. It provides great detail on foraging, farming, and coastal resources and their benefits, drawbacks, and challenges, as well as a description of the role these things played in shaping North Carolina's prehistoric societies.

James, Geord Wharton. *Indian Blankets and Their Makers.* Chicago: A. C. McClure, 1914.

This is one of several ground-breaking, turn-of-the-century studies of Native American culture and tradition that explores the deep symbolism in everyday tribal activities. The organization of the book is based on detailed observation and explanation of the blanket making process, but what makes this work so important is the connections made to beliefs and practices of Native Americans, specifically the Pueblo and Navajo tribes.

Jayne, Caroline Furness. *String Figures and How to Make Them: A Study of Cat's Cradle in Many Lands.* New York: Dover Publications, 1962.

This 1962 edition is an unabridged republication of a work first published in 1906. Caroline Furness Jayne traveled extensively, speaking with many people from many different cultures about their string figures or cat's cradle games. The book is a compilation of her many interviews, accompanied by detailed images and descriptions of how to make over 100 different string figures.

Jennings, Jesse D. *Prehistory of North America.* Mountain View, CA: Mayfield Publishing, 1989.

A short, but insightful, treatment of North American prehistory. According to the book's introduction, culture history is the traditional goal of archaeological study as an account of prehistoric ways of life. The main focus of its general treatment is the process of archaeological study and how it demonstrates change in prehistoric society, as well as assumptions about why those changes took place.

Josephy, Alvin M. *America in 1492: The World of the Indian People before the Arrival of Columbus.* New York: Vintage Books, 1991.

    This book explores the North American continent just on the eve of European contact. It is a multidisciplinary look at Native American culture and history as it was before Europeans arrived and began to stay in numbers. This is a collection of essays by leading scholars, it looks at different aspects of the pre-European world of Native Americans in an effort to accurately represent North America right before the beginning of Western settlement.

Key, David. "Walking with Ancestors: Discovery Rewrites American Prehistory." *Somos Primos* (July 5, 2005). Available from http://www.somosprimos.com/sp2005/spaug05/spaug05.htm.

    Somos Primos is the journal of a society dedicated to historical and ancestral research, heritage, and preservation issues. The specific article used in this book details the discovery of ancient footprints near Mexico City, analysis of the find, and dating of the footprints, which are at least 40,000 years old.

Lawrence, Bill. *The Early American Wilderness as the Explorers Saw It.* New York: Paragon House, 1991.

    This book is a primary-source look at early American wilderness and landscape as the first European explorers saw it. The evidence is taken from diaries, letters, and reports on what some of the first Europeans found. When they arrived, little, if any, European intervention would have taken place yet, so although this book records an entirely European perspective, it is about the earliest Western perspective possible.

Leblanc, Steven. *Prehistoric Warfare in the American Southwest.* Salt Lake City, UT: univ. of utab. press 1999.

    Leblanc demonstrates not only the rituals and reality of warfare, but also the prevalence of warfare in the American southwest, particularly focusing on the Anasazi. Although different tribes do not get equal treatment, this is only a result of a lack of evidence, not oversight. Leblanc details "military" structures within the tribes and argues that war was a predominant feature of Southwestern culture. He also ventures into explaining why: disappearing resources resulting from climatic change. The book does a good job of showing how integral natural resources were to the structure and stability of tribal culture, society, and interactions.

Lentz, David L., ed. *Imperfect Balance: Landscape Transformations in the Pre-Columbian Americas.* New York: Columbia University Press, 2000.

    The author's contention is that most people imagine the pre-Columbian landscape of the Americas to be perfect and undisturbed. David Lentz offers an alternate view that examines and describes the impact of native cultures on ancient ecosystems before

European contact. In order to do this, he consults experts in many fields, including botany, anthropology, paleontology, geology, and more, to create the most complete picture possible. Each section contains a botanical description of the environment coupled with case studies that discuss what the human element would have done to that environment.

Londrè, Felicia Hardison, and Daniel J. Watermeier. *The History of North American Theatre: The United States, Canada, and Mexico—From Pre-Columbian Times to the Present.* New York: Continuum Publishing, 1999.

The full work examines the history of North American theater from prehistory through Broadway, but for the purposes of researching precontact native culture, chapter 1 is especially useful. The focus of the chapter is an explanation of how dances and ceremonies contained a large element of performance in that socialization, communion between tribes, and community pride all played roles in the earliest known dance and ceremonial gatherings.

Martin, Paul S. *Indians before Columbus: Twenty Thousand Years of North American History Revealed by Archeology.* Chicago, IL: The University of Chicago Press, 1947.

Although this work is dated, it provides detailed, comprehensive information on Native American history in North America and on how archaeological study helped scientists come to those conclusions. There is a great deal of detail on each region of the continent and the regions are broken down even smaller for a more specific treatment. For each of the smaller areas, the author gives a summary of information on the local tribe or tribes.

McLauchlan, Kendra. "Plant Cultivation and Forest Clearance by Prehistoric North Americans: Pollen Evidence from Fort Ancient, Ohio, USA." *The Holocene* (July 10, 2002). Available from http://www.dartmouth.edu/~kmclauchlan/McLauchan%2003.pdf.

The abstract of this article states that archaeological records show that, as early as 2000–1500 B.C.E., Native Americans in the eastern United States domesticated a group of native plant species with starchy or oily seeds that helped support an extensive Woodland society. The evidence comes from 2000 year old pollen residue at Fort Ancient, Ohio, suggesting ancient cultivation practices in addition to ceremonial activities.

Meggers, Betty J. *Prehistoric America.* Chicago, IL: Aldine Publishing, 1972.

Although this is an older treatment of North American prehistory, it has fantastic perspectives on the settlement process (though this part is the most outdated), cultural development, and—most importantly for this environmental examination—adaptation to environments and the limits that environment imposed on culture. The subject of environmental cause, effect, and reaction involving Native Americans and their history and culture is often directly addressed, so some of these ideas were extremely useful.

Minnis, P. E. *Social Adaptation to Food Stress: A Prehistoric Southwestern Example.* Chicago: University of Chicago Press, 1985.

This work combines anthropology, archaeology, and evolutionary theory to explore how Southwestern tribes dealt with severe food shortages. He suggests that in responding to shortages, peoples developed increasingly more demanding in time and cooperation constraints. By looking at periods in a people's history, Minnis can inversely calculate times of food shortage and stress, based on these assumed behaviors.

Moss, Dr. Pius. "The Story of the Origin of the Arapaho People." *The Wyoming Companion.* Laramie: High Country Communications, 2006. Available from http://www.wyomingcompanion.com/wcwrr.html.

The Wyoming Companion transcribed Dr. Pius Moss's stories of his people, the Wyoming Arapaho, as handed down through oral tradition in his family. His father, Chief Black Coal, was an important tribal leader at the end of the 1800s, and this familial connection lends authority to his recollections of tribal history, culture, and tradition.

Muench, David. *Images in Stone: Southwest Rock Art.* San Francisco, CA: Browntrout Publishing, 1995.

David Muench traveled the Southwest with the goal of capturing the beauty and creativity of Native American rock art on film. By combining his expert photographic ability with an anthropologist's (Polly Schaafsma) expertise, Muench presents not only museum-quality photos of the rock art, but also accurate and engaging context and explanations of the peoples who created them.

Nabokov, Peter. *Native American Architecture.* London: Oxford University Press, 1990.

This book is the product of collaboration between an architect and an anthropologist, resulting in a multidisciplinary examination of design and building traditions across the North American continent. One of the most useful facets of this work is that the authors make a constant effort to connect a culture's buildings to the expression of culture itself as well as to their natural environment and how they interact and live in it. Each regional treatment ends with a look at present-day issues and concerns about remaining buildings and the traditions they come from, examining both revivals of building tradition and situations in which the traditions are in danger of being lost.

Neitzell, Jill E. *Great Towns and Regional Polities in the Prehistoric American Southeast and Southwest.* Albuquerque: University of New Mexico Press, 1999.

This is a collection of archaeological essays that examines socio-political developments in the prehistoric American Southwest and Southeast, two regions rarely discussed together. The contributors compare change in great towns, regional polities, and macroregions; document the diversity of intermediate-level societies; and search for underlying commonalities in diverse sites across the Southeast and Southwest. The chapters are presented in pairs, one dealing with each side of the continent, offering an interesting comparative perspective.

Official Web Site for the Cahokia Mounds State Historic Site. Available from http://www.cahokiamounds.com/cahokia.html.

This Web site is the official home of all available online information directly from the physical Cahokia site. Current research, activities, teaching resources, and historical presentation of the Cahokia story are available through this easily accessible site.

Opler, Morris Edward. *Myths and Tales of the Chiricahua Apache Indians (Sources of American Indian Oral Literature.* Lincoln: University of Nebraska Press, 1994.

This book is a transcription from collections of anthropological papers that not only preserves Apache tales and traditions, but also puts them into historical context of Apache beliefs and cultural history.

Page, Jake. *In the Hands of the Great Spirit: The 20,000 Year History of American Indians.* New York: Free Press, 2003.

Drawing upon the latest research and his own experiences living with Hopi Indians, the author looks at native life over the last 20,000 years. Only the first one-fifth of the book deals with Native American prehistory, and then comes discussion of European contact. Regionally speaking, the treatment is surface, but the book is meant to focus on larger trends in Native American history. It is one of the only books in publication that tries to look at the *entire* span of Native American history, and through these efforts, it offers some unique insights in the continuities and changes in native culture and society over large spans of time.

Philip, Neil, ed. *In a Sacred Manner I Live.* New York: Clarion Books, 1997.

Useful in this work is the collection of primary sources in the forms of quotes and pictures, although they focus largely on western North American tribes. The analysis (which is rather surface) and the pairing of visual and written sources (which is often incorrectly done) is less useful in higher level research as this book was written for junior high and high school age readers.

Prentiss, William C., and Ian Kuijt, eds. *Complex Hunter-Gatherers: Evolution and Organization of Prehistoric Communities on the Plateau of Northwestern North America.* Salt Lake City: University of Utah Press, 2004.

Contributors to this collection of essays explore prehistoric social organization, subsistence practices, and life/culture patterns of prehistoric natives of the North American plateau, then expanding on that basis to explore the general evolution and organization of complex hunter-gatherers.

Pringle, Heather. *In Search of Ancient North America: An Archaeological Journey to Forgotten Cultures.* Indianapolis, IN: Wiley Publishing, 1996.

The author took her own practical field experience and traveled the North American continent, spending time at archaeological digs and chronicling the history uncovered, but focusing on the scientists as the central point of the book. This work provides an insider's perspective of the difficulties and rewards of archaeology and how that plays into the writing of prehistoric North American history.

Raab, L. Mark, ed. *Prehistoric California: Archaeology and the Myth of Paradise.* Salt Lake City: University of Utah Press, 2004.

The editors suggest that honest evaluation of California prehistory has been skewed by the myth of eternal abundance. They present 13 archaeological studies whose evidence does not support this idea of endless bounty in the West Coast region. The essays look at things such as varying food availability, the ecological impact of prehistoric hunting, and changes in climate, among other compelling topics.

Sanders, William T. *New World Prehistory: Archaeology of the American Indian.* Englewood Cliffs, NJ: Prentice-Hall, 1970.

This book is another earlier work that looks at the prehistory of North American people. The focus is the application of cultural anthropology techniques to the study of prehistoric Native Americans. It is part of a larger series called *The Foundations of Modern Anthropology,* the focus of which is to examine the development of culture and cultural change in non-Western populations. The book's sections, rather than being organized geographically, are divided into themes or categories, such as agricultural evolution and the study of tribes and chiefdoms. This is one of the works that helped set the trend for treatment in Native American studies with the categorical organization, which leads to further study of commonalities across and between regions.

Schaafsma, Polly. *Indian Rock Art of the Southwest.* Albuquerque: University of New Mexico Press, 1986.

This book combines an anthropologist's examination and interpretation of Native American rock art with explanations of methods, tools, and materials used in their creation. It gives exceptionally detailed analysis of the Hohokam, Anasazi, Navajo, and Apache traditions, as well as a complex look at Pueblo tradition after 1300. Included in the work is also an introduction to hunter-gatherer societies, helping set a cultural stage for the artworks contained within the book.

Schlesier, Karl H. *The Wolves of Heaven: Cheyenne Shamanism, Ceremonies, and Prehistoric Origins.* Norman: Oklahoma University Press, 1987.

This work mostly describes in detail Cheyenne religious beliefs and ceremonies and offers rather brief but instructive and insightful information on the prehistoric connections to postcontact beliefs and practices.

Schusky, Ernest, John Adkins Richardson, and Sidney G. Denny. *The Ancient Splendor of Prehistoric Cahokia.* Bethany: Ozark Publishing, 1997.

This is a description and analysis of the Cahokia Mounds in southern Illinois. This is one of the few works that looks at Cahokia from an entirely prehistoric perspective. The book presents the Cahokian prehistoric society as "the most complex social and political culture of prehistoric North Americans." Cahokia is then compared with other contemporary sites in North America. Although the descriptions and analyses are mostly accurate throughout, the book is written for the layperson and aimed at a junior high and high school reading level.

Shetrone, Henry Clyde. *The Mound Builders: A Reconstruction of the Life of a Prehistoric American Race, through Exploration and Interpretation of their Earth Mounds, Their Burials, and Their Cultural Remains.* New York: Kennikat Press, 1930.

This is a very dated, although very complete, study of the mound-building tradition in the central United States. Written for the layperson, the book gives a background of scholarly assumptions at the beginning of the 20th century. It looks at history and culture with some treatment of economy, but largely focuses on material evidence, including a great deal of information about the architecture and possible symbolism of the mounds as archaeologists of the 1930s understood them. This work is especially useful in understanding the history of the archeological analysis of native North America.

"Table of Content: Native American Legend." *Manataka American Indian Council.* Available from http://www.manataka.org/Contents%20 Page.html.

This official Web site of the Manataka American Indian Council of Arkansas hosts a large collection of Native American legends compiled from across the Southeastern United State.

Valborg, Helen and Sri Raghavan Iyer, ed. "The Tipi." *Hermes Symbol Articles*. Theosophy Trust, 1982. Available from http://theosophytrust. org/tlodocs/articlesSymbol.php?d=TipiThe-0482.htm&p=23.

> Written by a scholar in the Hermetic Theosophy tradition, this article explores the tepee as a cultural reflection of the Native American world view. Analysis in this work is largely based on oral tradition and preserved quotations by Native American holy people.

Vierra, Bradley J. *Late Archaic across the Borderlands: From Foraging to Farming*. Austin: University of Texas Press, 2005.

> The 12 papers in this volume synthesize previous and ongoing research and offer new models to create the most up-to-date picture of life during the late Archaic across the North American borderlands. Some papers are specifically focused on topics such as stone-tool technology and mobility patterns, and others study the development of agriculture across regions within the borderlands, all in an effort to look at why human societies shift from nomadic hunting and gathering to settled agriculture.

Vilhjalmur Stefansson. *The Fat of the Land*. Hampshire: McMillan Company, 1956.

> Based on his observations in the late 1800s, Stefansson chronicles in depth his analysis of Inuit life and health. As an arctic explorer he took great care to record the anthropological details of the tribes he observed and interacted with, providing valuable information and insight into the Inuit peoples, the native society most successful at secluding themselves away from European contact.

Wayne, Robert. "Old World Origin of New World Dogs." *Science News* (2002). Available from http://www.sciencenet.org.uk/news/2002/1102/wolf.html.

> A research team at the University of California and Uppsala University in Sweden worked with zooarchaeologists from Mexico and Peru to combine archaeological and genetic evidence and analysis to determine that dogs have been in the New World for at least 10,000 years and that the dogs of that period were more genetically similar to dogs of the Old World than to wolves of the North American continent.

Weisman, Brent Richards. *Unconquered People: Florida's Seminole and Miccosukee Indians*. Gainesville: University of Florida, 1999.

> This book, written by a foremost authority on the Seminole Indians, answers the questions concerning who they were, where they came from, and comparison and contrast of cultural traits between the Seminole and Miccosukee tribes. Largely focused on the study of geographical, and hence environmental, effects on

native culture, the book includes a travel guide to publicly accessible ancient sites of the Seminole and Miccosukee tribes.

Women's International Center. *Spider Woman* (2005). Available from http://www.wic.org/artwork/spiderw.htm.

This web site focuses on providing specific information on women's participation in culture and history, as well as offering information on women's issues, organizational purpose, and further research sources. Included in this information is a collection of Native American stories and legends that tell of the role of women in different native societies.

Index

About the Author

STACY KOWTKO is assistant professor of history at Spokane Community College. She teaches Interdisciplinary Studies classes and American History classes. Her current research involves the history and culture of tourism by Americans.

The Greenwood Press
"Nature and the Environment in Everyday Life" Series

Nature and the Environment in Nineteenth-
Century American Life
Brian Black

Nature and the Environment in Twentieth-
Century American Life
Brian Black